THE JOURNAL OF THE ASSOCIATION OF MOVING IMAGE ARCHIVISTS

OVINGIMAGETHEMOVINGIMAGETHEMOVINGIMAGETHEMOVI

SPRING 2011

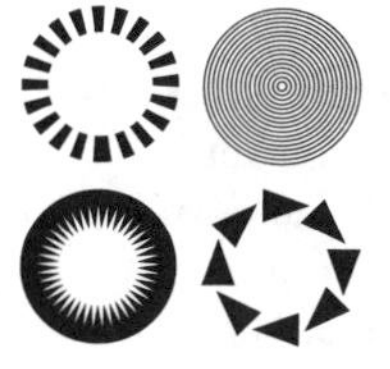

The Moving Image (ISSN 1532-3978) is published twice a year in spring and fall by the University of Minnesota Press, 111 Third Avenue South, Suite 290, Minneapolis, MN 55401-2520. http://www.upress.umn.edu

Published in cooperation with the Association of Moving Image Archivists (AMIA). Members of AMIA receive the journal as one of the benefits of membership. For further information about membership, contact Association of Moving Image Archivists, 1313 North Vine Street, Hollywood, CA 90028 (or e-mail amia@amianet.org or visit http://www .amianet.org).

Postmaster: Send address changes to *The Moving Image*, University of Minnesota Press, 111 Third Avenue South, Suite 290, Minneapolis, MN 55401-2520.

Inquiries and information about manuscript submissions should be sent to the editors, Marsha Orgeron and Devin Orgeron (marsha_orgeron@ncsu .edu and devin_orgeron@ncsu.edu). All manuscripts should be submitted as a Microsoft Word e-mail attachment, double-spaced throughout, using 12-point type, with one-inch margins, using the *Chicago Manual of Style*, 16th edition.

Please allow a minimum of four months for editorial consideration.

Address subscription orders, changes of address, and business correspondence (including requests for permission and advertising orders) to *The Moving Image*, University of Minnesota Press, 111 Third Avenue South, Suite 290, Minneapolis, MN 55401-2520.

Subscriptions: Regular rates, U.S.A.: individuals, 1 year (2 issues) $30; libraries, 1 year $75. Other countries add $5 for each year's subscription. Checks should be made payable to the University of Minnesota Press. Back issues are $22.50 for individuals and $56.25 for institutions (plus $5 shipping for the first copy, $1 for each additional copy inside the United States; $9.50 shipping for the first copy, $5 for each additional copy outside the United States). *The Moving Image* is a benefit of membership in the Association of Moving Image Archivists.

The Moving Image is available online through *Project* MUSE, http://muse .jhu.edu.

Founded in 1991, the **Association of Moving Image Archivists** is the world's largest professional association devoted to film, television, video, and digital image preservation. Dedicated to issues surrounding the safekeeping of visual history, this journal covers topics such as the role of moving image archives and collection in the writing of history, technical and practical articles on research and development in the field, in-depth examinations of specific preservation and restoration projects, and behind-the-scenes looks at the techniques used to preserve and restore our moving image heritage.

Scott MacQueen *Independent scholar*

Mike Mashon *Library of Congress*

Anne Morra *The Museum of Modern Art*

Charles Musser *Yale University*

Horace Newcomb *University of Georgia / Peabody Awards*

Margaret Parsons *National Gallery of Art*

David Pierce *Copyright Services*

Rick Prelinger *Internet Archive*

David Robinson *Giornate del Cinema Muto*

Robert Rosen *University of California, Los Angeles*

Ralph Sargent *Film Technology Company, Inc.*

Eric Schaefer *Emerson College*

Janet Staiger *University of Texas at Austin*

Jacqueline Stewart *Northwestern University*

Dan Streible *New York University*

Vanessa Toulmin *University of Sheffield / National Fairground Archive*

Gregory A. Waller *Indiana University*

Pamela Wintle *Human Studies Film Archives, Smithsonian Institution*

Patricia Zimmermann *Ithaca College*

REVIEWS

BOOKS

DVDS

Editors' Foreword

MARSHA ORGERON AND DEVIN ORGERON

The first issue of *The Moving Image* for 2011 marks two important milestones: the journal is embarking on its second decade of publication at the same moment that the Association of Moving Image Archivists (AMIA) is transitioning into its third decade of existence.

The journal and its sponsoring association have racked up substantial histories worth reflecting on at this juncture, and this issue commemorates the occasion with a substantial Forum section that records perspectives on how AMIA began, what the organization has accomplished, and what role it might play in the future. A society built around the archival profession owes itself a record of its existence, and we hope that these pages will begin to fulfill that function in a way that will prove useful for current and future generations of moving image archivists and scholars looking back to the organization's roots and development.

One refrain repeated throughout this issue's Forum concerns the international possibilities that AMIA might continue to explore as it evolves in the years to come. *The Moving Image* is, in fact, playing a pivotal role in this effort. For this reason, it seems especially appropriate that the articles in this issue are international in both scope and origin. Furthermore, the essays collected here revolve around the value of not just moving image holdings but paper archives, collections that allow these authors to reconstruct film histories that would otherwise have been unknowable.

Sarah Street's "Negotiating the Archives: The Natalie Kalmus Papers and the 'Branding' of Technicolor in Britain and the United States" is an account of the author's research at the Margaret Herrick Library in Los Angeles, where Kalmus's papers reside. Kalmus, a major figure in the history of color film, has been written about in a variety of contexts, perhaps most notoriously in Eleanore King Kalmus's at times rather one-sided 1993 book *Mr. Technicolor*. A collaboration between Technicolor's cofounder and president Herbert Kalmus and his second wife, *Mr. Technicolor* all but writes Natalie Kalmus out of the company's history. Street, on the other hand, demonstrates the underexplored reach of Kalmus's influence on British productions and on British popular culture more broadly. Street's research narrative is a familiar one to scholars who believe (and hope) that the archive will contain answers to pressing questions, and it offers those who have not been able to travel to the Herrick both a sense of the Kalmus collection's relevance and a reproduction of the complete finding aid for these materials. As often as not, archival research leads to new questions. Street's narrative, however, serves to remind us that the archival record is never complete and always needs to be read against a range of other texts. Street's work also indicates the degree to which the preservation of moving image culture involves a great deal more than the preservation of just moving images.

Eric Smoodin, in "Going to the Movies in Paris, around 1933: Film Culture, National Cinema, and Historical Method," takes this notion a step further. Smoodin's research, which takes its cue from other regionally focused studies of filmgoing habits, differs in both its subject and its approach. As Smoodin writes, "despite [an] abundance of possibilities for the movie enthusiast from the period and also the mythic status of Paris as a movie capital during the interwar years, we still know very little about going to the movies there in the 1930s." While Smoodin's research is archivally reliant (focused, as it is, on the journalism of the decade), perhaps equally interesting is his attempt to frame the city and its vast cinematic networks in archival terms. The implications here are twofold. On one hand, the city's inhabitants (and also the press) function like archivists, assigning value to films and influencing their movement. On the other hand, Smoodin's research reveals useful new contextual information for archives to consider as they ponder their own collections. His cinematic geography of the city, in other words, excavates meanings that have shifted, and these shifts, Smoodin suggests, are a critical part of the archival record.

The idea of cinematic geography takes on a different significance in **Louis Pelletier**'s "Useful Cinema, Film Genres, and Screen Networks: The Story of Canadian Films Limited (1919–1920)," which documents a nontheatrical film production company operating at a crucial moment in the history of useful cinema. Pelletier's exploration of the workings of Canadian Films Ltd. was made possible by a fortunate archival discovery of the organization's papers at the Municipal Archives of Montreal and the Bibliothèque et Archives nationales du Québec. Although the industrial, sponsored, and educational films made by this short-lived company are considered lost, the company's extensive papers allow Pelletier to illuminate a neglected aspect of Canadian film history. Pelletier's essay thus contributes to a growing body of scholarship focused on nontheatrical film, from which we are learning about the real extent of the motion picture's role in twentieth-century life. Because nontheatrical cinema has largely fallen under the radar or been deliberately neglected in many film histories—and, we might add, many archives as well—the unearthing and study of these films and the records associated with them will play a significant role in reshaping international film histories as well as film collecting and preservation practices in the decades to come.

Following the international pursuits of these authors is a special AMIA twentieth-anniversary Forum section, which was a true community effort. We owe thanks to AMIA's board of directors and especially to Dennis Doros, AMIA's resident idea man, for first suggesting the idea of commemorating the organization's anniversary in this fashion. We would also like to express our sincerest gratitude to the many people who read and commented on drafts of the Forum contributions, who offered fact- as well as memory-checking services, and who answered numerous queries, especially Laura Rooney, Greg Lukow (a gentleman possessed of both astounding recall and an impressive photographic record!), Janice Simpson, and Alan Stark. Thanks to all of the contributors to the Forum, who took time out of their busy schedules to dig up old files and memories and to reflect on them in writing.

What emerges from the Forum is a sense that at twenty years of age, AMIA remains a constantly evolving organization. Delving into the organization's history, this group of authors makes AMIA's growth and accomplishments tangible. But as these contributors subtly remind us, AMIA's biggest challenges lie ahead. Because the history we are all engaged in preserving and documenting in various ways is itself not static, AMIA's organizational goals, methods, and priorities are also always shifting. This Forum section charts many of those changes not just to celebrate the organization's progress but to offer perspectives that members may use as the organization segues into another decade of existence.

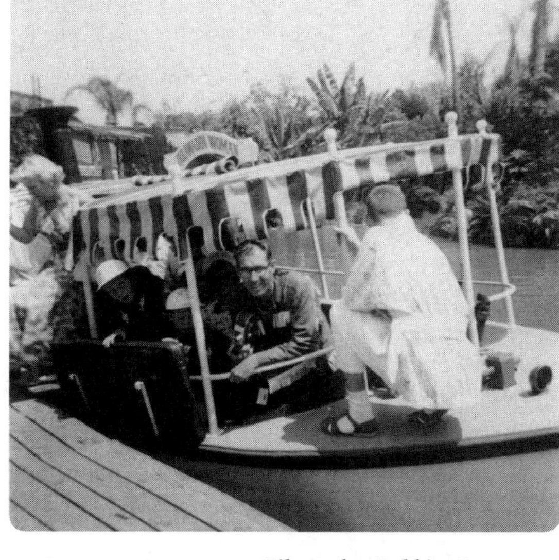

Filmmaker Robbins Barstow (center) holding a 16mm movie camera on the Disneyland Jungle Boat Cruise (1956). Photo courtesy Robbins Barstow.

The ten contributions (note how many were penned by past presidents of the organization, and even the current one!) that conclude this issue offer an array of insights about the organization's efforts in its first twenty years, while also anticipating the role it may play in the future. The pieces cover a significant, though obviously not comprehensive, range of subjects: from AMIA's founding and early days to assessments of the organization's international efforts to a behind-the-scenes account of archival screening nights at the annual conference to the history of the local television project to AMIA's considerable efforts to create scholarship programs to a meditation on the value of AMIA for an amateur archivist to musings on the role the organization might play in the transition to digital archiving. Like AMIA's annual conferences (we write this introduction fresh from the 2010 meeting in Philadelphia, the first held jointly with the International Association of Sound and Audiovisual Archives), these contributions are a testament to the breadth of AMIA's aims and the diversity of its constituency.

We are especially honored to publish in these pages contributions from **Sam Kula**, who passed away in September 2010, and from **Robbins Barstow**, who passed away in November 2010. Dwight Swanson paid tribute to Robbins on the Home Movie Day Listserv, writing,

Robbins got very active in the film preservation community in his later years, attending the AMIA conference in Rochester as well as the Orphan Film Symposium and the Northeast Historic Film Symposium, where his love for filmmaking made him many friends and admirers. Robbins joined the Amateur Cinema League in the 1930s and made one of his most famous films (and one of the very first fan films), *Tarzan and the Rocky Gorge,* in 1936. His other masterpiece, 1956's *Disneyland Dream,* about winning a trip with his family to the newly opened Disneyland park, was named to the National Film Registry in 2008.

One of the most unique things about Robbins was the way in which he kept his films alive for decades after their creation. He edited his 16mm films [and] then transferred them to video at the Wethersfield public access TV station, adding his own narration. He distributed his films first on VHS, then DVD, and then finally on the Internet Archive. . . . Robbins donated a portion of his films to the Library of Congress several years ago (something which made him extremely proud), and the remainder will be going to the Center for Home Movies collection at the Library of Congress, as well as going on Archive.org, according to his wishes.[1]

When we first approached Robbins about contributing a piece to this is-sue's Forum section, he responded, "I am an amateur moving image archivist. Before learning of and joining AMIA a few years ago, I thought I was just a home movie saver, having started 16mm filmmaking as a boy in Hartford, Connecticut, in 1932, at the age of 13."[2] He also humorously told us that because he was ninety years "of age," his essay would not be long but that he was honored to contribute to the organization's official publication. Robbins was, indeed, tremendously proud of his late-in-life affili-ation with AMIA, and his dedication to making, saving, and sharing film should be an inspiration to us all.

It is a testament to Sam Kula's character and his dedication to this profes-sion that he chose to work on his contribution to *The Moving Image* during the final months of his life, and we are grateful for the opportunity to record his thoughts here. Immediately following his passing, Rick Prelinger described Sam as "a relentlessly positive mentor" on the AMIA Listserv (September 11, 2010). Our always upbeat e-mail interactions with Sam during what must have been immensely trying times for him affirm his spirit as well as the depth of his tremendous regard for the field of moving image archiving. Ray Edmondson's tribute to Sam, which was read at the AMIA Awards and Scholars Luncheon at the November 2010 conference in Philadelphia, speaks to Sam's standing in the field:

Sam left us on September 8, just two months ago, his final battle faced with courage and his characteristic sense of humor. Many of us have electronically shared our memories of Sam, who, as a leader, teacher, mentor, and personal friend, had such a pervasive impact on our profession for half a century. He was a link with its pioneering days, having worked as deputy to Ernest Lindgren at the National Film Archive in London before moving to the American Film Institute, where I encountered him on my first overseas trip in 1973. Sam's later career took him to the National Archives of Canada, where he was director of the National Film, Television, and Sound Archives and where, among other things, he was responsible for the rescue of the Dawson collection, one of the most spectacular film discoveries in archiving history. As a writer, too, Sam has left his legacy: his books on appraisal have become part of the standard literature of our field. . . .

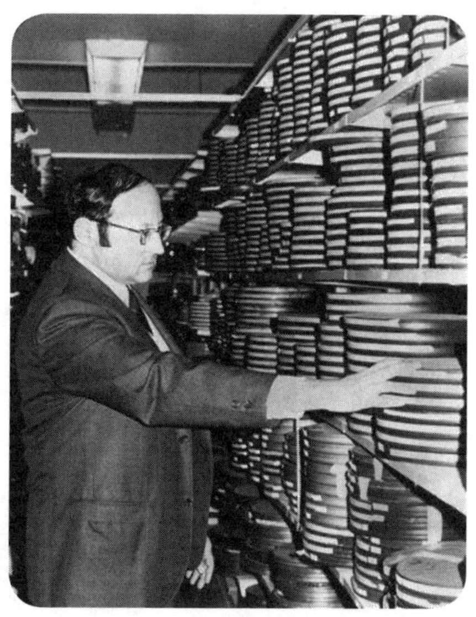

Sam Kula at the National Archives of Canada in the 1970s, credited to the *Ottawa Citizen*. Courtesy Jocelyn Kula.

Sam was an advocate and an internationalist, and he saw the profession in those terms. He was involved in the creation of AMIA and its predecessors, and he later served for four years as its president. He was a founding member of the board of the AV Preservation Trust of Canada. His stature and lifetime achievement were recognized when the association conferred on him the Silver Light Award in 2006. But he had a special feel for the Internationalization Task Force, as it was then called, of which he and I were the first cochairs, as well as AMIA's involvement in the [Coordinating Council of Audiovisual Archive Associations] and in building its links with kindred associations. That's why this year's conference was so important to him. He saw the need to direct AMIA's vision outward and fulfill its potential as an international forum.[3]

It is especially fitting that Kula's work is published posthumously in these pages since his words also graced the inaugural issue of *The Moving Image* in spring 2001. In the wittily titled Forum piece "Mea Culpa: How I Abused the Nitrate in My Life," Kula wrote what is actually a lovely appreciation of nitrate to which readers may wish to return now, a full decade after its publication.

NOTES

1. Dwight Swanson, Home Movie Day Listserv, November 9, 2010.
2. Robbins Barstow, e-mail correspondence with Marsha Orgeron, January 15, 2010.
3. Excerpted from Ray Edmondson, "Here's to You, Sam: A Tribute to Sam Kula from Ray Edmondson," presented at the AMIA–IASA conference, Philadelphia, November 2–6, 2010. From e-mail correspondence with the editors, November 7, 2010.

NEGOTIATING THE ARCHIVES

SARAH STREET

The Natalie Kalmus Papers and the "Branding" of Technicolor in Britain and the United States

Based on research for a project on color films in Britain, this essay presents a case study of the Natalie Kalmus Papers in the Margaret Herrick Library, Los Angeles, highlighting Kalmus's role in exploiting Technicolor in the U.K. market and as a color advisor for British production. Credited as "color consultant" on most Technicolor films from 1933 to 1949, Natalie Kalmus was the ex-wife of Technicolor cofounder Herbert Kalmus. Though she often worked with others and delegated responsibilities, recent scholarship demonstrates that, contrary to opinion that downplayed her role in film history, she most certainly influenced how Technicolor was used for many years.[1] In her position as head of the Color Advisory Service, she developed guidelines, advocating a theory of *color consciousness* through the use of charts for each film that operated like a musical score and associated color intensity with dominant moods or emotions.[2] Kalmus produced a chart after reading a script, after which consultations would take place with producers and members of a studio's art and costume departments, and further adjustments would be made on the set and into postproduction. In addition to cinematographers, art directors were key production personnel who negotiated the details of working with color in collaboration with Kalmus and Joan Bridge, who was also credited as "color director" on many British films.[3] Kalmus thus oversaw the exportation of Technicolor into Britain in the mid-1930s, working firsthand on several productions.

My search for primary documentation involved locating Kalmus's papers, which I hoped might answer questions about the extent of her influence, particularly on British films, and her dealings with Technicolor Ltd., the British side of the operation, formed in 1935. The extent of Kalmus's involvement with British films is a key issue in film history, as is the nature of the work she did with the Color Advisory Service, which producers had to use as part of their contract to use Technicolor. Primary archival documentation on this topic did not, in the main, survive, and in the absence of a Technicolor Ltd. archive, the Natalie Kalmus Papers were a route toward understanding a major link in the company's international activities.

The Natalie Kalmus collection spans the years 1930–48 (see the description at the end of this article). It was a gift to the Herrick in 1992 by Ron Haver, who was the head of the film program at the Los Angeles County Museum of Art and a noted film historian, collector, and preservationist. The collection is lacking in some areas, while being surprisingly rich in others. Though the collection is cataloged according to a particular correspondent, organization, film title, or type of documentation (e.g., fan mail or radio broadcast transcripts), it is necessary to read everything because you can never be sure what a file might actually contain. The fields in which I was interested related to a number of key themes, including Kalmus's professional work generally, how the

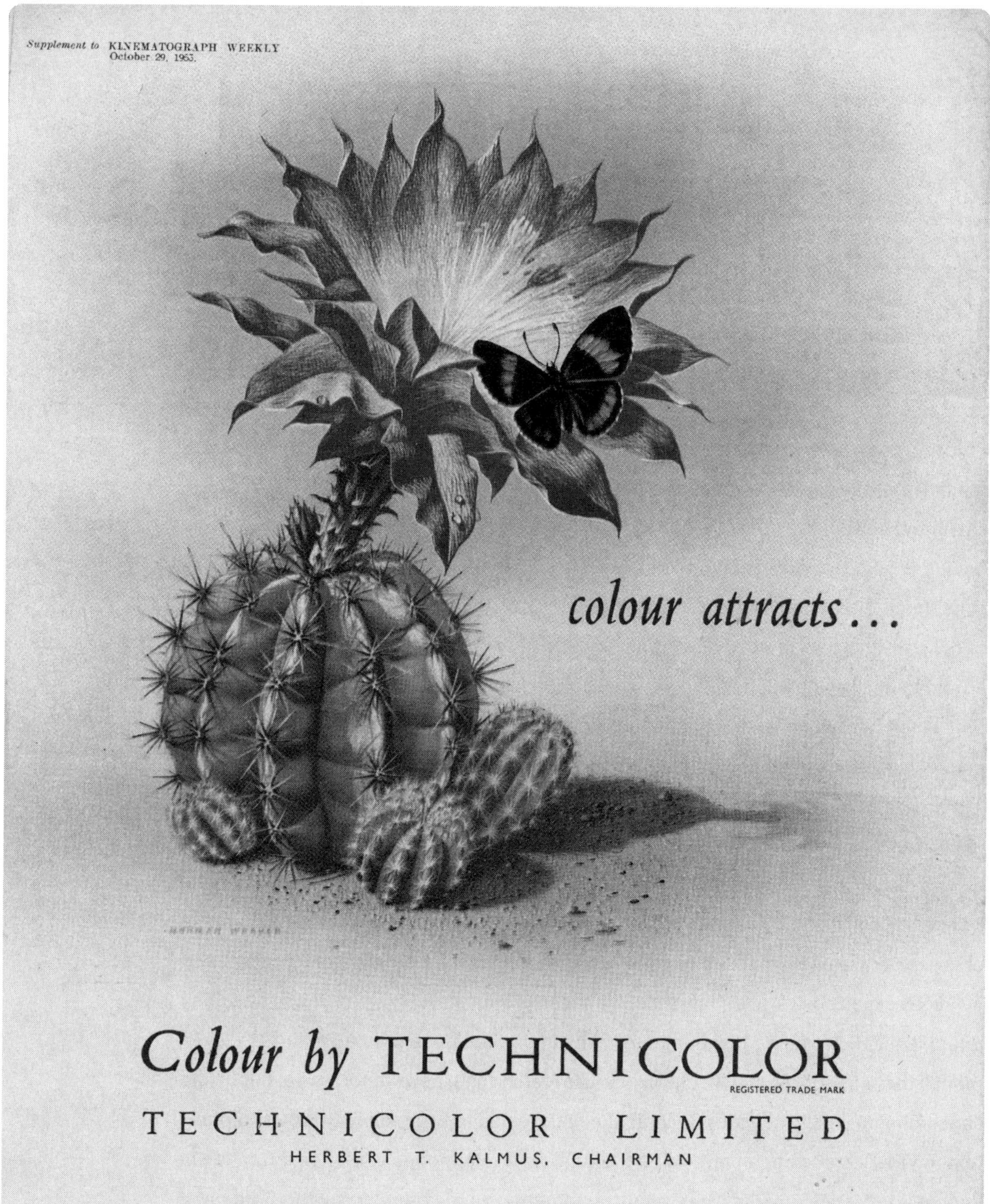

Advertisement for Technicolor Ltd. From *Kinematograph Weekly*, October 29, 1953.

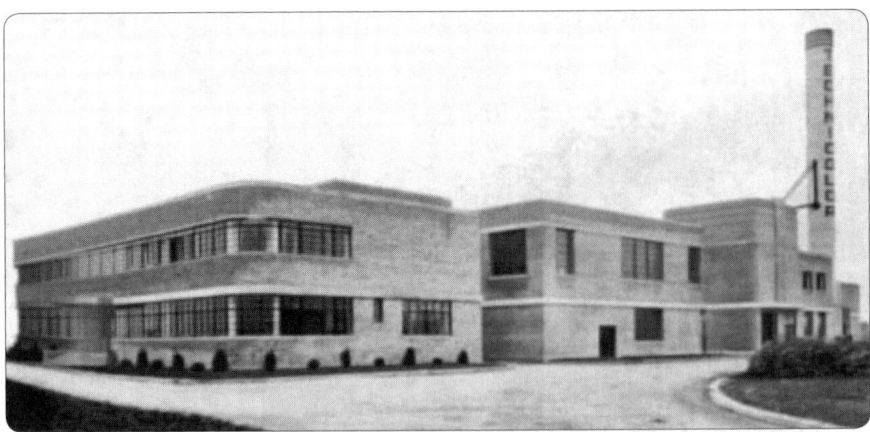

Technicolor Ltd. offices and lab (Bath Road, Harmondsworth, West Drayton, Middlesex, England), circa 1937.

Color Advisory Service operated in relation to British filmmakers, and evidence about the company's technical innovations in the form of reports circulated by the company and occasional commentary in letters. I also considered it important to gain a sense of Kalmus's overall place in women's film history and, finally, to learn more about her personal history. She is an interesting example of a woman in a key position in Technicolor, occupying a fairly unique technical role at a time when Hollywood was concerned about expanding the lucrative English-speaking market in the face of European protectionist policies.[4]

It was highly promising to find that primary documentation from the 1930s and early 1940s had survived since previous research on film trade papers indicated that this was a crucial period before Technicolor had established its monopoly. Although the British box office was dominated by Hollywood films, British filmmakers took advantage of the expertise offered by Technicolor to assist their own strategies for domestic and overseas expansion. At the same time, American producers were encouraged by British quota legislation to fund bigger-budget films that could be registered as British, even though they had substantial American input. In March 1936, news reports were published concerning the first three-strip Technicolor feature film to be made in Britain and plans to build the Technicolor laboratory on the Bath Road, Harmondsworth, West Drayton in Middlesex. Technicolor Ltd. and the new laboratory were cofunded by the Prudential Assurance Company, Gerrard Industries, London Film Productions, and the Technicolor Corporation. Herbert Kalmus was chairman of the board of Technicolor Ltd. It made commercial sense for a laboratory in Britain to make release prints of American films for the U.K. and European markets as well as to process British Technicolor films. As Herbert Kalmus recalled, the British laboratories had to be identical to those in Hollywood "so that an interchange of matrices and other facilities could become the practice."[5]

While these plans were being made, Natalie Kalmus arrived in London to supervise the use of the process in *Wings of the Morning* (Harold Schuster; produced by New World Pictures, a subsidiary of Twentieth Century Fox, 1937). She confidently predicted that in two years, every major feature film would be made in color.[6] Her color consciousness article, first published in an American technical journal, detailed her approach to designing screen color based on principles of harmony, strategic juxtaposition, and awareness of complementary colors. This piece received widespread coverage in Britain, demonstrating the extent to which her guidelines were in currency at the same time as the process had been exported and the British company established.[7]

One of the main themes I was interested in researching was the extent and nature of her contribution to the creation of Technicolor as a successful color process and as an economic enterprise. Technicolor cameras and processing were not available on the open market, a restrictive policy that ultimately contributed to its ascendancy. Cameras were leased, and processing took place in Technicolor laboratories. It was also a requirement for productions to use the Color Advisory Service, which applied Kalmus's principles in preproduction and on the set. As head of the Color Advisory Service, Natalie Kalmus was a contracted employee with Technicolor.[8] The Kalmus collection contains a memo on the services provided that was geared toward proving how Technicolor's expertise could save producers time and money, particularly during preproduction planning. The service involved advising on the correct shades of colors, contrasts, costumes, and sets, per the color consciousness article. Samples of materials and colors from previous Technicolor films were provided so that unnecessary photographic tests could be avoided. Particular attention was paid to how the costumes worn by stars related to their on-screen characters as well as to the mood or tone of a scene. Advice was given on how to avoid distracting colors so that audience interest was always maintained in the principal players. Kalmus argued that it was necessary to establishing good color "flow," based on her belief in the efficacy of "warm" and "cool" colors in relation to mood and characterization.[9]

The company therefore depended on studios using its equipment and personnel, thus establishing a mutually dependent relationship with studios. This inevitably led to some friction. The difficulties of negotiating over color control are more extensively documented for the United States than Britain. As early as 1931, for example, studio correspondence files include cases such as *Manhattan Parade,* in which Warner Bros. ignored Technicolor's advice on costumes so that "the colors were not favourable for the Technicolor process. Such a thing is a handicap toward what we aim to do—make a good picture of pleasant colors." Furthermore, the plea was made by Technicolor that "we must know and study the color relation between the sets, the furniture, the drapes and the costumes to obtain proper separation of values and harmony of colors. With due respect for the art director's architectural conception of a set, Technicolor's art department should be given the privilege of choosing the colors of the walls, decorations, wallpaper etc. The same thing applies to costumes."[10] Difficulties were also encountered when Fox Movietone resisted advice from Technicolor's experts on a series of fashion short films in 1939, resulting in their colors being in "bad taste."[11] A file on Orson Welles's unfinished film *It's All True* (1942) shows how Natalie Kalmus assisted Bob Brower on color control before giving him the responsibility of going to Rio de Janeiro to work on the film's production. Brower, a consultant at the Color Advisory Service, complained that Welles was very difficult to work with and about general mismanagement, even though RKO was generally pleased with Technicolor's work.[12]

There is also evidence in the Herrick papers of Kalmus being involved at quite a detailed level in British productions. She prepared charts for *The Divorce of Lady X* (1938), the first feature film in Technicolor produced by Alexander Korda's London Film Productions, which was photographed and sent to England in 1935. In an unusual record of how this actually worked, she advised in a long memo how the company should work with the photographs in anticipation of her arrival to supervise the production:

> I have shipped to you for Mr. [Vincent] Korda today a print in color of color charts which were photographed for his guidance in the use of our photographic process. Included with the print there is a set of the colored cards of which the charts were composed. Each one is numbered to correspond with its number on the chart, and the formula for mixing each color is written on the back of each card and on a separate list as well. By reconstructing the charts and comparing them with the projected print a general idea of the process of translation can be gained.[13]

The authoritative tone of such correspondence, as well as its particular details, confirms that Kalmus worked well with art directors, including Vincent Korda. As an indication of the increasing respect for her services, before embarking on her second trip to Britain in 1937, Kalmus bargained for a higher salary for working on some short films.[14] When she crossed the Atlantic on the *Queen Mary* in February 1937, Kay Harrison, managing director of Technicolor Ltd., arranged for her arrival to be celebrated by a brass band wearing "red coats." Although this was clearly a publicity stunt, Harrison's letter to

Kalmus noted this detail perhaps with irony because in a way, she was being welcomed as an ambassador for Technicolor.[15]

Although most greeted Kalmus's presence in Britain enthusiastically, this was not always the case. The script of *Sixty Glorious Years* (1938; U.S. title *Queen of Destiny*) was sent to Kalmus, and there is correspondence with Maude Churchill, wardrobe mistress, regarding a number of possible laces dyed particular shades that were submitted as swatches to Kalmus for her selection and then the chosen ones returned.[16] On the other hand, Freddie Young, who worked with Bill Skall as first cameraman on the film, recalled Natalie Kalmus visiting the studio when *Sixty Glorious Years* was being shot and declaring the shade of the exterior blue sky to be "wrong" on the basis of "instinct." His view was that she failed to take into account the impact of studio lights, which made any such judgment problematic. He concluded that she was ignorant and persuaded producer Herbert Wilcox to thereafter ban her from the studio.[17] This is typical of subsequent responses to the Color Advisory Service, with cinematographers in particular being disrespectful of Kalmus's knowledge and all too willing to interpret recommendations as interfering with their own expertise. As British producers and directors grew more confident working with color after the Second World War, this criticism increased, inflected with nationalist discourses that claimed that a British school of Technicolor was being developed. In this particular case, however, it is likely that Young exaggerated antipathy toward Natalie Kalmus because when *Sixty Glorious Years* was finished, Herbert Kalmus sent a cable to Kay Harrison congratulating him, and Natalie, in particular, for doing "a wonderful color job."[18] The papers therefore provide intriguing glimpses of the intricacies involved in operating the Color Advisory Service, glimpses not so easily conveyed by a simple screen credit at the end of a film.

Kalmus acknowledged that others followed her guidelines and was appreciative of many British films in this respect. In relation to Herbert Wilcox's *Irene* (U.S., 1940), starring Anna Neagle, a very popular British star who was married to Wilcox, the papers reveal Kalmus's admiration for the famous "Alice blue gown" sequence shot in Technicolor. Films introducing color intermittently or for a particular sequence such as this were always handled carefully lest the sudden introduction of color cause too much distraction from the narrative. Kalmus explained the approach taken in Irene:

> The method employed was to do all the backgrounds for the entire sequence in neutral gray, the murals in gradations from white through gray and black, and the costumes of all players, except Miss Neagle's, in grays or in predominant neutral values of color. Thus when the moment arrived for the transition

from black and white to color, the change in color tone in the background
and surrounding players was so slight as to lend exceptional emphasis to
the entrance of Miss Neagle in her gorgeous Alice blue gown, making her the
centre of interest from a color point of view. Thus Miss Neagle alone has a
great change in color tone at the moment of transition and the effect on the
audience is breath-taking.[19]

This account was then published in Technicolor's in-house magazine, *Technicolor News
and Views,* also held in the Herrick Library.[20] This source contains a picture of Natalie
Kalmus and Anna Neagle at a luncheon of the Women's Press Club when Neagle was
visiting Hollywood in 1942, providing more evidence of the good relationship that had
been established between Technicolor and British companies and stars.[21] This somewhat contradicts cinematographer Freddie Young's account of Herbert Wilcox, Neagle's
producer and husband, agreeing with his opinion of Kalmus as interfering and ignorant,
particularly in view of the "Alice blue gown" sequence's textbook application of her color
consciousness principles. This positive appreciation of the impact of the Color Advisory
Service was echoed in numerous articles in the *British Journal of Photography* to the
extent that Kalmus's principles were recommended to amateur home movie enthusiasts,
many of whom were beginning to experiment with color.[22]

 Although the documents on her dealings with Technicolor Ltd. are not volu-
minous, they nevertheless reveal a productive and mutually respectful relationship
with Kay Harrison. Though Kalmus might have enjoyed being in Britain for many social
reasons, such as going to the races, the idea that she was not much involved with British
productions can, to some extent, be challenged by reading letters from the beginning of
the Second World War.[23] Soon after she had returned to Hollywood following the production of the first British three-strip films, Harrison wrote that they missed her expertise
and that her presence "alone made it possible for this company to have efficient color
direction during the initial stages of its development."[24] Natalie Kalmus replied with
details of how she was busy in Hollywood keeping up to date with the latest technical
developments, including monopack film:

 I am so enthusiastic and thrilled about it that the extra work, which runs into
 long hours, is more entertaining than tiring. I wish I could tell you more about
 it but mum is the word for the present. I am also busying myself learning every
 new trick of the trade, particularly the changes that have been brought about
 by the use of our fast negative. I am also following the trick work on different

pictures very carefully. This I know will be very useful to us in England. . . . I want you to be assured of my willingness to cooperate with you in any way that it is possible for me to be helpful, and to reassure you that you can call on me any time you need me. I have no fear whatever about being in England in these times of war.[25]

She did not return to England for some years but instead advised from Hollywood, where she continued working not only on fiction films but also on industrial shorts that were beginning to use color. With this example, we get a sense of her technical interests as well as her special attention to British production at a key time in Technicolor's development of its overseas operations. Records exist of other figures who worked with color, for example, Bernard Happé, who managed Technicolor's laboratory in Britain for many years.[26] These are primarily of a technical nature, but in the absence of surviving records of Technicolor Ltd., they are also a valuable source of information about working conditions, particularly during the Second World War. In this respect, they usefully complement the production-orientated correspondence between Natalie Kalmus and Kay Harrison held at the Herrick Library by covering the war's impact on postproduction color processing.

Some documents are tantalizing, including a record that Natalie Kalmus received the script of *The Life and Death of Colonel Blimp* (1943), Powell and Pressburger's controversial wartime feature, and that she "revised and finished the color synopsis" for the film in June 1942.[27] Unfortunately, this synopsis is missing, as are the elusive charts, but that it was done indicates that she had input into a film that is normally regarded as the color achievement of cinematographer Jack Cardiff, director Michael Powell, and production designer Alfred Junge. Junge's archive in the Harry Ransom Humanities Research Center in Austin, Texas, does not contain any correspondence with Natalie Kalmus; instead, it has a detailed account of how Junge designed sets for *Colonel Blimp* with Technicolor in mind. A dovetail approach whereby one archival source complements another is particularly fruitful. Putting the two sets of documents together, a broader picture emerges as to how color control was the responsibility of many interdependent professionals throughout a production, not least Kalmus herself. Looking for traces of authorship regarding color is complex, requiring the realities of each stage of a Technicolor production to be fully understood, including the role of the laboratories in postproduction. This method has been productively applied to Hitchcock's work, which, by acknowledging the collaborative expertise involved in films he directed, greatly extends our understanding of the nature of his authorship.[28]

The Natalie Kalmus Papers are also rewarding in other related areas, particularly the public presentation and marketing of Technicolor as well as the attendant gender issues that her career raised. Kalmus was generally regarded as the Technicolor expert who also knew about art, a combination that attracted a degree of curiosity that was partly to do with her gender. As one trade press commentator reported after interviewing her, "Mrs. Kalmus I found a most delightful and enlightened character. . . . Indeed I'd like to see her in Technicolor herself for she's by no means a flat personality. It is clear that she has the technical side of the game at her fingertips and can be depended on not only to look after that angle but the creative color angle as well."[29] This kind of reportage continued throughout her career, and Technicolor clearly took advantage of her star value as an ambassador for the process who was in a fairly unusual position as a woman heading a complex and key operation in the company's development.[30] It suited them to publicize her technical knowledge for this purpose, on one occasion putting her name on an article written by a male colleague in the company.[31]

Her work attracted widespread reports in fan magazines, and she encouraged tie-ins between Technicolor and department stores by advising on color combinations for new fashion ranges; she also gave radio interviews. She was admired for her dedication to and knowledge of Technicolor, one commentator observing after meeting her, "Her vitality is incredible, almost electric in its force. You can feel it when you are anywhere near her. It's exhausting if you are not in tune with her."[32] For those not intent on criticizing her recommendations as interference in a production, her expertise was important in the creation of Technicolor as a brand. Together with Herbert, Natalie made a technical process a household name, with both personalities performing different but crucial showmanship functions for the company. One article described Herbert as the "Techni" and Natalie the "Color" of Technicolor.[33]

Technicolor found it expedient to deploy Kalmus's color expertise on many occasions in advertising, and in this she was tied to their general strategy of controlling every aspect of the process, including validating her approach to color consciousness not only in films but in everyday life. The documents relate in this regard primarily to the United States, but reports in the United Kingdom show a similar spread of knowledge about Technicolor as a process and inculcator of color consciousness in everyday life and commerce.[34] The Herrick file on fan mail, for example, includes letters from people whose viewing was immeasurably improved by an appreciation of Technicolor.[35] Influencing audience tastes was a key goal of the company, so these letters are evidence of how propagandizing color consciousness was a key marketing strategy and intimately related to the rhetoric deployed by Natalie Kalmus in interviews and on radio broadcasts.

The letters contain many enthusiastic comments such as "I enjoy Technicolor movies enormously and hope the day will come when they are all made in Technicolor. In fact movies that I did not find quite so entertaining, I thought were worth while seeing just for the Technicolor."[36] One correspondent declared that he was more interested in the quality of colors than anything else: "My mind, precisely trained in engineering, often brushes aside the dramatic influences of the picture to analyze the color play of the production. Undoubtedly, I reason, some massive intelligence is behind the combination of hue there."[37] Similarly enthusiastic comments were made by respondents to sociologist J. P. Mayer's surveys of cinema audiences in Britain, conducted in the 1940s and published in two books. These constitute fascinating contemporary accounts of audience behaviors and preferences among children and adults.[38] As a public figure and advocate of color, Kalmus's influence extended beyond film production to advising women to wear particular colors to go with their hair and mood; for example, a platinum blonde was urged to wear blues and somber colors rather than pink. Further evidence of the construction of Kalmus's public persona is provided by transcripts of radio interviews when she is asked about color generally, about her work with Technicolor, and for advice on the importance of color, particularly in the immediate postwar period.[39] In hindsight, it is easy to see Technicolor dominating the color film market, although at the time, the company did not take its success for granted and was keen to keep ahead of competitors such as Dufaycolor in the United Kingdom.[40]

Intriguingly, the creation of her public persona involved facilitating tie-ins with department stores. A folder containing correspondence with J. H. Hugues, merchandise manager for A. Harris and Company of Dallas, Texas, in 1943–44, demonstrates how her views on color extended beyond Hollywood. Having read her color consciousness article, Hughes sought her advice on how to tie in Technicolor with the colors of his incoming spring collections. She replied, "The word Technicolor is banned for use outside of the corporation, but it is permissible to use my name in your booklet." The collections were duly advertised as "Natalie Kalmus colors." On this basis, particular colors were selected and approved; she changed the description of one from "True Blue" to "Serene Blue," which further popularized her views on cool and warm colors. The costume display was erected in the store in February 1944, with coverage in *Vogue* and *Harper's Bazaar*. In gratitude for her cooperation, and after inquiring with Kalmus's secretary about a desirable gift, she received an alligator purse and perfume.[41] Examples such as this make it clear that Kalmus was a sort of ambassador for the company in technical and aesthetic terms, and in this arena, her gender was convenient. She was also consulted by makeup companies such as the House of Westmore and Max Factor, the latter having a special relationship with Technicolor as adviser to the company on makeup foundation.[42]

Natalie Kalmus thus facilitated the branding of Technicolor as more than a motion picture process. Living life in Technicolor extended beyond the studio and outside the movie theater. Tie-ins were also a feature of marketing Technicolor films in the United Kingdom. For example, reports on *The Divorce of Lady X* showed that color was indeed seen to be a notable feature by exhibitors, with one manager of a cinema in Nuneaton linking with a dyers and cleaners shop as well as with local decorators to show how Merle Oberon's gowns and the sets reproduced a range of colors that could be applied to everyday fashion and interior design.[43]

As noted earlier, I hoped to gain from the documentation at the Herrick a sense of Natalie Kalmus's role in women's film history. During this period, women's involvement in film production was limited, far more so than during the silent era. Kalmus's role was, however, rather unique, making it difficult to find a comparative frame of reference as one might with editing, directing, or production design. What emerges from the papers is that Technicolor used Kalmus's expertise and public persona very much as a means of marketing the process, what it stood for, and its ambitions to invade public consciousness beyond motion pictures. Commentators were fascinated by her apparently powerful position, as when "Find the Woman," a 1941 radio broadcast, introduced her as "a brilliant, beautiful woman whose knowledge of colors and their relation to moving images is helping to pave the way to an all-color screen. Petite, utterly feminine, she is, nevertheless, the supreme dictator of color technique in Hollywood . . . and the world over. She schedules her day so she can supervise as many as six films in production or preparation at one time."[44] The admiration of her artistic, technical knowledge and hard work featured in other publicity, as well.

Tie-ins with consumer products worked extremely well with her advocacy of color consciousness as a way of negotiating the modern world, her insistence on nongarishness establishing a code of taste around color that gravitated toward careful, artistic choices rather than nonnaturalistic "super-abundance."[45] These principles were taught to others with whom she worked. Joan Bridge is an intriguing figure in the British context since she did a similar job but did not provoke such criticism. Having worked with Dufaycolor in the 1930s, she subsequently collaborated with Natalie Kalmus or was the sole Technicolor adviser on many British feature films. Bridge was admired by British cinematographers such as Ossie Morris, who never accorded Natalie Kalmus the same courtesy.[46] A woman doing the job of color advisor was therefore not necessarily problematic on a film set, and so it is likely that criticism of Kalmus arose more from specific difficulties people experienced when working with her that were exacerbated by a perception that she represented external regulation. Her importance is that she was the first person to work as a color consultant in the motion picture industry, and her guidelines informed the company for many years, whether or not she personally supervised their application. Her gender also assisted Technicolor in many ways, not least in perpetuating particular cultural associations between women and color.[47]

Aspects of Kalmus's personal life are documented only in part in the Herrick collection. Again, there are intriguing omissions, which presumably were never part of the archive, as there are with many such collections that contain little personal information. Her correspondence with Herbert Kalmus is generally friendly, and he seems fully supportive of her career. Personal differences apart, they were linked by their enthusiasm for Technicolor and worked hard to enhance its commercial and public profile. But the documents are mainly from the 1930s, before the controversy over their secret divorce made headlines in the late 1940s.

There is no correspondence relating to the lawsuit in which Natalie claimed a monetary settlement in 1948. Herbert and Natalie had divorced in 1921, but they continued to live in the same house, and most people assumed that they were still married. To find more information on this, it was necessary to consult the Herrick's press clipping files on Natalie Kalmus. These document how, in 1944, relations between the couple began to break down. Herbert's affairs and his relationship with Eleanore King, whom he married in 1949, were the background to Natalie filing the lawsuit, claiming that she was entitled to a financial settlement because their divorce in 1921 was invalid (on the grounds that they had lived as man and wife subsequently, sharing a house in Bel Air, California, for which, as documents in the Kalmus collection reveal, Herbert paid household expenses).[48] The *LA Times* reported that the court had declared the divorce to be legal, and Natalie was not therefore entitled to further financial support. Kalmus had in fact been paying her alimony until 1945, and she also received a salary from the Technicolor Corporation, from which she retired in 1948.[49]

Though the archive has no material on these matters, it does have a file of Natalie Kalmus's horoscopes. One might wonder why these were kept in an archive that otherwise contains materials more central to Kalmus's professional career. The dates for the file are significant, 1944–48, years when Kalmus was undergoing personal crisis. It is likely that people were trying to exploit her vulnerability and belief in superstition, so the horoscopes are of definite value when trying to understand the pressures on a woman in her public position at this time.[50] Subsequent years were also dominated by controversy as she descended into professional and personal decline. She died in 1964, aged eighty-four, in a hospital near Boston where she had been a patient for two years.[51]

In 1993, Eleanore King Kalmus, Herbert's second wife, published a scurrilous account called *Mr. Technicolor.* It was a combination of Herbert Kalmus's autobiography with considerable additions and commentary by Eleanore. Though it acknowledged the importance of Natalie Kalmus's work with Technicolor, admitting that "the practices she established in her department during the mid-1930s strongly affected the art of color motion pictures," Herbert Kalmus emerges as "the genius who invented Technicolor and forever changed the history of cinema," a powerhouse of brilliant ideas and financial acumen who was dragged down by his increasingly unstable wife.[52]

Natalie Kalmus has gone down in history as the name credited on all those films, yet from Eleanore's book, this was a symptom of her controlling and demanding personality, which Herbert merely wished to placate, though he did accord generally with her views on color consciousness. In my quest to understand the history of color films in Britain, I have come across other accounts that seek to marginalize her from the historical record. Cinematographers are the most dismissive. On the other hand, the work of color consultancy and assistance, especially from people such as Joan Bridge, was more appreciated, and one must understand that for many, Natalie Kalmus represented American interference in their professional competences. The papers, however, reveal that managers such as Kay Harrison were grateful for Kalmus's input at a crucial point when British companies were beginning to produce in color. The pre–World War II advances in color were very important determinants of subsequent developments, especially in the short film market and in popularizing amateur formats such as Kodachrome. The papers thus provide a corrective to standard accounts of Technicolor's working methods.

Color consciousness, or the desire to control color, was not just the whim of Natalie Kalmus. Many contemporaries were similarly concerned about deploying color in particular ways that posed no threat to the dominant forms of narrative cinema. Kalmus and others shared a fascination with how color could enhance a film drama, and she clearly captured the public imagination. In this respect, the archive at the Herrick is significant, detailing the role she played in advertising the process and disseminating a certain ideology around color. Although lacking in key respects—there are no charts, only fractions of correspondence with Technicolor Ltd., and no financial information or correspondence with people with whom we know she worked closely such as Joan Bridge—the papers have been useful in my research, even though a lot of material seems to have disappeared, destroyed, perhaps, by Natalie or Herbert Kalmus.[53] Yet the papers are tantalizing in their glimpses of the way Technicolor operated and how the three-strip process was developed, with Natalie Kalmus strategically involved in disseminating Technicolor as a brand name.

The company's gradual monopoly of the color film market was made possible by overcoming specific technical problems that had stymied other rival systems, but there is no doubt that effective marketing and the inculcation of color consciousness in the popular imagination also played a huge role. The Herrick does have a separate Technicolor collection, but this is not a complete corporate archive.[54] It has very little relating to films made in Britain and certainly does not further illuminate the role of Natalie Kalmus.[55] Yet what remains in her papers perhaps indicates what she valued most about her career: her professionalism, her role in advocating the work of Technicolor, and the importance of color consciousness in everyday life. She must have been proud of her links with Technicolor Ltd. and seems to have admired British films and—contrary to what many would have us believe—British attempts to be creative with color design. Visitors to the projection room in the Kalmus's Bel Air home were shown examples of notable British Technicolor films, including *The Thief of Bagdad* (1940) and *The Great Mr. Handel* (1942).[56] Such knowledge, which could only be gleaned from the papers in the Herrick collection, tells us a lot about how individuals seek to control their images. What she left for posterity in the form of her papers has not, however, limited the perpetuation of myths around her activities, the color consultancy service, and her personal life. Yet the Natalie Kalmus Papers have helped me contextualize her work in conjunction with other papers, interviews, the film trade press, and the films on which she collaborated with other key professionals in the quest for color in British cinema.[57]

DESCRIPTION OF THE NATALIE KALMUS PAPERS FROM THE MARGARET HERRICK LIBRARY, SPECIAL COLLECTIONS

The Natalie Kalmus collection[58] spans the years 1930–48 (bulk 1939–48) and encompasses 0.8 linear feet. The collection contains information on early 1940 Technicolor films, including camera department crew calls for forty films ranging from *For Whom the Bell Tolls* (Paramount, 1943) to *Victory through Air Power* (United Artists–Disney, 1943); Eastern unit work; a 1940 exhibition reel; and advance schedules. There is some business correspondence between Herbert and Natalie, primarily in the form of telegrams sent when he was on business trips. Other correspondence is between Kay Harrison in the Great Britain offices of Technicolor and interoffice memos for the color control department, including a list of services provided. Two productions have correspondence:

It's All True (unrealized/RKO, 1942) and *Queen of Destiny* (RKO, 1940), also known as *Sixty Glorious Years*. Miscellany includes fan mail, horoscopes, household bills, personal correspondence, testimonials by Kalmus for House of Westmore, and the manuscript for an article by Kalmus on color photography.

Natalie Kalmus Papers

Production files

1.f-1   *It's All True*—miscellaneous 1942.
Includes: press release; memos regarding difficulty in shipping equipment to Rio de Janeiro, Brazil; handwritten letter from Bob [Brower] to Natalie Kalmus with details of shooting the Carnival, February 17, 1942; handwritten letter from Mr. Brower regarding his possible return to Hollywood and the "unfortunate situation" of the film, March 4, 1942; handwritten account of how Orson Welles and [Phil] Reisman held up a plane with a diplomatic mission.

1.f-2   *Queen of Destiny*—miscellaneous 1938.
Includes: letter from Maude Churchill, wardrobe mistress, with sample of net pinned to page, April 28, 1938; copy of memo from F. George Gunn with information about the crew and also discusses *Over the Moon,* April 29, 1938. Note: Released in Great Britain as *Sixty Glorious Years* (1938).

1.f-3   *This Is the Army*—miscellaneous undated.
Contains: notes; credits; breakdown of musical numbers.

Subject files

1.f-4   A. Harris & Co. 1943–1944.
Includes: letter from J.H. Hughes to Natalie Kalmus saying he wanted to draw on her book for his spring line, November 16, 1943; carbon of letter from Ms. Kalmus to Mr. Hughes saying he could use her name for publicity but not the word 'Technicolor,' December 16, 1943; letter from Mr. Hughes to Ms. Kalmus with enclosed swatches, January 20, 1944.

1.f-5   Christmas 1933–1935.
Includes: list of gifts and cards sent by Dr. and Natalie Kalmus, 1933–1934; handwritten note.

1.f-6   Correspondence 1930–1948.
Includes: letter to Florenz Ziegfeld listing recommended changes for the color of costumes for *Whoopee,* January 26, 1930; note from John Harkrider to Natalie Kalmus asking if she would like to have lunch, October 4, 1935; letter from Serge Oukrainsky to Mrs. Kalmus asking for an interview, October 6, 1935; letter from Alexander Oumansky to Mrs. Kalmus, October 24, 1935; letter from Walter Ross to Mrs. Kalmus, October 21, 1935; letter from W.H. Vilas, Wilding Picture Prods., to Mrs. Kalmus with enclosed treatment for short about Elizabeth Arden, July 18, 1940; copy of letter from H.T.K. to Morgan Hobart, August 13, 1940; carbon of letter from Gerry F. Rackett to Mrs. Kalmus discussing work on industrial films, August 17, 1940; carbon of memo from Mr. Hobart to Mr. Rackett with enclosed script for slide film, August 21, 1940; carbon of 4-page memo from Mr. Hobart to Mr. Rackett describing meetings with various businesses about proposed industrial films, August 28, 1940; letter from Mr. Harkrider to Mrs. Kalmus asking for shots to be used in a pageant for the United War Fund, October 5, 1942; telegram from Mrs. Kalmus to Jan de Hartog about the success of *Skipper,* February 12, 1948.

1.f-7   Dannenbaum, Ray 1942.
Includes: copy of letter from A.B. Hecht, Popular Photography, to Margaret Ettinger saying they will publish Ray Dannenbaum's article, 'The Black and White of Color Photography,' under Natalie Kalmus' byline, September 25, 1942.

1.f-8   Durenceau, Andre 1930–1931.
Includes: reports by Andre Durenceau with information about *Manhattan Parade* and his difficulty working at Warner Bros. since they did not want to take the advice of Technicolor's Art Department, November 24, 1931; handwritten letters from Mr. Durenceau.

1.f-9   Fan mail 1939–1948.
Includes: letters from servicemen; complaints about use of color.

1.f-10   Harman, Hugh 1945–1947.
Includes: notes by Natalie Kalmus regarding *King Arthur* test reel, 1945; letter from Mrs. Kalmus to Luise Corkran saying that the Rank Organization was not interested in the film but that Richard Stilwell, a financier, would be coming to Hollywood to talk to Hugh Harman about the project, November 4, 1947.

1.f-11   Harrison, Kay 1935–1944.
Includes: letter from Kay Harrison to Natalie Kalmus relaying questions from

Vincent Korda, August 12, 1935; letter from Robert Riley to Mrs. Kalmus with estimated costs for two-reel musicals, October 7, 1936; memo from Mr. Riley to Mrs. Kalmus with costs for the Warner Bros. short *The Song of a Nation,* October 26, 1936; letter from Mr. Harrison to Mrs. Kalmus discussing upcoming productions, including *Lawrence of Arabia, Over the Moon* and *Jamaica Inn,* September 28, 1937; copy of cable from Herbert Kalmus to Mr. Harrison saying that while progress was being made "on a new process which it is expected will eventually eliminate the necessity of special cameras and three negatives" there was still no definite date, April 5, 1938; cable from Mr. Harrison to Mr. Kalmus discussing *Lawrence of Arabia* and the breakdown of talks with Paramount, November 28, 1938; letter from Mr. Harrison to Mrs. Kalmus discussing the war and a possible production, November 23, 1939; handwritten letter from Heather Harrison to Mr. and Mrs. Kalmus about her children going to the U.S., July 9, [1940]; letter from Mr. Harrison to Frank R. Oates discussing the war, the Blitz and the upcoming elections in the U.S., September 13, 1940.

1.f-12   Horoscopes 1944–1948.
Contains: horoscopes for Natalie Kalmus [and Mr. Kalmus?] by Isidor Oblo and David Sturgis.

1.f-13   Household 1939–1942.
Contains: bills and monthly breakdowns of money spent by Natalie Kalmus and reimbursed by Dr. Kalmus.

1.f-14   Kalmus, Herbert T. 1934–1941.
Includes: carbon of letter to Herbert Kalmus discussing work at the plant and saying they would be making a test of Katharine Hepburn for *Joan of Arc,* May 22, 1934; copy of memo by Mr. Kalmus regarding his discussion with Samuel Goldwyn about doing a color sequence for the next Cantor picture, July 19, 1934; carbon of letter from Mr. Kalmus to Natalie Kalmus discussing Henri Jaffa's work on *Nothing Sacred,* his discussions with labor unions and general business news, August 19, 1937.

1.f-15   Kalmus, Natalie 1941–1948.
Includes: canceled checks; miscellaneous notes and memos; copies of articles "The Importance of the Correct Use of Color in Every Day Life" and "Motion Pictures in Colors" by Natalie Kalmus.

1.f-16   Kalmus, Natalie—telegrams 1937.
Contains: handwritten drafts of telegrams sent by Natalie Kalmus when she

was working in England, covering the period from February 3, 1937 through July 3, 1937.

1.f-17   Lewis, George F. and Bess 1935–1945.
Includes: personal correspondence; letter from Bess Lewis to Natalie Kalmus enclosing photos of her son and grandson, March 1941.

1.f-18   Manuscript undated.
Contains: synopsis of *Copper Dusk* by Natalie Kalmus, 10 pages; typed story, *Copper Dusk: A Hawaiian Love Tale,* by Natalie Kalmus, 100 pages.

2.f-19   Miscellaneous 1932–1945.
Includes: announcement by Pearl Eaton of the opening of her new studio, January 1932; synopsis by Dianna Beresford of *The Lost Ecstasy* by Mary Roberts Rinehart; research notes.

2.f-20   *Musical Moments* 1931.
Contains: story and continuity for *Musical Moments: Hungarian Rhapsody No. II* by Leslie Balogh Bain, December 28, 1931, 14 pages.

2.f-21   Personal bills 1935–1944.
Contains: breakdown of charges for Natalie Kalmus, primarily of a personal nature but there are also business expenses included.

2.f-22   Radio 1933–1942.
Contains: transcript of interview with Mrs. Kalmus conducted by Eleanor Barnes for radio station KRKD, February 15, 1933; script drafts for [segment?] of "Find the Woman" on KNX-CBS, January 24, 1941; note regarding broadcast on KMTR, February 22, 1942.

2.f-23   Riley, Robert 1940–1945.
Includes: memo from R. Riley with attached copy of February 13, 1940 memo by Darryl Zanuck saying the color for *Swanee River* was bad and inconsistent and that he wanted *Maryland* to have some realism, February 15, 1940; carbon of letter from Riley to Natalie Kalmus discussing the films being shot, September 10, 1941.

2.f-24   Screenings 1942–1945.
Includes: lists of films shown, and occasionally guest lists, for screenings at Bel Air projection room.

2.f-25   Smith, Donald and Betsy 1939–1946.
Includes: a letter from Donald Smith to Natalie Kalmus speaking about the opening of the new Technicolor office building, May 5, 1939; clippings about his wedding.

2.f-26   Steno notebooks 1939.
Contains: two notebooks [of Vi Shaw?] with Natalie Kalmus' dictation, covering the period from March through June 1939 [mostly in shorthand].

2.f-27   Sutton, Ezilda 1941.
Includes: telegram from Margaret Faulconer to Natalie Kalmus regarding a proposed series of color chart shorts by Ezilda Sutton, January 29, 1941.

2.f-28   Technicolor—camera crew calls 1942.
Contains: carbon copies of daily camera department crew calls from January 7, 1942, and July 31 through December 31, 1942 with call time, location, number of cameras, and cameramen for *America* (September–November); *Arabian Nights* (July–December); *Battle of Midway* (September); *Best Foot Forward* (December); *Black Swan* (July–September); *Coney Island* (September–December); *Crash Drive* (July–December); *Defense Against Invasion* (October); *Desert Song* (July–November); *Dixie* (October–December); *Dubarry Was A Lady* (August–December); *Fighting Engineers* (September–November); *Fitzpatrick Travel Talks Trip No. 2* (August–September); *For Whom the Bell Tolls* (July–December); *Forest Rangers* (November); *Hello Frisco Hello* (October–November); *Horses are Human Too* (August); *Horses, Horses, Horses* (September); *Indian Temples* (August); *Jungle Book* (January); *Lady in the Dark* (November–December); *Lassie Come Home* (July–November); *Mormon Trails* (December); *My Friend Flicka* (July–November); *My Gal Sal* (January); *Neptune's Daughter* (November); *Pioneers* (July–December); *Private Miss Jones* (October–December); *Saludos* (September); *Salute to the Marines* (September–December); *A Ship is Born* (July–August); *Sporting Dogs* (September); *Springtime in the Rockies* (July–August); *Thunder Birds* (July–August); *To the Shores of Tripoli* (January); *U.S. Gypsum Slide Film* (August); *Victory Through Air Power* (October); *White Savage* (October–December); *Women in Sports* (November); *Wood Goes to War* (November–December); *Young and Beautiful* (December). Note: Each daily crew call lists multiple films in production. The month notation refers to the shooting period for that film.

2.f-29   Technicolor—Color Control Dept. 1938–1944.
Includes: carbon of letter from Henri Jaffa to G.F. Rackett regarding Richard Mueller's work on the Fox Fashion Short No. 1 in New York, November 7, 1938;

carbon of memo from Rackett to Herbert T. Kalmus explaining the situation with Fox Movietone News and the Fashion Forecast series, October 19, 1939; copy of memo from R.W. MacCuaig to Mr. Kalmus breaking down the time worked on *Billy the Kid* and *Blossoms in the Dust,* February 14, 1941; letters of appreciation.

2.f-30   Technicolor—correspondence and memos 1940–1947.
Includes: copy of letter from H.T.K. to G.F. Rackett discussing general business matters, October 1, 1940; copy of letter from Mr. Kalmus to Donald G. Smith regarding the possibility of hiring Francis Coradel-Cugat, March 4, 1943; memo regarding *The Reluctant Dragon,* November 20, 1945.

2.f-31   Technicolor—daily notes 1942.
Contains: handwritten notes from March 7 through September 15, 1942.

2.f-32   Technicolor—Eastern unit work 1940–1942.
Includes: copy of a letter from Natalie Kalmus to Donald Smith, August 18, 1942.

2.f-33   Technicolor—exhibition reel 1940.
Contains: memos from George A. Cave to Natalie Kalmus regarding a Technicolor sales reel; two scripts.

2.f-34   Technicolor—miscellaneous 1929–1948.
Includes: notes about working on *King of Jazz* and *Paramount on Parade,* 1929; article titled '*Irene* Outstanding from Point of View of Color,' April 5, 1940; production shooting schedule, April 26, 1948; camera dept. schedule, May 7, 1948; proposed business organization for Frank Wilt's *Song of Egypt,* undated.

2.f-35   Technicolor—schedules 1942–1943.
Contains: advanced schedules for July 8, 1942 to July 29, 19[42]; December 31, 1942; January 27, 1943; February 17, 1943; February 27, 1943 to April 8, 1943.

2.f-36   Travel 1948.

2.f-37   Westmore (House of) 1937–1944.
Includes: material regarding testimonials issued by Mrs. Kalmus.

2.f-38   *Who's Who in the Western Hemisphere 1943.*
Includes: biographical sketch of Natalie Kalmus.

NOTES

1. See Scott Higgins, *Harnessing the Technicolor Rainbow* (Austin: University of Texas Press, 2007), 39–47.

2. Natalie Kalmus, "Color Consciousness," *Journal of the Society of Motion Picture Engineers*, August 1935; repr. Angela Dalle Vacche and Brian Price, eds., *Color: The Film Reader* (London: Routledge, 2006), 24–39.

3. For a detailed discussion of British Technicolor, see Sarah Street, "'Color consciousness': Natalie Kalmus and Technicolor in Britain," *Screen* 50, no. 2 (2009): 191–215.

4. Sarah Street, "The Hays Office and the Defence of the British Market in the 1930s," *Historical Journal of Film, Radio, and Television* 5, no. 1 (1985): 37–55.

5. Herbert Kalmus, with Eleanore King Kalmus, *Mr. Technicolor* (Chesterfield, NJ: Magic Image Filmbooks, 1993), 112.

6. *Kinematograph Weekly*, May 7, 1936, 14.

7. See, e.g., the article by Kalmus that quotes her "color consciousness" ideas in *The Cinema*, January 2, 1936, xxix.

8. Kalmus, *Mr. Technicolor*, 203.

9. Natalie Kalmus Papers, Margaret Herrick Library, Academy of Motion Picture Arts and Sciences, Los Angeles, CA (hereinafter NK Papers), 2, f-29, Technicolor Control Department, 1938–44.

10. NK Papers, memo, Andre Durenceau file, 1-f.8.

11. NK Papers, Color Control Department, 2, f.29, interoffice memo from G. F. Rackett, October 19, 1939.

12. NK Papers, *It's All True* (RKO) file, 1.f-1.

13. NK Papers, Kay Harrison folder, 1.f-11, NK to KH, September 24, 1935.

14. NK Papers, Kay Harrison folder, 1.f-11, NK to KH, November 16, 1936.

15. NK Papers, Kay Harrison folder, 1.f-11, cable, KH to NK, February 27, 1937.

16. NK Papers, *Queen of Destiny* folder, 1.f-2, Maude Churchill to Natalie Kalmus, April 28, 1938.

17. Freddie Young, Broadcasting Entertainment Cinematograph and Technicians Union (BECTU) Oral History Project interview no. 4, April 1, 1987.

18. NK Papers, 1.f-2, cable, Herbert Kalmus to Kay Harrison, October 15, 1938.

19. NK Papers, miscellaneous, 2.f-34, NK notes, April 5, 1940.

20. *Technicolor News and Views* 2, no. 4 (1940): 1.

21. *Technicolor News and Views* 4, no. 3 (1942): 2.

22. *British Journal of Photography* 89, no. 4270 (1942): 87.

23. Art director L. P. Williams's BECTU Oral History Project interview no. 381, August 12, 1993, claims that Natalie Kalmus spent much of her time in England at the races.

24. NK Papers, Kay Harrison folder, 1.f-11, KH to NK, October 10, 1939.

25. NK Papers, Kay Harrison folder, 1.f-11, NK to KH, November 2, 1939. Monopack film (a single film based on Eastman Kodak Kodachrome film that was exposed in a conventional camera) was a very significant innovation because it meant that special three-strip cameras only manufactured by Technicolor were no longer necessary, even though Technicolor processing methods continued to be used.

26. These are available in the BFI Special Collections library.

27. NK Papers, Daily Notes, 2.f-31, June 8–13, 1942.

28. Will Schmenner and Corinne Granof, eds., *Casting a Shadow: Creating the Alfred Hitchcock Film* (Evanston, IL: Mary and Leigh Block Museum of Art and Northwestern University, 2007).

29. *The Cinema,* report in "Onlooker" section, April 30, 1936, 1.

30. See *Photoplay* article with Kalmus declared as "Technicolor's first star!" and described as "one of the most romantic figures of the day"; *Photoplay* 37, no. 5 (1930): 67.

31. NK Papers, Ray Dannenbaum folder, 1.f-7. The file has details of an article, "The Black and White of Color Photography," written by Dannenbaum that was published under Kalmus's name in *Popular Photography,* September 25, 1942.

32. John K. Newman, "Profile of Natalie Kalmus," in John Huntley, *British Technicolor Films* (London: Skelton Robinson, 1949), 148.

33. See the portrait of Natalie Kalmus by Ida Zeitlin, "Great Women of Motion Pictures," *Screenland* 38, no. 4 (1939): 75.

34. See, e.g., *British Journal of Photography* 89, no. 4285 (1942): 226–27.

35. NK Papers, Fan Mail, 1939–48, 1.f-9.

36. NK Paper, Rose de Tourville folder, 1.f-9, April 6, 1941.

37. NK Papers, Captain Marshall Waller folder, 1.f-9, Pueblo, Colorado, April 22, 1943.

38. J. P. Mayer, *The Sociology of Cinema* (London: Faber, 1946), and *British Cinemas and Their Audiences* (London: Dennis Dobson, 1948).

39. NK Papers, Radio folder, 2.f-22.

40. In the 1930s, Dufaycolor was tipped by many as a very appropriate color technology for British films. Several short advertising and animation films were made, along with a feature film. Technical difficulties and the impact of the war, however, curtailed its development, and the company was never able to seriously threaten Technicolor. See Brian Coe, *The History of Movie Photography* (London: Ash and Grant, 1981), 125–26.

41. NK Papers, A. Harris & Co. folder, 1.f-4.

42. NK Papers, House of Westmore folder, 2-f.37, and see Sarah Berry, *Screen Style: Fashion and Femininity in 1930s Hollywood* (Minneapolis: University of Minnesota Press, 2000), 121–26.

43. *Kinematograph Weekly* 261, no. 1647 (1938): 48.

44. NK Papers, Radio folder, 2-f. 22, "Find the Woman" broadcast, January 24, 1941, KNX-CBS Pacific Net Know Manning.

45. Kalmus, "Color Consciousness," 25.

46. Interview with Ossie Morris by Sarah Street and Liz Watkins, August 6, 2008.

47. See Steve Neale, *Cinema and Technology: Image, Sound, Colour* (London: Macmillan/BFI, 1985), 151–55.

48. NK Papers, "Household," 1939–42, 1.f-13.

49. *LA Times*, December 11, 1948.

50. NK Papers, Horoscopes, 1.f-12.

51. *Variety*, April 15, 1964.

52. Kalmus, *Mr. Technicolor*, 198. The quotation about Herbert is from the book's front cover jacket.

53. *Mr. Technicolor* cites an example of Herbert Kalmus's lawyer destroying correspondence and Natalie Kalmus "withholding" a key "nasty" letter in the 1948 dispute. Ibid., 203.

54. A recent donation of Technicolor papers to George Eastman House, Rochester, may well contain corporate materials, but as yet, this collection is uncataloged and unavailable for research purposes. It is unclear whether there are materials relating to relations with the United Kingdom.

55. See http://www.oscars.org/library/collections/special/index.html for the Natalie Kalmus and Technicolor Special Collections. There are also notebooks on technical aspects of Technicolor's development at George Eastman House. See Ulrich Ruedel, "The Technicolor Notebooks," *Film History* 21, no. 1 (2009): 47–60.

56. NK Papers, Screenings, 1942–45, 2.f-24.

57. In the color project on which this work is based, we have interviewed Chris Challis, Ossie Morris, Ronald Neame, Paul de Burgh, and other film restorers and archivists. We have also consulted the BECTU Oral History Project interview tapes, available at the BFI, London.

58. The inventory and scope and content note for the Natalie Kalmus papers are reproduced here, with permission of the Margaret Herrick Library.

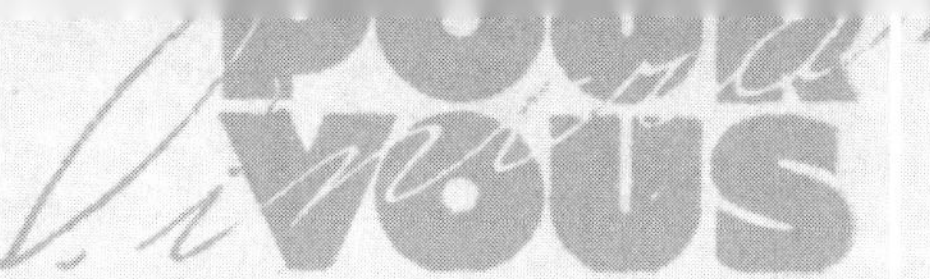

GOING TO THE MOVIES IN PARIS, AROUND 1933

ERIC SMOODIN

Film Culture, National Cinema, and Historical Method

During the week of October 13, 1933, filmgoers in Paris could watch Fritz Lang's *The Testament of Dr. Mabuse* (1933), Max Ophuls's *Liebelei* (1933), Josef von Sternberg's *Blue Angel* (1930), and Frank Capra's *Forbidden* (1932) as well as *I Am a Fugitive from a Chain Gang* (Mervyn LeRoy, 1932), *King Kong* (Cooper and Schoedsack, 1933), and Jacques Tourneur's *Toto* (1933). They might see Eddie Cantor in *The Kid from Spain* (Leo McCarey, 1932) and Boris Karloff in *Frankenstein* (James Whale, 1931) and also go to any number of films that have long been forgotten: *La Voie sans disque* (Léon Poirier, 1933), for instance, or *Madame ne veut pas enfant* (Landau and Steinhoff, 1933), or *Rumba* (director, date unknown). In fact, with at least two hundred movie theaters in Paris at the time, a dedicated fan might see several films in the same day, with screenings running from nine o'clock in the morning until well past midnight. In the ninth arrondissement alone, that fan could walk into the Paramount Theater on 2 Boulevard des Capucines for a 9:30 A.M. show of *Un soir de récreillion* (director, date unknown), end the day down the block with a 3:00 A.M. screening of *Tire au flanc* (Henry Wulschleger, 1933) at the Olympia at 28 Boulevard des Capucines, and watch two or three movies in between at theaters just a few steps away.[1]

Despite this abundance of possibilities for the movie enthusiast from the period, and also the mythic status of Paris as a movie capital during the interwar years, we still know very little about going to the movies there in the 1930s. Richard Abel has provided a full sense of the film distribution systems and exhibition experience throughout France during the period just before World War I. Abel as well as Christophe Gauthier have unearthed and examined the history of the cine clubs and specialized movie theaters that showed avant-garde, documentary, or animated films in Paris and elsewhere in France during the teens until about 1930.[2] From 1894 until the end of World War I, we have Jean-Jacques Meusy's encyclopedic rendering of all manner of film theaters in the city, including descriptions of the streets where they were located, in the aptly titled *Paris-Palaces*.[3] But for that period between the wars, perhaps because of the emphasis placed on Paris as a site for alternative cinema and for the dedicated cinephile rather than the film fan, little attention has been paid to the average moviegoer and to the theaters along the grand boulevards and in the neighborhoods that specialized in commercial, feature-length films.[4]

An examination of filmgoing in Paris, of the theaters and the audiences that went to them and the films they saw there—or what we might more broadly call film culture—helps explicate the related developments of the cinema and urban space during the period. But my goal here is not simply to celebrate that flâneur on the Boulevard des Capucines strolling from theater to theater, nor to assert the links between film, modernity, and the growth of cities, an often repeated but extremely vexed aspect of film studies over the last two decades.[5] Rather, a look at Paris yields information that is both empirically and historiographically significant. Despite the city's importance in film history, we still do not understand many of the basic aspects of the cinema in Paris such as the number of theaters and their locations. And the close analysis of the ways films were exhibited and then moved through the city makes Paris itself, in the sense of a singular film culture, a problematic area of study. Examining films and filmgoing in Paris makes us take our local study of the city to the micro level, to the neighborhoods within the city and the differences and similarities, in terms of film preference or audience, from one to the other. The city's film audience, from the working-class Menilmontant to the Jewish center of the Marais to the bourgeois quarters in the middle of the city, becomes a fragmented one, signifying not so much the "Parisian" as the individual neighborhood itself.

Studying the varied audiences of Paris, the movies they watched, and the theaters where they saw them also illuminates significant changes in the practices of film studies. Increasingly over the last twenty-five years, the field has refined its understanding of the movie audience. I have written about this shift elsewhere, but for a number of reasons, the field has moved away from an idea of a spectator mostly determined by the film itself, with one viewer much the same as any other. As Annette Kuhn has written, approaches to film viewing that developed in the 1960s and 1970s were "predominantly about a spectator addressed or constructed by the film text."[6] While these typically psychoanalytic approaches still circulate, the prevailing belief is that issues of film viewing, and relationships between viewer and film, are far more complex and that empirical audiences are much more differentiated than can be accounted for by the notion of the textually produced viewer.

In a 1995 essay, "The Place of the Spectator" ("La place du spectateur"), Christian-Marc Bosséno established some of the broad contours for studying the historical film viewer and for shifting the emphasis from that which took place on the screen to "the theater itself" *(á la sale elle-même)*. Bosséno posed a series of questions for conducting research on the audience: "Who went to the cinema, and why? How and under what technical and material conditions did they see films?" and later, "When can we date the death of the 'grand public' and the birth of specialized, micro audiences?"[7]

In asking about micro audiences, Bosséno had in mind those spectators who were particularly interested in art films, or documentaries, or feature films. But one of the means for answering Bosséno's question, and for understanding these empirical spectators, has been to move away from the notion of the mass audience, the "grand public," and to engage in regional and local analyses. As a result, the city and the town have become central to contemporary audience studies, much more so, in fact, than the nation. There might be nothing new about this emphasis on the local, as the 2001 translation and publication, in *Screen,* of Emilie Altenloh's 1914 dissertation regarding filmgoing in Mannheim, Germany, suggests. More recent scholars, such as Kathryn Fuller-Seeley, Gregory Waller, Lee Grieveson, and Ben Singer, have not only produced historiographies of local film habits, from the 1890s through World War II, but have also elucidated the varied audiences within a town or city.[8] In U.S.-based film studies, scholars have analyzed the perceived tensions between city and town during the period in relation to taste in film and consumption practices so that we might examine the full range of filmgoing habits in such places as New York, Milwaukee, or Campbellsville, Kentucky, to name three test cases in a recent collection on the movie audience.[9]

And yet in film studies, Paris has gone largely unexamined.[10] In fact, as a French example, we probably have greater knowledge of modes of film exhibition and consumption in much smaller French locations than we do of the capital. Renaud Chaplain has examined the practices in Lyon, for instance, while Pierre and Jeanne Berneau have performed a similar study of Limoges from the beginning of cinema until the end of World War II and Sylvie Rab has analyzed interwar film practices in Suresnes, the Parisian suburb.[11] But Paris remains a compelling case study because it functioned as a center of both national and international production, as one of the largest sites of filmgoing in Europe, as a center of intellectual interest in cinema, and as the location of some of the most important film journalism on the continent.

By making sense of the information about movies in Paris, we can also start to reconsider our ideas about national cinema. Since the 1930s and until fairly recently, film studies, at least as practiced in the United States and Great Britain, has made the term *national cinema* seem self-evident, with historians showing a clear sense of what French cinema might indicate, or German, or American, for that matter. National cinema has meant, unproblematically, the films of a particular country. That is, national cinema has been defined textually as the narrative and visual mechanisms of large bodies of films: French poetic realism in the 1930s, for example, or the French New Wave in the 1950s. But as I have argued before, we might also develop an understanding of national cinema based not so much at the point of production, through analyses of the films made, but at the point of reception—the ways in which audiences participated in film culture, the opportunities they had to see films, and the broad discourses about movies from such media as print journalism.[12]

Such an examination helps us understand the national in both internationalist and fragmented terms. We can study the place of French cinema and French film culture in the rest of Europe as well as the United States and also their reach to France's colonies. But we can examine as well the similarities and differences between Parisian film culture and that of other areas in France, metropolitan, rural, and in between, to develop a more nuanced sense of French cinema.

In the case of Paris alone, by concentrating on the details of reception, we acquire a way of reading that city, in the manner of de Certeau's "rhetoric of walking," from the ground, in terms of the spatial arrangement of film culture, for instance, the location of theaters and the movement of films through the city.[13] My imaginary flâneur or flâneuse in the ninth arrondissement, then, as well as invoking a literary and cinematic trope from Walter Benjamin, Walter Ruttman, and others of the city dweller strolling through the streets, also provides a means for reexamining Paris through the everyday routes of film culture and the options of the city's film enthusiasts for seeing movies. Studies of urban mobility, by art historians and literary theorists, typically have focused on representations of cities made by the artists and authors who walked through them: Manet's stroll on Haussmann's Boulevard Malesherbes in the Paris of the early 1860s or Dickens's evocations of London.[14] Theorists and historians of urban space have questioned the gendered dimension of these walks through modern streets and have recovered the possibilities for women as well as men to meander through the city.[15] The important advance of film studies, however, has been to move beyond the study of representations of cities and the options of individuals to explore them and to analyze the movements through space of the products of culture and of significant numbers of cultural consumers.

THE ARCHIVE OF PARISIAN FILM EXHIBITION

Addressing cinema and film exhibition in Paris at the point of reception means reading through a range of primary materials from France and elsewhere. My focus on just a few years in the early 1930s for this study is historiographically motivated, in terms of the assumptions of film studies, but is also random. In most French film histories from the last two decades, the period marks what Colin Crisp has called the beginning of the "classic French cinema," which developed with the conversion to sound technology in the late 1920s and lasted for about thirty years.[16] Historians have usually applied this classicism to modes of film style, but we can also presume that the development of rules governing representation or narrative indicates the possibility of the same precision in other systems connected to the cinema, for instance, exhibition.

As a means of understanding these systems, the daily journalism of 1930s

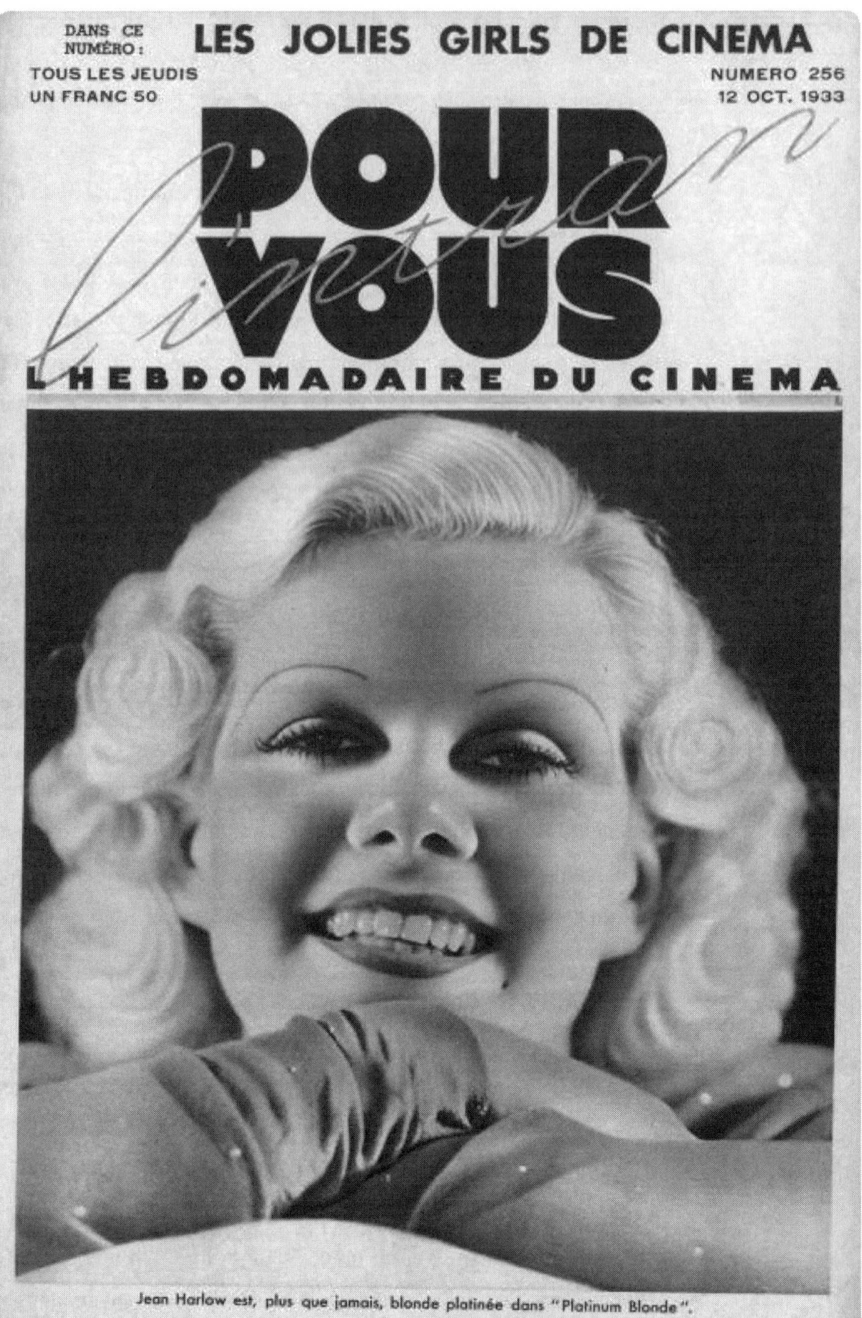

Pour Vous, no. 256, from October 12, 1933, with Jean Harlow in *Platinum Blonde* on the cover.

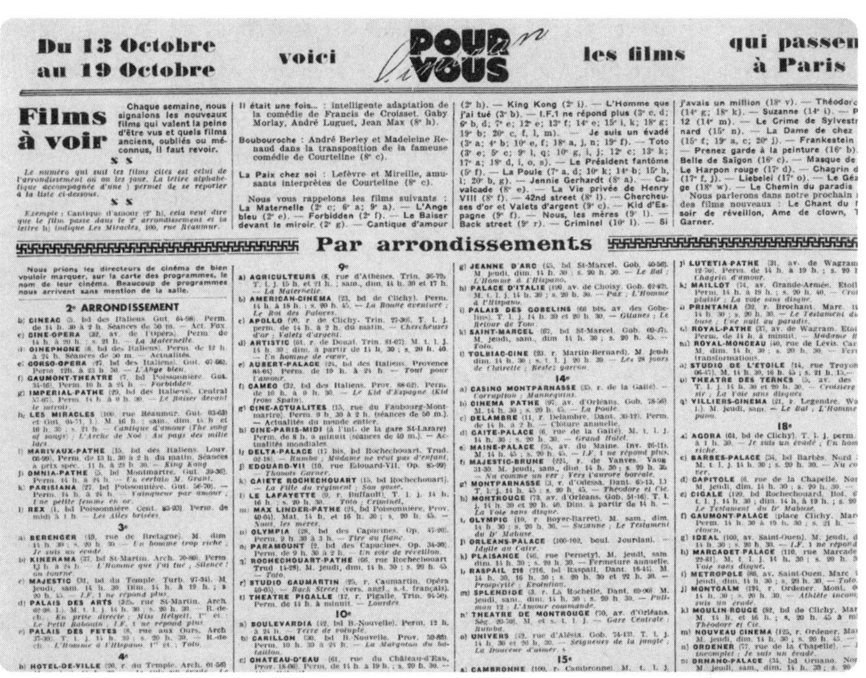

A fragment of the film listings
for Paris in *Pour Vous,* no. 256.

Paris as well as France gives us important information about film culture broadly and audiences and exhibition more narrowly. But these newspapers are often difficult to find, at least for the scholar in the United States, and usually are not fully indexed. In addition, many of the newspapers from the period that have been preserved are more national in scope than local. Although they often concentrated on Paris, they provided coverage for all of France, and so film listings, even for a city of Paris's importance, were incomplete. Because of this, my archive of materials includes American sources. Newspapers and magazines from the United States reported on the Parisian film scene regularly during the 1920s and 1930s, and for the film historian working in the United States, these materials are readily available and often indexed in such databases as ProQuest Historical Newspapers.

Indeed, the extensive coverage by the pre–World War II American press makes the early 1930s a compelling period for study. But my analysis of these years is also by happenstance because of my own chance discovery, almost a decade ago in a Paris shop stacked floor to ceiling with old magazines, of a film tabloid, *Pour Vous,* from October 12, 1933, with a complete listing of the city's films and theaters for the week that started the next day. Over the years, I have acquired more issues of *Pour Vous*, and a complete set is available on microfilm. And unlike any other French source I have found, including newspapers from the period, *Pour Vous* ran full listings of the commercial films playing in the city every week for all of 1933, and more sporadically before and after, under the headline "Voici les films qui passent á Paris" ("Here Are the Films Playing in Paris").[17]

Pour Vous was just one of many movie magazines and journals that flourished in Paris and in the rest of France during the period. In detailing the specialized magazines and newspapers about film from the late teens through the early 1930s, Crisp lists, among others, *Ciné Pour Tous, Ciné Magazine, Mon Ciné, Ciné Revue, Ciné Miroir, Ciné France,* and *Ciné Combat.* Paramount Pictures, the American movie studio, distributed its own journal, *Mon Film,* to advertise the movies that the company made in France—and in French—during the first years of the conversion to sound. And it was one of France's leading newspaper entrepreneurs, Léon Bailby, the director of the daily *Intransigeant,* who founded *Pour Vous,* which appeared from 1928 until 1940.[18] Though it was a national periodical, *Pour Vous* asserted the centrality of the Parisian film scene and the Parisian audience and the peripheral status of the film culture in other regions in France and the colonies. Many issues from the early 1930s include the section "On the Screens in the Four Corners of France," with information about Marseille, Lyon, Cherbourg, and Lille, for example, and also detailing such North African locations as Oran and Morocco.[19] But always, the focus was on Paris, with its listings of films that played in the city and the theaters that showed them.

The period covered by my examples from *Pour Vous* marked the founding of the major film archives in the cultural or political capitals of Europe and the United States: the BFI opened in London in 1933, the Reichfilmarchiv in Berlin in 1935, the Film Library of MoMA in New York in the same year, and the Cinémathèque Française in Paris in 1936. Though the various archives certainly responded to periodic calls to preserve different forms of national film heritage, they also helped make their cities centers of international film culture. The Cinémathèque Française, of course, while emphasizing French cinema, preserved and exhibited films from around the world. In 1947, founder Henri Langlois wrote proudly of his success in saving German, Russian, and American films, among others. Almost immediately after its founding, the Cinémathèque brought these film experiences not just to Paris but to the world, with the London Méliès Exposition, for instance, and the French Retrospective in Venice in the late 1930s.[20] Langlois also understood that the museum must not just preserve and exhibit a film repertory but also the technologies of cinema and its documents.

So the city and the cinema came to be linked through the film archive, with that archive itself asserting the importance of a broad sense of film culture, including films, cameras, and projectors and also the primary materials of the film industry and film journalism. Indeed, this film journalism helped found the archive, at least in Paris. Colin Crisp has written of the important role played by editorials in *Pour Vous,* in 1932 and 1933, when first Lucienne Escoubé and then Nino Frank called for the creation of a national cinémathèque before it was too late and before the loss of even more silent films in particular.[21]

This era is a significant one in French cinema for a number of reasons, from the 1934 liquidation of the vertically integrated conglomerate Gaumont-Franco Film-Aubert to the 1935 collapse of Pathé to the formation of the Popular Front.[22] But the coincidence of the historically engaged film journalism of *Pour Vous* and other sources and the development of major film holdings in American and European cities, including Paris, signal this period as particularly important for the restoration and preservation of film culture. An analysis of the cinema of Paris in the early 1930s, then, as well as the film journalism that covered the city coincides with the development of an understanding of the centrality of the cinema to urban, national, and international cultures. Along with the cinémathèque, the city and the film tabloid become archival sources, providing films and explaining them to the audiences of the period and helping restore to us the habits, practices, and politics of film viewing and film exhibition.

Understanding the city in this way, and examining exhibition practices and audience preferences there, helps change our attitudes about the film archive in general. *Preservation* becomes a more complicated term, referring not just to the films but to other materials, for instance, the writing about cinema or film posters or products related to movies. Preservation also takes on architectural and archaeological importance, as we can see the significance of saving or restoring, most typically through documentary evidence, the contours of streets or neighborhoods, so that they can be studied as aspects of film history that yield as much information as the films themselves.

THE STATISTICS OF FILMGOING IN PARIS

The information in *Pour Vous* indicates that there were movie theaters in nineteen of Paris's twenty arrondissements, all except the first, which is taken up primarily with the area around the Louvre. Most of the large, first-run theaters were clustered in the more well-heeled neighborhoods, in the second arrondissement on the Boulevard des Italiens (at 5, 6, 15, 27, and 29) and the Boulevard Poissonière (at 1, 7, and 27) and in the eighth, on or near the Champs-Elysées, although there were others in neighboring areas such as the sixth and seventh. The number of theaters in the arrondissements varied, from only two in the fourth to eighteen in the ninth, which included the area around the Rue Pigalle, and nineteen in the eighteenth arrondissement, around Montmartre, one of the more peripheral neighborhoods of the city. These numbers were tied to population density, but not strictly. The eighteenth arrondissement was, throughout the 1930s, the most highly populated area in Paris, while the first typically had the fewest inhabitants. The ninth arrondissement, however, with its eighteen theaters, as well as the second, sixth, and seventh were on the low end of the Parisian population scale. The first-run theaters in those areas almost certainly had more seats than the average theater in the eighteenth, and so it becomes difficult to determine exactly the link between movie theater space—in the broad sense of number of theaters and number of theater seats— and the population of a particular arrondissement.[23]

Most of these theaters ran their programs from noon or 2:00 P.M. until 8:30 or 9:00 P.M., typically every day, although in some cases only on two days a week, usually Thursday and Sunday. A few theaters opened as early as 9:00 A.M., and some had their last screenings at midnight or even as late as three o'clock in the morning. Matching an American model, these theaters seem either to have been in chains or independent. We can locate several major concerns, such as the Pathé theaters or Gaumont or Palace (with the Gaumont-Palace in the eighteenth arrondissement, apparently with links to both chains, the largest movie theater in Paris). Pathé had its theaters throughout the city, often with several in the same arrondissement, as in the second, with an Imperial-Pathé, a Marivaux-Pathé, and an Omnia-Pathé. There were also theaters owned by American motion picture firms or their French subsidiaries—the previously mentioned Paramount, for example, in the ninth arrondissement. Chains typically had connections with production companies, with Gaumont theaters, logically enough, often but not exclusively showing Gaumont films and Pathé connected to both Pathé-Natan and Paramount, the American movie studio. In the sixteenth arrondissement during the week of October 13, the Victor Hugo–Pathé showed *Tout pour rien* (René Pujol, 1933), a Pathé film, while the Mozart-Pathé screened *Madame Butterfly* (Marion Gering, 1932), a movie from Paramount. But the chain also booked prestige films from other companies; audiences that week could go to the Marivaux-Pathé in the second arrondissement to see *King Kong,* a first-run American film from RKO.[24]

Just as in the United States, more and more French theaters showed double (and sometimes triple) bills throughout the 1930s, with many exhibitors responding to the Pathé theater chain's aggressive July 1933 commitment to programs of multiple films.[25] In Paris during that week in October, the major first-run theaters still only showed single films, but in neighborhoods with mostly subsequent-run exhibition sites, audiences could easily see two films for the price of one. In the third arrondissement, three of the five theaters showed two films and usually maintained that practice from week to week. On the Boulevard St. Martin in the third, the Kinerama paired two reissues of Hollywood films from 1932: Ernst Lubitsch's World War I melodrama *The Man I Killed,* with the Harold Lloyd comedy *Movie Crazy* (Clyde Bruckman), after having shown Marlene Dietrich in *Shanghai Express* (Josef von Sternberg, 1932) the previous week, along with *Idylle au Caire* (Heymann and Schünzel, 1933), the French version of a film from UFA, the German studio.[26] In the ninth arrondissement, five of nine theaters showed double bills, whereas five of twelve theaters reporting programs that week from the fourteenth, near the southern edge of Paris, presented two films each.

Parisian theaters had been wired for sound by October 1933, and almost all of them showed, if not exclusively current films, then films that had been released before in Paris, in 1931 or 1932. One theater, however, still showed mostly silent films from the previous decade. In the tenth, the Boulevardia treated Greta Garbo fans to *Wild Orchids* (Sidney Franklin, 1929) and then changed the program the following week to Douglas Fairbanks in *Thief of Bagdad* (Raoul Walsh, 1924).[27] Even if they did not show double bills, Parisian theaters provided a mixed bill of movies, with documentaries and short subjects accompanying the features so that the American film *Igloo* (Ewing Scott, 1932), about the Arctic, and the Laurel and Hardy two-reeler *The Music Box* (James Parrott, 1932) played alongside other films in the neighborhoods, while the Disney cartoon *Father Noah's Ark* (1933) showed on a first-run bill with the Dietrich film *Song of Songs* (Rouben Mamoulian, 1933) at the fashionable Les Miracles theater in the second arrondissement.[28]

THE AMERICAN PRESS, ALCOHOL, AND AIR-CONDITIONING

I will return to *Pour Vous* later, for a discussion of historiographic practice. But as a complement to the statistical information in the French movie tabloid, newspapers from the United States provide us with significant empirical data about Parisian theaters and the movies they showed. The American press gives us, as well, ample anecdotes and impressions and also typically corresponds to the conventions of American nonfiction from the period for reporting on Europe. Many of these entries on filmgoing in Paris repeat one of the clichés of much American travel literature, of a sort of unfathomable Frenchness and the complete difference of the French from the Americans.

Examples from the weekly magazine the *Literary Digest* typify this balance of information and incredulity. The *Digest* compiled the best of middle- and high-brow journalism from a number of sources and, in 1929, ran an article titled "Why Paris Goes to the Movies," which acquainted readers with reporter Quinn Martin's recent "European Tour of Movie Houses."[29] One of the ongoing problems in film studies is that of determining precisely what people did at the movies. We know that they watched films and that they ate food, but we do not know much else: how intently they watched, how much they talked, what other activities took place at theaters, and how that activity might be connected to first-run or subsequent-run theaters, or to seats in the balcony or orchestra sections, or to time of day. From Martin, though, we get the amateur anthropologist's view of the bizarre practices of the natives, as he noted, first, that "the French go to the movies to rest." When Martin dropped into a theater to see a reissue of the British film *The White Shadows* (Graham Cutts, 1923), which was "preceded by a number of talking short subjects," the theater was only one-quarter full, and the audience "sat there reading newspapers and eating sandwiches." Apparently the lights remained on during the movies there, at least high enough to let viewers read, but at another theater on Martin's tour, the Gaumont, the ambience may have been much darker, as "half the audience appeared to be drowsing" and the "other half was making love on its own."[30]

Two years later, in April 1931, the *Digest* provided more information about when and how Paris viewers used theaters to make love and to rest, although here the source is perhaps no better than Martin, the amused tourist. In this case, the *Digest* cited a long-standing French satirical magazine, *Le Crapoiullot,* and a special issue on "Pictures of Paris." The view from *Le Crapouillot,* then, was probably both distanced and ironized, as the magazine complained about the "continuous performance" in theaters, "which open at nine in the morning and grind off reel after reel until two the next morning." *Le Crapouillot* then gives the sense of filmgoers less concerned about showtimes than with dipping into a theater when it was most convenient to them, as "spectators are just as likely to enter the theater at the middle or end of a picture as at the beginning." This casual viewer, though, had strong feelings about the movies being shown, and especially about film product from Hollywood, as the critic in *Le Crapouillot* wrote that "I have . . . had the satisfaction of seeing honest folk leave a boulevard cinema at midnight, and stop to dissuade, in loud and unmistakable terms, those in the waiting line that they would lose both their time and money seeing and listening to an imbecility" from the United States.[31]

Thus in one essay we have the mythic binary of the French filmgoer, the flâneur who goes to the cinema at the beginning, middle, or end of a program and the dedicated cinéaste who engages strangers in debate about movies. *Le Crapouillot* may not have been the most reliable source for information about film in Paris, given its emphasis on humor and satire, but there were other, perhaps more sober sources that indicate the potential for some extreme behavior by an audience. Also in 1931, the *New York Times* ran an Associated Press report and headlined it, somewhat incongruously, "Movie Riot and Wheat Price Linked."[32] When an unnamed theater on the Boulevard des Italiens showed a newsreel with information about a proposed increase in the price of wheat, "a riot of protest" ensued, and "several persons among the audience . . . made a concerted rush to the stage and tore down" the screen. The ongoing "uproar" forced the theater manager to "reimburse all patrons for the price of their seats" and temporarily close the theater.

That this constituted news indicates that it was at least somewhat out of the ordinary. But the wheat riot almost certainly did not take place at a cine club or at a special screening of an experimental film, in the manner of the famous, and famously violent, opening of Luis Buñuel and Salvador Dali's *L'âge d'or* (1930).[33] Viewers at those sites might be expected to react more impulsively to the avant-garde movies they saw. The Boulevard des Italiens bordered two major areas for Parisian commercial film culture, the second and ninth arrondissements, and several important movie theaters were on it.[34] The audiences reacting so violently to the newsreel that night were probably there to watch a first-run film or a film that had only just left first-run theaters. These were average fans, if indeed that term can ever be used to characterize any group of movie viewers, and so the riot, or at least the possibility of one, was likely one small point on a continuum of audience behavior in Paris in the 1930s.

There was much more to the *Times* coverage than just the wheat riot, making that newspaper stand out as the best source for data and opinion about film culture in the city. As part of the paper's extensive international reporting, particularly from urban centers around the world, the *Times* had its man in Paris, Herbert L. Matthews, who wrote regularly on the films there, the audiences who watched them, and the theaters where they saw them. A quarter century later, Matthews's liberal cosmopolitanism would lead him to Cuba and to an infatuation with the revolution lead by Fidel Castro, which he chronicled for an American audience.[35] In the 1930s, though, he was less the political leftist and much more the cultivated man about town in Paris, reporting on the arts scene and taking the movies very seriously.

Matthews, as well as some of his colleagues at the *Times*, took a special interest in the city's movie theaters. Reporting during late summer 1932, Matthews lamented that few new films were showing and that audiences were dwindling, in part because "Parisian theaters do not employ the water-cooling system which entices so many sweltering New Yorkers off the streets and into the gigantic ice-boxes of Broadway." Of course, air-conditioning was one of the important advances of movie theaters in the

United States in the post–World War I period, one that has not been given the attention of other technological innovations, such as the conversion to sound later in the decade, but that nevertheless marked a major difference between theaters in the United States and those in France.[36] Despite this American advantage, Matthews took pains to point out that "there are many cinemas here as modern, as large and as attractive as those along Broadway." He then mentioned the Paramount, in the ninth arrondissement, and approvingly wrote that it was "not nearly so pretentious as its namesake in New York," and also the Gaumont-Palace, "which was recently done over in modernistic style." Moreover, "there are film houses along the Champs-Elysées of a smaller, more intimate sort which yield to none, anywhere, in attractiveness and comfort."[37]

So Matthews provides us with the range of theaters in the more elegant neighborhoods and approves of a more modest style than one might find in theater architecture in New York. In next giving us some particular details of Parisian film culture, at least in the chic quarters, he more fully rounds out his comparison with the United States and finds American theaters wanting. Matthews reports that theaters in Paris have a fifteen-minute intermission between feature films on a double bill or between shorts and the main feature or the stage show and the film. And Parisians apparently put that intermission to good use, as did Matthews, the Prohibition-era journalist happily working in Europe. "There is one great convenience which Paris houses have, and the best of them in New York do not have," Matthews wrote, "and that is a bar—a real, old-fashioned bar where . . . the audience can go for refreshments that are indeed refreshments."[38] Thus in weighing the comforts of cool air and the comforts of a cool drink, Matthews preferred the latter and therefore favored the French theatrical model.

About six months later, in January 1933, Matthews began a report by writing about "an almost feverish activity in getting cinema theaters built," noting that "three were completed and opened within the last month, and several others are nearly ready for use." The buildings that marked this boom were "as fine as anything of the kind to be seen in New York." For the most part, and quite unlike many of the downtown urban theaters in the United States, the style of the new theaters in Paris leaned "toward small, exclusive, intimate edifices, with either no balconies or just a tiny one far in the back." Theater architects in Paris emphasized "comfort and roominess, with splendid bars for the intermission," and their style was markedly "modernist . . . even to the extent of being slightly freakish about it."[39]

The Raspail 216, named for its address in the fourteenth arrondissement, was one of those theaters, and it opened with Danish director Carl Theodor Dreyer's 1932 horror film *Vampyr*. Dreyer's movie is now widely considered an art film, more suited to the university or the museum, but this German–French coproduction was originally released commercially. Matthews provides us with an eyewitness account of the audience response to the film, a response that seems in keeping with the somewhat obscure narrative of *Vampyr.* Those viewers, sitting in the Raspail's "seats of white leather," were "either held . . . spellbound as in a long nightmare or else moved . . . to hysterical laughter."[40]

Other new theaters played more conventional films. Shortly after the Rex opened on the Boulevard Poissonière in the second arrondissement, it had great success with "that veteran comedian of the French stage, Max Dearly." The film was *L'Amour et la Veine* (Monty Banks, 1932), and it had been produced by the same man who built the theater, Jacques Haïk. Matthews showed much more interest in the theater than in the film, and he gave readers a sense of the Rex's appeal. "Outwardly it is a simple building in white stone," Matthews wrote, adding that "it is the inside that is unique." The theater seated four thousand "in an orchestra and two wide, sweeping balconies," and though this might have compared to the largest downtown theaters in the United States, the Rex catered specifically to Continental sensibilities. "What Europeans consider to be more suitable to their tastes," Matthews said, "the carpets, decorations, stairways, doors and the like, are not striking or rich or colorful, but simple and comfortable, and even elegant." The ceiling was especially so, as it was "made into a representation of the heavens at night—a Summer's night on the Riviera." All of this fell under the authority of an American manager, Francis Mangan, apparently brought in from the United States to add some New York–style showmanship to Haïk's palace. The Thirty-six Rex Mangan Stars performed there as part of the stage show, as did sixteen rhythm dancers "doing their mechanically perfect cavorting."[41]

From Matthews and other *Times* reporters from the early 1930s, we learn, then, about an expansion in theater construction in Paris during the period that marked the conversion to sound cinema. Paris entrepreneurs emphasized small theaters, perhaps out of economic necessity or perhaps because of the city's spatial constraints, but the occasional new film palace still appeared on the grand boulevards. We can learn just how big these palaces were, from the four thousand seats of the Rex to the twenty-five hundred of the Marignan, which opened on the Champs-Elysées in 1933.[42] According to the *Times,* this boom in building theaters brought twenty-three new movie houses to Paris between 1930 and 1932 and seven to the suburbs just outside the city.[43]

Matthews also recorded responses to films, although here his remarks may be compromised by his continuing insistence on fully nationalist film preferences, with French—and primarily Parisian—audiences always apparently looking for the "truly French" motion picture.[44] Despite this, Matthews noted that Parisians particularly liked many early-1930s Hollywood films, all dubbed into French, such as *Frankenstein, Dr. Jekyll and Mr. Hyde* (Rouben Mamoulian, 1932), *The Crowd Roars* (Howard Hawks, 1932), with James Cagney, as well as Lubitsch's *The Man I Killed,* Frank Capra's aviation epic *Dirigible* (1931), Greta Garbo in *Mata Hari* (George Fitzmaurice, 1931), and three Marlene Dietrich films directed by Josef von Sternberg: *Shanghai Express* (1932), *Dishonored* (1931), and *Morocco* (1930). Among subtitled films, two gangster movies, *Scarface* (Howard Hawks, 1932) and *Public Enemy* (William Wellman, 1931), as well as the Eddie Cantor film *Palmy Days* (Edward Sutherland, 1931), Harold Lloyd's *Movie Crazy,* and two literary adaptations, *Arrowsmith* (John Ford,

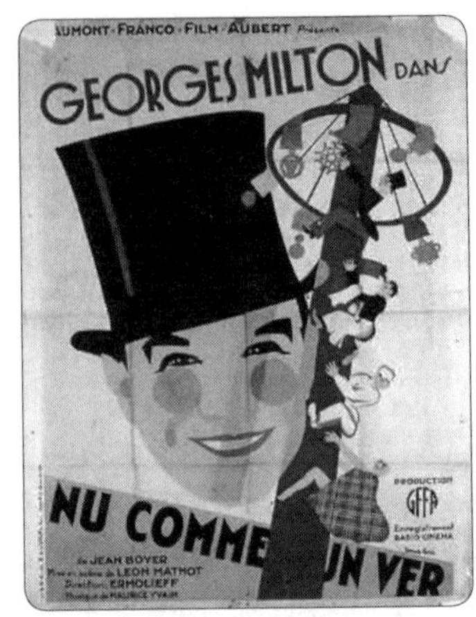

Georges Milton in *Nu comme un ver,* which attracted large crowds to the Rex Theater.

1931) and *Murders in the Rue Morgue* (Robert Florey, 1932), were particularly successful. Cross-cultural incomprehension, however, seemed to make a Hollywood adaptation of Maugham's *Rain* (Lewis Milestone, 1932), with Joan Crawford, a failure among Parisian fans, who were also left cold by Mae West's films. These same moviegoers loved the latest film with French star Georges Milton, *Nu comme un ver* (Léon Mathot, 1933), even though it would be safe to assume that "no American would enjoy" this French picture.[45]

POUR VOUS AND "LES FILMS QUI PASSENT"

Milton's movie brings us back to our filmgoer in the ninth arrondissement, on the Boulevard des Capucines, and also back to the French source, *Pour Vous*. That tabloid reports that *Nu comme un ver* had opened at the Rex, the theater that Matthews had so detailed, on September 8, 1933, and, if our film enthusiast in the ninth arrondissement had wanted to see it then, the film was playing just a few blocks away in the second, on the Boulevard Poissonière.[46] Other films playing that week in this exclusive district included two Marlene Dietrich films, *The Blue Angel* and *Song of Songs* (Rouben Mamoulian, 1933). *No Other Woman* (J. Walter Ruben, 1933), with Irene Dunne, was showing there as well, at the Ciné-Opèra, and yet another American film, *Madame Butterfly* (Marion Gering, 1932), played at the Omnia-Pathé. *Nu comme un ver* was not the only French film playing in the area—Pierre Colombier's *Theodore et Cie* (1933), for instance, was showing at the Marivaux-Pathé.[47]

    After one week, and despite Matthews's assertion of the film's popularity, *Nu *comme un ver* seems to have disappeared from Paris theaters, with this one-week open-ing run not unusual among films in the city but not the rule either.[48] *No Other Woman* remained at the Ciné-Opèra, and *The Blue Angel* was in the midst of a sensational showing at the Corso-Opéra. The film that helped make Dietrich an international star had opened there at least some months before and would not leave the theater until November (it is difficult to tell whether this was a subsequent run for Sternberg's film or a continuation of its first run). By the week of October 6, *Nu comme un ver* had returned to theaters across the city, in fashionable areas and also farther out toward the periphery, in the sixth, eleventh, fifteenth, and seventeenth arrondissements, and was also showing in four theaters in the twentieth. One week later, the run had contracted, and the film showed only in the fourteenth, seventeenth (in a different theater from the week before), and eighteenth, and by October 20, the film had once again fallen out of circulation.[49]

The example of just one film lets us pose a series of general questions about the film culture of Paris during the early 1930s. Were there many other films that moved through the city in the same way as *Nu comme un ver*? How common was it for a single film to play in more than one theater in the same neighborhood? Indeed, what, if any, were the predictable distribution and exhibition patterns across the city? What were the connections between films and the theaters and neighborhoods in which they played? What was the place of a film like *Nu comme un ver* in a city full of films from other coun-tries, and how might the variety of films there affect our notions not just of the cinema in Paris but of French cinema and of national cinemas more broadly?

Pour Vous as well as other French sources allow us to consider these issues. As one would expect, the daily journalism from Paris gives us a great deal of data about the movies there, and a few examples from one of the most famous and available newspapers from the period, *Le Figaro,* serve as useful evidence. The paper always ran brief reviews of films and stories about them when they first appeared in the city. On October 25, 1931, for instance, filmgoers learned that the latest Janet Gaynor film from Hollywood, *Daddy Long Legs* (Alfred Santell, 1931), had just opened at the Edouard VII in the seventh arrondissement and that Jean Renoir's "audacious" new film, *La Chienne* (1931), was bound to be "greatly discussed as well as at least occasionally condemned."[50]

Films less well known to us also opened that week: *Le Chanteur inconnu* (Vik-tor Tourjanksy, 1931), for example, as well as *Le Petit Ecart* (Henri Chomette, 1931). The newspaper marked each of these films "P" for *parlant,* or "talking," probably indicating that silent films were still at least somewhat common in Paris in 1931, both as revivals and as silent versions of sound productions.[51] Photos of the stars of the week often ac-companied the brief reviews, in this case one of Gaynor from her film and also the French actress Madeline Renaud from *Serments* (Henri Fescourt, 1931). Advertisements for movies hint at the range of important films in the city and indeed in any single theater. On October 31, 1931, readers saw an illustration of an airplane that had crashed nose first to the ground and learned that Frank Capra's *Dirigible,* dubbed into French, would begin its exclusive run at the Marigny the following Tuesday, replacing the far more intimate—and nontalking—Charles Chaplin film *City Lights* (1931).[52] These ads and this information about movies appeared on an entertainment page, with a crossword puzzle and news about concerts, music hall performances, circuses, sporting events, and organization meetings (Le Club féminin d'aviation in the October 31, 1931, *Le Figaro,* next to the advertisement for Capra's film). But *Le Figaro* provided theatrical listings only sparsely, with schedules given for just a few venues for seeing films because of the paper's mission of providing news and information for all of France.

During the week in October that began this essay, *Pour Vous* reported that all those films in Paris numbered about 150 among the 200 or so theaters in the city. The movies were mostly feature length, but there were also shorts and documentaries, and six of the theaters showed only newsreels.[53] I have been able to identify about 110 of the films playing that week, with forty-eight of them coming from French film companies. Hollywood accounted for thirty-four of the films, while at least nine were produced in French, and either in France or in Hollywood, by American film studios (Paramount mostly, but also Warner Bros. and Universal).

Indeed, assigning national origins to films from the period can be troubling, given the practice at the time of companies from Germany, Great Britain, and the United States to produce multiple-language versions of movies or original films in French and also the possibility of multinational productions. *The Private Life of Henry VIII* (Alexander Korda, 1933), a prominent British film, was playing in Paris at the time, but there were also three British films that had been produced in French and with French actors. Audiences also had the chance to see at least one Italian–French coproduction, a Spanish–French film, and a French–Belgian coproduction.[54] There were three German films in Paris that week, although there were a number of films that were either German films made in French for a French audience or Franco-German coproductions. Showing that week in Paris, *L'Etoile de Valencia* (1933) typified this blending of national styles, workers, and economies. Directed by French filmmaker Serge de Poligny, *L'Etoile* starred French leading man Jean Gabin and German actress Brigitte Helm (famous for her appearance as Maria in *Metropolis* [Fritz Lang, 1927]) and was produced by UFA, the German studio. The version of *Dr. Mabuse* that Parisian audiences saw that week was almost certainly the fully French one, directed by Fritz Lang but with the assistance of French filmmaker René Sti and with a mostly French cast.[55]

If we concentrate on just the week of October 13, we get no sense of the movement of films across Paris and of the various patterns of film distribution and exhibition in the city. Examining the week before and the week after helps show these patterns and the varying possibilities for audiences to attend movies at first-run theaters and in the neighborhoods. Beginning with the larger, first-run film theaters, a standard emerges based, apparently (and naturally enough), on audience interest. In the grand theaters in the second arrondissement, each new film played for at least a week, in the manner of *Nu comme un ver.* At the Rex on the Boulevard Poissonière, audiences could see the just-opened American film *Zoo in Budapest* (Rowland V. Lee, 1933)

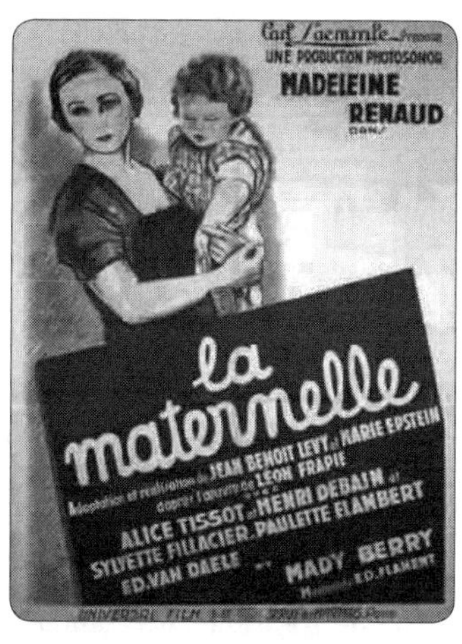

Poster for *La Maternelle,* the film that drew audiences to the Cinèac week after week in 1933.

the week of October 6 and then two new French films: *Les Ailes brisées* (André Berthomieu, 1933) the following week and *L'Abbé Constantin* (Jean-Paul Paulin, 1933) the week after that.[56] At the Cinèac, nearby on the Boulevard des Italiens, Jean Benoît-Lévy and Marie Epstein's *La Maternelle* (1933) drew large crowds continually and so showed there for all three weeks and more (as did two Dietrich films, *The Blue Angel* at the Corse-Opèra and *Song of Songs* at Les Miracles).

The same pattern persisted in other major venues. In the eighth arrondissement, Capra's *Platinum Blonde* (1931) as well as another American film, *Jennie Gerhardt* (Marion Gering, 1933), showed at the same theaters for the same three-week period. But the Pepenière, which seems to have shown subsequent-run as well as first-run films, switched from *Conduisez-moi, Madame* (Herbert Selpin, 1932) to *Les Deux "Monsieur" de Madame* (Jacquin and Pallu, 1933) to *The Testament of Dr. Mabuse.* So far, then, the system in France seems fully as rational as that in the United States, which has been examined so extensively during the last two decades.[57] The most important theaters showed films, typically but not always in their first run, for one week, unless audience demand remained high, in which case, the theater held options for subsequent weeks. In keeping with an American model, we might expect, then, to see a system of "zones" and "clearances," in which a film would be shown exclusively at one theater and nowhere else within a zone that might encompass the entire city and then disappear for a week or more—the clearance—before opening at another venue.

A closer look at exhibition practices reveals other possibilities. *La Maternelle,* as well as showing in the second, also played for that three-week period in theaters in the sixth and ninth arrondissements, in the latter case in two theaters just a healthy but not uncomfortable walk away from each other, up the Avenue de l'Opéra to the rue d'Athènes.[58] A Jean Epstein film, *L'Homme à l'Hispano* (1933), in wide release, played at two theaters each in the fifth and thirteenth arrondissements during the week of October 13 as well as at other theaters throughout the city. In fact, it was not uncommon for two theaters in the same neighborhood to play the same film; in just one other example, on October 6, three theaters in the eleventh arrondissement exhibited the American film *I Am a Fugitive from a Chain Gang*. From week to week, films might also move from one theater to another within a neighborhood. In the thirteenth arrondissement, *Moi et l'Impératrice* (Hollaender and Martin, 1933), a film produced in French by UFA and starring Charles Boyer, moved from the Cinèma des Bosquets, where it played on October 13, to the Edens des Gobelins for the week of October 20, while during the same period, *Rumba* shifted from the Casino de Grenelle to the Splendide-Cinèma just a few blocks away in the fifteenth arrondissement.

KING KONG IN PARIS

Two films with overlapping theatrical engagements in Paris demonstrate the extremes of film exhibition there. As noted earlier, the Marivaux-Pathé in the second arrondissement hosted the Paris opening of *King Kong* on September 15, 1933. When the film first appeared, in a dubbed version, *Pour Vous* gave it only a lukewarm review, calling it more of a "photographic curiosity" because of its famous stop-motion animation than a film that might inspire "fear" or any other emotion.[59] But the film was a popular one in Paris and stayed exclusively at the Marivaux for almost two months, a lengthy, although not unprecedented, first run. *King Kong* had replaced *Théodore et Cie,* a film much less well known to us now than *Kong* but that starred the great French performer Raimu and also played exclusively at the theater for about three months. After leaving the Marivaux in early November, *King Kong* did not appear on any Parisian screen at least until the beginning of 1934, a first run that indicates that films might indeed have a "clearance" period in Paris before playing in the neighborhoods and that almost certainly was coordinated, at least in part, by RKO, the film's American production company.

Another film, without the caché of *King Kong* but significant nonetheless, presents a different model. *Toto* premiered in Paris in three theaters on October 6. Jacques Tourneur directed the film, and although this was an early motion picture for him, and well before the distinguished films noirs and horror movies he made in Hollywood, Tourneur certainly would have been known at the time as the son of one of Europe's more distinguished filmmakers; Maurice Tourneur had been directing movies in France and the United States since before World War I. The star of *Toto,* Albert Préjean, began in films in the early 1920s and was well known for his roles in such René Clair films as *Paris qui dort* (1925) and *Un chapeau de paille d'italie* (1928). Pathé-Natan, one of France's leading film studios, had produced *Toto,* and so this was, indeed, an important film for French audiences, if not a release on the same level as *King Kong* or *The Blue Angel* or *La Maternelle.*

Possibly because of this, the film seems to have opened in the neighborhoods rather than in the grand movie palaces. It initially played near the southeastern border of the city in the sixteenth arrondissement and in two theaters on the northeastern edge of the seventeenth, both of which paired *Toto* with a short subject by Maurice Tourneur, *Lidoire* (1933), another Pathé movie, as if trying to capitalize on the familial connection between the filmmakers. The film lasted only one week in those theaters, but on October 13, *Toto* opened in fourteen others. Ten of those venues were bunched very close together around the Montmartre and Pigalle sections of the city, more or less outlying areas in the hierarchy of Parisian cinemas, despite the previously mentioned and densely packed number of theaters there. *Toto* continued moving throughout the city the following week. The film still seems to have been playing at fourteen theaters, but all of them different from the week before, and by this time, *Toto* had made it to the interior of the city, in theaters in the third and fifth arrondissements, although it still remained, typically, on the geographical edges of Paris.

The system that brought *King Kong* to Parisian audiences looks familiar to anyone with knowledge of the fully rationalized Hollywood mode of distribution and exhibition of the period. The options for seeing *Toto,* however—almost three dozen different venues in a three-week period—look random and ill advised. In fact, seeing how *Toto* moved through the city, and noting the differences between that film and *King Kong,* the temptation is to assume that Parisian practices simply exemplified the legendary chaos and economic instability of the French film industry of the 1930s.[60]

But there may be some other possibilities. In just one practical example, and as Matthews noted in one of his *New York Times* dispatches, cited earlier, Parisian theaters seem to have been smaller than their American counterparts, and if this was the case, then it probably made sense to show a film in more than one theater in the same or neighboring arrondissement to attract a wide audience. Other ways of understanding Parisian exhibition raise significant historiographic issues, however, and make us reconsider our understanding of the relationships between film culture and the nation, on one hand, and the neighborhood, on the other.

Pour Vous itself highlights these issues. The tabloid, of course, had a national circulation and perhaps even beyond, to other French-speaking countries and regions, and typically emphasized French films and film culture. But with its concentration on Paris, *Pour Vous* announced that French and Parisian film cultures were identical. In extending the reach of that culture to other parts of France, Europe, and the world, the periodical showed as well just how differently French cinema might be understood, and French film culture experienced, in different places. That section in so many of the issues, "On the Screens in the Four Corners of France," with its articles on different French cities as well as on such French-language European areas as the Savoy and such North African locations as Oran and Morocco, notes the different films playing in different regions, the ways in which variations in weather might bring people to theaters or keep them away, or the new theaters being built.

This section asserts the reach of a French national film culture even to the colonies (and those colonies themselves constituting a "corner of France"), while also indicating the differences in available films, or theater architecture, or the perceptions of varied audience desires and preferences from region to region.[61] Readers learned, for example, that viewers in Mostaganem, in Oran, were particularly taken by the American film about Africa, *Trader Horn* (W. S. Van Dyke, 1931), because they so enjoyed movies about "mysterious voyages" *(voyages inconnus)*; that audiences in Nîmes, in France, should not be "underestimated" *(sous-estimer)*, presumably by Parisians, and that they would indeed fully appreciate the great German film *Maedchen in Uniform* (Leontine Sagan, 1931); and that film fans in Le Mans were staying away from theaters, probably because exhibitors there depended too much on programs put together by the large movie firms. This section also provided information about international distribution practices, as readers learned that Renoir's *La Chienne* was only just appearing in Morocco in July 1932, after having opened in France in fall 1931.[62]

Thus France's control of cinema in the colonies did not necessarily mean that colonials experienced French films and French film culture in the same manner as Parisians. Even in terms of France alone, we need to analyze much more fully the idea of local film cultures rather than a national one, with such an analysis providing a different understanding of the place of the city in film history. With some of the notable exceptions mentioned earlier—work by Kathryn Fuller-Seeley, for instance, and Gregory Waller—film historiography, as practiced in the United States and Great Britain, and at least since the early 1990s, has concentrated on the links between cinema and cities and, in the words of Leo Charney and Vanessa Schwartz, has viewed late-nineteenth- and early-twentieth-century "metropolitan urban culture [as] leading to new forms of entertainment and leisure activity."[63] The cinema has emerged as the form par excellence of these activities, and through readings of Simmel, Benjamin, Kracauer, and others, modern scholars have made Baron Haussmann's revamped Paris of the late-nineteenth and early-twentieth centuries one of the models of this new urban experience, which itself led to new forms of national culture. But a study of cinema in Paris and also other cities in France during the early 1930s shows the need to reconfigure this assessment. As we can see from some of the discussions in *Pour Vous* of Paris, Nîmes, and Le Mans or of Marseille, Lille, and Cherbourg, as well as other locations, there were marked differences, both real and imagined, between metropolitan areas that at first glance seem unproblematically French.

Cities and other locations, moreover, produced multiple film cultures. In Paris, this meant not only the possibility of different audiences for commercial and avant-garde films but also varied expectations, desires, and pleasures from neighborhood to neighborhood. Exhibition patterns in Paris, as in any city, indicate different ways of viewing films within the city itself, from the extravagant floor shows of the first-run theaters to the more intimate pleasures of neighborhood venues. Moreover, and rather than signifying the chaos of the French film industry, the seemingly random exhibition of *Toto* in 1933, concentrated week after week in different theaters around Montmartre and Pigalle, seems to indicate that film preferences can be isolated to neighborhoods rather than broad metropolitan areas and so demonstrates the geometric precision of film distribution throughout the city, taking into consideration, as it did, microlevels of audience desire.

If this was the case, if we return to our filmgoer on the Boulevard des Capucines, it becomes possible that this movie enthusiast would have stayed right there, in that neighborhood on the southern edge of the ninth arrondissement, rather than venturing to see a movie like *Toto* playing just due north in the eighteenth. If we then leave the neighborhoods and return to the issues of the global and the regional that helped introduce this essay, the example of Paris and the possibilities for seeing films there provide new options for considering national cinema. In the manner of Ruth Vasey, Andrew Higson, and others, we of course need to think of the nation in internationalist terms. As just one example, the French cinema of the period had significant impact in all the country's colonies, while also reaching areas of less influence such as the United States. But audiences also experienced that cinema in particular ways, depending on location, and movie fans may well have understood audiences even in nearby cities and towns as quite different from each other. The brief example from *Pour Vous* about cinephiles in Nîmes seems to indicate this and so makes the idea of a cohesive "French" cinema from the period practically impossible.

We can only make these assessments of the international, the national, and the local if we shift our methodological focus and study materials in addition to, or other than, the films themselves. In the case of Paris, the French film journalism from the 1930s provides us with invaluable data about filmgoing there: the locations of theaters, the times of shows, and the flow of movies across the city. The scope of film-related journalism in France at the time, so often centering on Paris, informs us of the ways in which many of the film viewers in that city had their understanding of movies, movie stars, and gossip, for instance, mediated by the periodicals they read. *Pour Vous,* along with other newspapers and magazines, specialty or otherwise, gave audiences the information they needed for seeing films and also many of the terms for understanding and enjoying them.

These materials make the movie theater, and the progress of movies through the city, central to any consideration of the period's film history. Our filmgoer in the ninth arrondissement might plan a day or week or month around the movies and their movement from theater to theater, choosing whether to stay in the neighborhood or venture out, to see *King Kong* now or much later, to watch *The Blue Angel* for the third or fourth time, or to enjoy or avoid the more fleeting and very local pleasures of *Toto.* The listings of the theaters and their programs in *Pour Vous* give us the beginnings of both a geography and sociology of film viewing in Paris, allowing us to analyze many of the relations of spectators to the movies they saw, the conditions in which they saw them, and when and where they were able to watch films. "Les films qui passent" itself evokes movement and flow, from the verb *passer,* and the name of the tabloid made this movement of films specifically "for you," the film viewer. For the modern film scholar, *Pour Vous* and the rest of the archive of primary materials considered here let us chart some of the relations of the city to the nation and the world and begin to determine the multiple film cultures that produced the Parisian cinema of the 1930s.

NOTES

I am indebted to Caren Kaplan for her careful reading of many drafts of this article. I also would like to thank the anonymous readers of *The Moving Image* for their valuable suggestions.

1. "Voici les films qui passent à Paris," *Pour Vous*, no. 256 (October 12, 1933): 15 (hereinafter *PV*).

2. Richard Abel, *The Ciné Goes to Town: French Cinema 1896–1914* (Berkeley: University of California Press, 1994), 9–58; Abel, *French Cinema: The First Wave, 1915–1929* (Princeton, NJ: Princeton University Press, 1984), 251–60; Christophe Gauthier, *La passion du cinéma: Cinéphiles, ciné-clubs et salles specialisées à Paris de 1920 à 1929* (Paris: Association française de recherche sur l'Histoire du cinéma, 1999).

3. Jean-Jacques Meusy, *Paris-Palaces: ou le temps des cinémas (1894–1918)* (Paris: CNRS Éditions, 1995).

4. For a new historiography of Parisian culture, including cinema, during the 1930s, see Dudley Andrew and Steven Ungar, *Popular Front Paris and the Poetics of Culture* (Cambridge, MA: Belknap Press of Harvard University Press, 2008).

5. See, e.g., Ben Singer, *Melodrama and Modernity: Early Sensational Cinema and Its Contexts* (New York: Columbia University Press, 2001), and Leo Charney and Vanessa R. Schwartz, eds., *Cinema and the Invention of Modern Life* (Berkeley: University of California Press, 1996). For a critique of the idea of modernity being synonymous with the urban, see Kathryn H. Fuller, *At the Picture Show: Small-town Audiences and the Creation of Movie Fan Culture* (Washington, DC: Smithsonian Institution Press, 1996).

6. For an examination of the shift in film studies from an emphasis on texts to an interest in audiences, see my introduction, "The History of Film History," in *Looking Past the Screen: Case Studies in American Film History and Method*, ed. Jon Lewis and Eric Smoodin, 1–33 (Durham, NC: Duke University Press, 2007). See also Kathy Fuller-Seeley, "Introduction: Spectatorship in Popular Film and Television," *Journal of Popular Film and Television* 29, no. 3 (2001): 98–99. Annette Kuhn writes of the spectator "constructed by the film text" in her book *Dreaming of Fred and Ginger: Cinema and Cultural Memory* (New York: New York University Press, 2002), 3–4.

7. Christian-Marc Bosséno, "La place du spectateur," *Vingtième Siècle: Revue d'histoire* 46 (April–June 1995): 143–54. See p. 143 for the shift from the "screen" to the "theater" and p. 144 for the list of questions: "Qui va au cinéma et pourquoi? Comment et dans quelles conditions techniques et matérielles voit-on les films? Quelles sont les conditions et les modalités de reception des oeuvres? Á quel moment le public cesse-t-il d' 'aller qu cinéma' (pour la nouveauté de l'expérience ou le seul plaisir, ou tout simplement parce que le cinéma est un lieu de sociabilité de première importance durant plusieurs décennies) pour 'voir des films' (j'entends des films choisis, selon

des critères de goût qui restent à déterminer, socialement et esthétique)? Où passé la frontière entre celui qui 'va au cinéma' (le *cinemagoer,* comme dissent les Anglo-Saxons) et celui pour qui la vision d'un film est une expérience artistique et intellectuelle, ou même, dans le cas des 'cinéphiles' les plus enragés, un mode de vie et une foi? De quand date la mort du 'grand public' et la naissance de micro-audiences spécialisées?"

8. Emilie Altenloh, "A Sociology of the Cinema: The Audience" (1914), trans. Kathleen Cross, *Screen* 42, no. 3 (2001): 249–93; Kathryn H. Fuller-Seeley, ed., *Hollywood in the Neighborhood: Historical Case Studies of Local Moviegoing* (Berkeley: University of California Press, 2008); Gregory Waller, *Main Street Amusements: Movies and Commercial Entertainment in a Southern City, 1896–1930* (Washington, DC: Smithsonian Institution Press, 1995); Lee Grieveson, *Policing Chicago: Movies and Censorship in Early-Twentieth-Century America* (Berkeley: University of California Press, 2004); Ben Singer, "Manhattan Nickelodeons: New Data on Audiences and Exhibitors," *Cinema Journal* 34, no. 2 (2001): 5–35.

9. The three case studies come from Melvyn Stokes and Richard Maltby, eds., *American Movie Audiences: From the Turn of the Century to the Early Sound Era* (London: BFI, 1999). See Judith Thissen, "Jewish Immigrant Audiences in New York City, 1905–14," in ibid., 15–28; Leslie Midkiff DeBauche, "Reminiscences of the Past, Conditions of the Present: At the Movies in Milwaukee in 1918," in ibid., 129–39; and Gregory Waller, "Hillbilly Music and Will Rogers: Small-town Picture Shows in the 1930s," in ibid., 164–79.

10. There is some scattered evidence about "average" movie audiences in Paris. The most important comes from 1947, and from a corporate source. The postwar incarnation of the Gaumont corporation, the Sociètè Nouvelle des Etablissements Gaumont, commissioned a study on the audiences that attended the company's most important Paris theater, the Gaumont-Palace. The result, one of the first in France based on modern polling methods, documented when audiences went to the movies, whether they entered the theater after programs had already begun, whether they typically liked Gaumont films, what they were willing to pay to go to the movies, and a great deal of other information. See "Etude du comportement des specateurs du Gaumont réalisée en 1948," *Les Cahiers de la Cinémathèque* 63/64 (December 1995): 143–49.

11. Renaud Chaplain, "Les exploitants des salles de cinéma lyonnaise: Des origins à la seconde guerre mondiale," *Vingtième Siècle: Revue d'histoire* 79 (July–September 2003): 19–35; Pierre and Jeanne Berneau, *Le spectacle cinématographique á Limoges de 1896 á 1945: Cinquante ans de culture populairie* (Paris: Association française de recherché sur l'Histoire du cinéma, 1992). See also Jean A. Gili's preface to the volume (7–13), in which he cites studies of such places as Marseilles, Toulon, and Nice; Sylvie Rab, "Le cinéma dans l'entre-deux-guerres: une politique culturelle municipale impossible? L'exemple de Suresnes," *Le Mouvement social* 184 (July–September 1998): 75–98.

12. For my discussion of new approaches to national cinema, see my essay "American Madness," in *America First: Naming the Nation in US Film*, ed.

Mandy Merck, 65–82 (London: Routledge, 2007). For a recent and significant rethinking of national cinema, and particularly in terms of internationalizing our notion of the term, see Andrew Higson, *Waving the Flag: Constructing a National Cinema in Britain* (Oxford: Oxford University Press, 1995), and Ruth Vasey, *The World According to Hollywood, 1918–1939* (Madison: University of Wisconsin Press, 1997).

13. Michel de Certeau, "Walking in the City," in *The Cultural Studies Reader*, ed. Simon During, 151–60 (London: Routledge, 1993). The "rhetoric of walking" appears on p. 158.

14. Theodore Reff, "Manet and the Paris of Haussmann and Baudelaire," in *Visions of the Modern City: Essays in History, Art, and Literature*, ed. William Sharpe and Leonard Wallock, 135–67 (Baltimore: Johns Hopkins University Press, 1987); Deborah Epstein Nord, "The City as Theater: From Georgian to Early Victorian London," *Victorian Studies* 31, no. 2 (1988): 159–88.

15. Indeed the flâneur has typically been figured as a man. For a critique of the gender politics of the use of this figure, see Janet Wolff, "The Invisible Flâneuse: Women and the Literatures of Modernity," *Theory, Culture, and Society* 2, no. 3 (1985): 37–46. See also Mary Ryan, *Women in Public: Between Banners and Ballots, 1825–1880* (Baltimore: Johns Hopkins University Press, 1992).

16. See, e.g., Colin Crisp, *The Classic French Cinema: 1930–1960* (Bloomington: Indiana University Press, 1997), and Alan Williams, *Republic of Images: A History of French Filmmaking* (Cambridge, MA: Harvard University Press, 1992).

17. The film listing always appeared on p. 15 of the 16-page tabloid.

18. For a discussion of film journalism in France between the late teens and early 1930s, see Crisp, *Classic French Cinema*, 216–22. Crisp discusses the founding of *Pour Vous*, and Bailby's interest in cinema, on p. 220. Abel, *French Cinema*, also examines film journalism from about the same period on pp. 245–50.

19. E.g., *PV*, no. 190, from July 7, 1932, 14, listed such locations as Reims, Versailles, Sète, Le Mans, Nancy, and Nîmes as well as Oran and Morocco.

20. Henri Langlois, "The Cinémthèque Française," *Hollywood Quarterly* 2, no. 2 (1947): 207–9.

21. Crisp, *Classic French Cinema*, 231, discusses the calls in *Pour Vous* for a cinémathèque. The piece by Escoubé appeared in the March 31, 1932, issue, Frank's on June 3, 1932.

22. For an analysis of the demise of Gaumont and Pathé, see Crisp, *Classic French Cinema*, 31–36. For an examination of the impact of the Popular Front on French cinema, see Andrew and Ungar, *Popular Front Paris*.

23. In 1931, the population of the eighteenth arrondissement was around 289,000, whereas the first had only 42,000 inhabitants. The fifth, sixth, and ninth had 118,000, 100,000, and 103,000, respectively. See "Paris Arrondissements: Post 1860 Population and Population Density," *Demographia*, http://www.demographia.com/db-paris-arr1999.htm. For work on relations between urban population densities and movie theaters, although in an American context, see Singer, "Manhattan Nickelodeons." For work on city population, theaters, seating capacities, and film attendance, all in a British context, see John Sedgwick, "Cinemagoing in Portsmouth during the 1930s," *Cinema Journal* 41, no. 1 (2006): 52–84.

24. *PV*, no. 256, October 12, 1933, 15.

25. For a discussion of the development of multiple-film programs in France, see Crisp, *Classic French Cinema*, 15–17. Just as in the United States, these programs were not uncontroversial. Many film distributors and producers argued against them and also argued against film screenings that began after midnight. There were various injunctions passed in France against multiple film programs and early-morning screenings in the 1930s, but none was ever implemented. See Crisp, *Classic French Cinema*, 17.

26. *PV*, no. 256, October 12, 1933, 15; no. 255, October 5, 1933, 15.

27. *PV*, no. 256, October 12, 1933, 15; no. 257, October 19, 1933, 15.

28. *Igloo* played at the Clichy-Legendre in the seventeenth arrondissement, with the feature film *L'Homme à l'Hispano*, while *The Music Box*, called *Livreur, sachez livrez* in France, showed at the Palermo-Cinèma in the eleventh arrondissement, with *Rumba.*

29. "Why Paris Goes to the Movies," *Literary Digest*, March 9, 1929, 21–22.

30. Ibid., 21.

31. "Paris Raps Our Movie Methods," *Literary Digest*, April 11, 1931, 17.

32. *New York Times*, "Movie Riot and Wheat Price Linked," January 19, 1931, 11 (hereinafter *NYT*).

33. *L'âge d'or* first showed at Studio 28 on the rue de Tholozé in the eighteenth arrondissement. The same theater also screened conventional commercial films. For a discussion of the violence at the opening of *L'âge d'or*, see Georges Sadoul, *Dictionnaire des Films* (Paris: Editions du Seuil, 1976), 9: "After the opening screenings at Studio 28, fascist groups ransacked the theatre while yelling 'Death to Jews.'" ("après les premières représentations au Studio 28 des organizations fascists saccagèrent la salle au cris de 'Mort aux Juifs'").

34. During the 1930s, theaters on the Boulevard des Italiens, which runs through two Parisian districts, included the Cinèac, in the second arrondissement, and the Aubert-Palace and the Cameo, in the ninth. All typically played first-run films.

35. For an examination of Matthews's career as well as his experiences reporting on Castro, see Anthony DePalma, *The Man Who Invented Fidel: Castro, Cuba, and Herbert Matthews of the New York Times* (New York: Public Affairs, 2007).

36. Douglas Gomery, one of the few film historians to discuss air-conditioning, writes that "Balaban & Katz's Central Park Theater, opened in 1917, was the first mechanically air cooled theater in the world," and then further examines the Balaban and Katz theater chain's efforts to bring the technology to other sites. See Gomery, *Shared Pleasures: A History of Movie Presentation in the United States* (Madison: University of Wisconsin Press, 1992), 53–54.

37. Herbert L. Matthews, "The Screen in Paris," *NYT*, September 18, 1932, X4.

38. Ibid.

39. Herbert L. Matthews, "Paris Views New Films and Theatres," *NYT*, January 15, 1933, X4.

40. Ibid.

41. Herbert L. Matthews, "A Glimpse at the Cinema of Paris," *NYT*, April 2, 1933, X4.

42. Matthews wrote about the Marignan in "The Cinema in Paris," *NYT*, June 11, 1933, X2. The Marignan was "less pretentious than the Rex, but its simplicity and comfort make it quite as attractive." The Gaumont-Palace, in the eighteenth arrondissement, was even larger than the Rex, with around six thousand seats.

43. *NYT*, "More Theatres in Paris," April 23, 1933, E3. This report noted increases in all forms of Parisian theatrical venues, from 509 in 1930 to 641 in 1932. In addition, 1932 "saw 12 street fairs in Paris, and 156 in the suburbs," while "ten gambling halls opened," and the city hosted "two hundred and thirty-seven open air concerts."

44. For a discussion of the French preference for French films, see, e.g., Herbert L. Matthews, "Paris Screen Notes," *NYT*, May 1, 1932, X4.

45. Herbert L. Matthews, "The Cinema in Paris: To Dub or Not to Dub Films—Successful Original American Pictures," *NYT*, June 4, 1933, X2.

46. *PV*, no. 251, September 7, 1933, 15.

47. "Voici les films qui passent á Paris," *PV*, no. 251, September 7, 1933, 15.

48. *PV*, no. 252, September 14, 1933, 15.

49. My listings from *Pour Vous* begin on June 9, 1933, when *The Blue Angel* was already playing at the Corso-Opèra. "Voici les films qui passent á Paris," *PV*, no. 238, June 9, 1933, 15. On November 24, 1933, the film finally was replaced by *Maedchen in Uniform*, the Leontine Sagan film that also enjoyed a long run at the Corso. "Voici les films qui passent á Paris," *PV*, no. 262, November 23, 1933, 15.

50. "Les Présentations," *Le Figaro*, October 25, 1931, 8. The reviewer called *La Chienne* "an audacious film that people will talk about a great deal, that will be debated constantly and occasionally condemned" ("un film audacieux dont on parlera beacoup, qui sera discuté toujours, condamné parfois").

51. Charles O'Brien, *Cinema's Conversion to Sound: Technology and Film Style in France and the U.S.* (Bloomington: Indiana University Press, 2005), 68–89, discusses the sound categories of films in France at this time. Besides *film parlant*, there was also *film sonore*, that is, the film that "had been shot silent and then supplemented with a separately recorded soundtrack."

52. *Le Figaro*, October 31, 1931, 9. The advertisement referred to Capra's film as the "grand film Américan parlant français."

53. In the second arrondissement, the Cinèphone and the Cinèac showed only newsreels, with the latter presenting only those made by Fox, the American film company. In the ninth, the newsreel theaters were the Cinè-Actualités and the Cinè-Paris-Midi. The Pathé-Journal showed Pathé newsreels in the tenth, and the Cinè-Paris-Soir, probably associated with the newspaper *Paris-Soir*, showed newsreels in the eleventh

54. The Italian–French coproduction was *Je vous aimerai toujours* (1933), directed by Mario Camerini and starring French actors Lisette Lanvin and Alexander D'Arcy. The Spanish–French film was *Pax* (1932), directed by

Francisco Elias and starring Gina Manes and Camille Bert. The French–
Belgian film was *Le Mariage de Mlle Beulemans*. It is also possible that, for
instance, the Italian–French coproduction was more fully an Italian film
made in multiple languages.

55. Films made by American, German, and British corporations, produced in
French and often in France, were relatively common during the early 1930s.
Metro-Goldwyn-Mayer, for example, made its French films in Hollywood,
whereas Paramount made French films at the Joinville studio outside Paris.
Germany companies produced the most French films, made them at the
Neubabelsburg studio near Berlin and at the Epinay studio in France. During
this period, René Clair, Julien Duvivier, and Jacques Feyder all made films
for German concerns. See Crisp, *Classic French Cinema*, 24. I would like to
thank Jan-Christopher Horak for information about the French version of *The
Testament of Dr. Mabuse.*

56. *PV*, no. 255, October 5, 1933, 15; no. 256, October 12, 1933, 15; no. 257,
October 19, 1933, 15. These same volumes, dates, and page numbers apply,
throughout this section, to all the listings for this three-week period.

57. For information about exhibition strategies and practices in the United
States during the period, see Tino Balio, *Grand Design: Hollywood as a
Modern Business Enterprise, 1930–1939* (Berkeley: University of California
Press, 1995), esp. Chapter 4, "Feeding the Maw of Exhibition," 73–107.

58. The two theaters in the ninth arrondissement showing *La Maternelle*
were the Cinè-Opéra and the Agriculteurs. In fact, the film had opened
in both the sixth and ninth arrondissements, at the Bonaparte and at
Agriculteurs, on September 8. The film began its simultaneous run at the
Cinè-Opéra on September 22, when it replaced the Irene Dunne film *No
Other Woman.* "Voici les films qui passent á Paris," *PV*, no. 251, September
7, 1933, 15, and no. 253, September 21, 1933, 15.

59. Lucien Wahl wrote the review of *King Kong* for *Pour Vous*, in "Les films
nouveaux," no. 252, September 14, 1933, 6. "I don't believe that *King Kong*
creates anxiety or inspires fear or emotion. It's a photographic curiosity" ("Je
ne crois pas que *King Kong* crèe de l'angoisse, inspire la peur ou l'émotion.
C'est une curiosité photographique.").

60. A very partial list of these problems would include the French film
industry's inability to exploit fully the foreign market during the early sound
era; egregious government taxes on the motion picture industry; and the
inability of film firms to stay in business (in 1933, fifty-eight film production
companies faced bankruptcy, and by 1935, both Pathé and Gaumont
had collapsed). Colin Crisp has written the most effective history of the
magnitude of the problems facing the French film industry at this time. In
his *Classic French Cinema*, see p. 19 for details about France's conversion to
sound as well as the country's foreign markets; for the effect of tax issues on
the industry, see pp. 17–18; see p. 21 for information about firms going into
bankruptcy and p. 31 for the collapse of Gaumont and Pathé. Crisp discusses
the problem of postmidnight screenings on p. 17. Other histories of French
national cinema also discuss the industry's chronic problems. In Williams,
Republic of Images, see Chapter 3, "The Golden Age of Sound Cinema,"
157–212. For a more measured view of the industry's problems during the

1930s, see Yann Darré, *Histoire sociale du cinéma français* (Paris: Éditions La Découverte, 2000), 49–58.

61. In France and the United States, there has been only sporadic historical interest in charting the film cultures of France's colonies. See, e.g., Harold Salemson, "A Film at War," *Hollywood Quarterly* 1, no. 4 (1946): 416–19 (about Tunisia); Roger Aubry, "Le Cinéma au Cameroun," *African Arts* 2, no. 3 (1969): 66–69; and Peter Bloom, *French Colonial Documentary: Mythologies of Humanitarianism* (Minneapolis: University of Minnesota Press, 2008).

62. All these examples come from one issue. "Sur les écrans des quatre coins de la France," *PV*, no. 190, July 7, 1932, 14.

63. Charney and Schwartz, Introduction to *Cinema and the Invention of Modern Life*, 3.

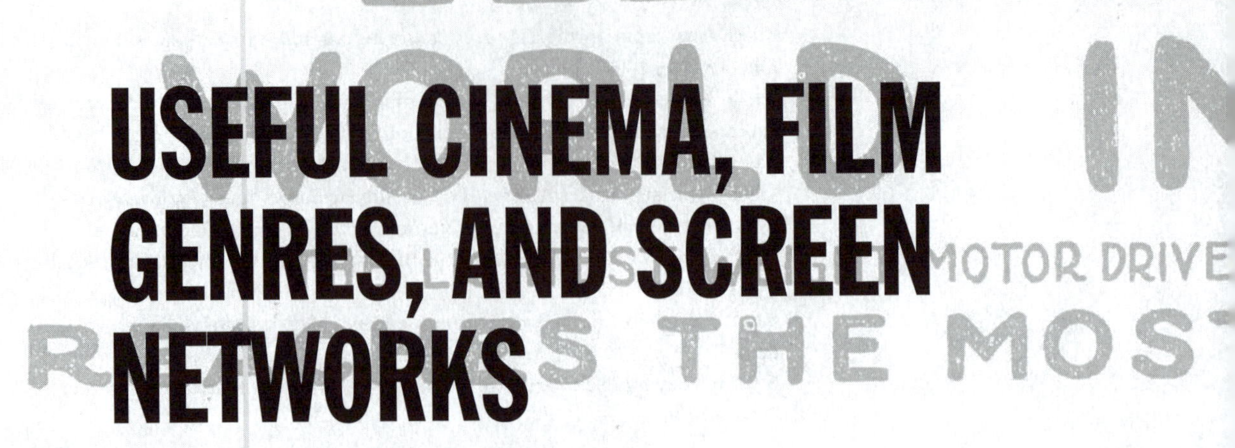

USEFUL CINEMA, FILM GENRES, AND SCREEN NETWORKS

LOUIS PELLETIER

The Story of Canadian Films

Limited (1919–1920)

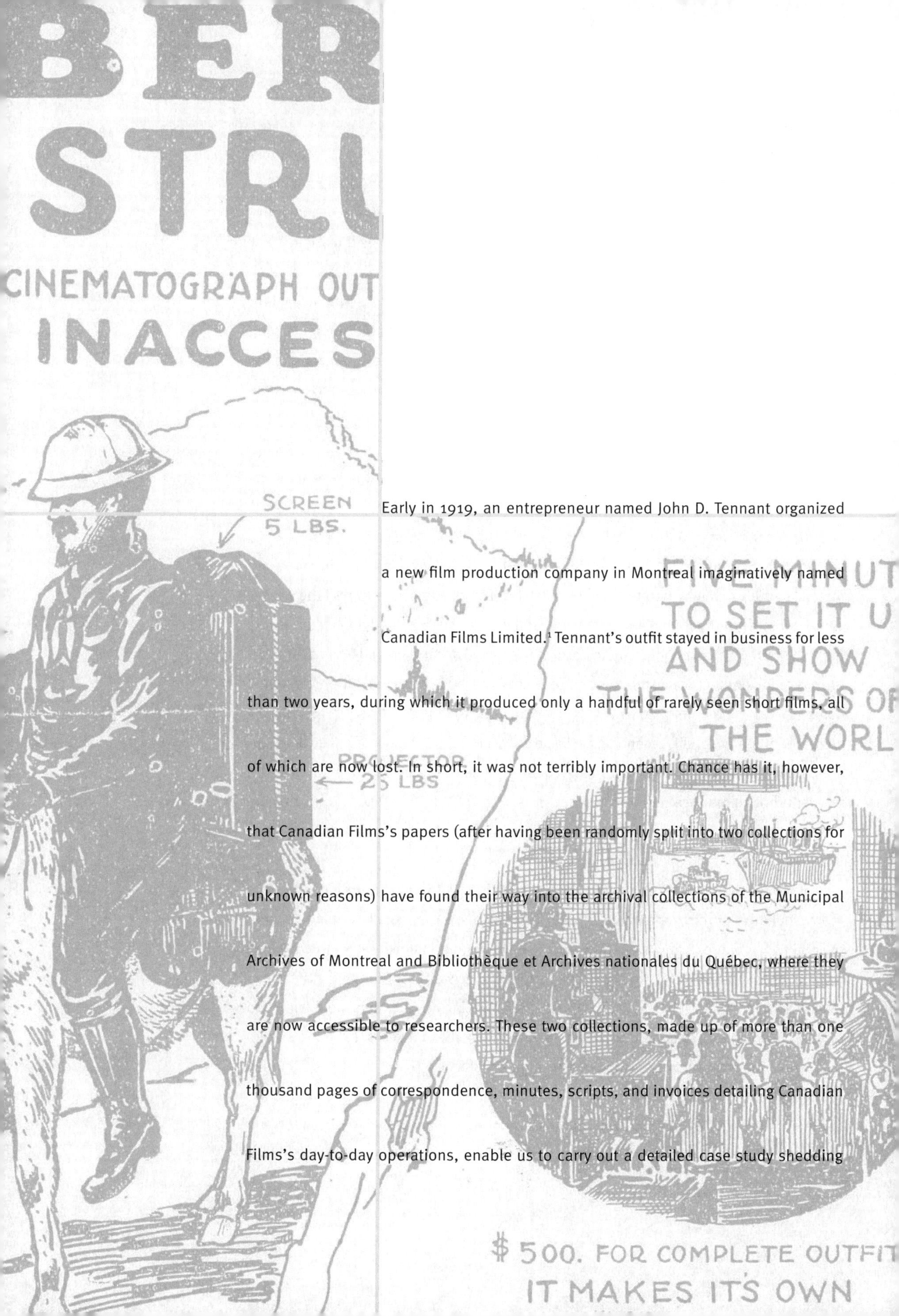

Early in 1919, an entrepreneur named John D. Tennant organized

a new film production company in Montreal imaginatively named

Canadian Films Limited.[1] Tennant's outfit stayed in business for less

than two years, during which it produced only a handful of rarely seen short films, all

of which are now lost. In short, it was not terribly important. Chance has it, however,

that Canadian Films's papers (after having been randomly split into two collections for

unknown reasons) have found their way into the archival collections of the Municipal

Archives of Montreal and Bibliothèque et Archives nationales du Québec, where they

are now accessible to researchers. These two collections, made up of more than one

thousand pages of correspondence, minutes, scripts, and invoices detailing Canadian

Films's day-to-day operations, enable us to carry out a detailed case study shedding

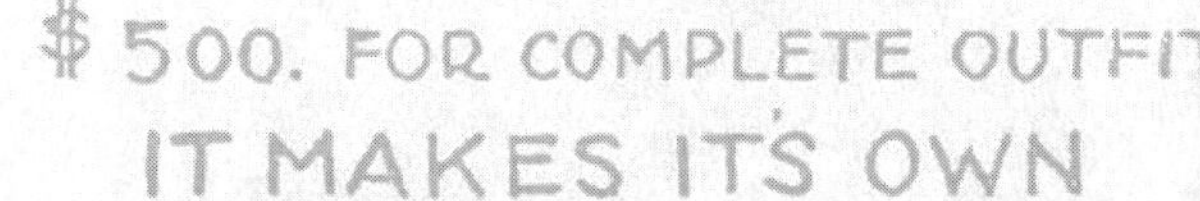

much light on a crucial yet underdocumented period in Canadian film history.

Though Tennant's company may not have been the only or—by far—the most important organization attempting to put Canadian content on Canadian screens in these years marked by a strong push toward vertical integration and American control of the nation's film industry, it likely struggled with the same issues as the other, more accomplished Canadian film producers, who have, for the most part, failed to leave much of a record, filmic or otherwise. Canadian Films's story thus grants us fascinating insight into the activities of pioneering Canadian film producers as well as into their evolving relationships with investors, sponsors, and cultural elites. As such, it complements the first surveys of early Canadian film production undertaken during the last few decades by Peter Morris, André Gaudreault, Germain Lacasse, Pierre Véronneau, and Charles R. Acland.[2]

The story of this short-lived company mostly dedicated to the production of industrial, sponsored, and educational films further brings to the fore many of the trials and challenges associated with the early years of what Haidee Wasson and Acland have labeled "useful cinema."[3] Canadian Films's story indeed confirms that whereas commercial narrative cinema had fully entered its classical phase by the turn of the 1920s, contemporary nontheatrical film production and exhibition remained a most decidedly preinstitutional phenomenon. It more particularly lacked a standardized format suited to the needs of nontheatrical exhibitors and sponsors on a budget, as the portable systems using safety base 22mm, 28mm, and 35mm film marketed in the 1910s had all failed to gain wide acceptance. This technological issue contributed to the much-delayed development of nontheatrical screen networks. Canadian Films therefore had to face up to the fact that though many reformers and educators across North America were embracing the educational and persuasive potential of film, most schools and institutions were still unequipped for film projection.

Canadian Films's story will moreover enable us to delve a little deeper into the articulation of film genres and screen networks. The company's leading concern over its two-year life span was to find and/or develop suitable markets for its modest productions. The main difficulty faced by Canadian Films was that though the theatrical market was, for the most part, out of its reach, the Canadian nontheatrical field remained largely undeveloped, despite its sudden growth during the war years. It will be argued that one of the main tactics developed by Canadian Films to circumvent the difficulties brought about by the scarcity of nontheatrical exhibition sites relied on the production of films that could be identified with different genres associated with different screen networks. Canadian Films thus hoped that its productions could be simultaneously or successively disseminated through different theatrical (commercial moving picture theaters) and nontheatrical (classrooms, boardrooms, etc.) networks. It consequently set out to devise formulae that rendered possible the production of texts permitting a relatively broad range of readings determined by a variety of reception contexts.

My overview of Canadian Films's short life will be followed by a brief inquiry into the history of Associated Screen News, another production company created in Montreal in 1920, which will simultaneously demonstrate the wisdom of this production policy and foreground Canadian Films's unfocused application of it. Unlike Tennant at Canadian Films, Associated Screen News's experienced management understood the importance of planning, of identifying beforehand the combinations of networks through which each particular film would be distributed. Through this policy, Associated Screen News gained the trust of sponsors and investors and managed to contribute to the development of both the Canadian film industry and the nontheatrical film market, while its courageous (or was it foolhardy?) predecessor fell into oblivion.

Of course, Canadian Films and Associated Screen News were not the first film producers to stumble on this commercial tactic relying on the production of polysemous texts. As Rick Altman has demonstrated, even the producers associated with classical Hollywood exploited the fact that genre is not always clearly inscribed in the filmic text itself but is largely a function of the discourse surrounding the film. Altman remarks in particular that "whereas film reviews almost always include generic vocabulary as a convenient and widely understood shorthand, film publicity seldom employs generic terms as such. Indirect references to genre are of course regularly used, but they almost always evoke not a single genre but multiple genres."[4] This practice obviously aimed to avoid reducing a film's potential audience from the outset by explicitly associating it with a specific genre and thus with a reduced niche market.

Canadian Films's eventual decision to launch the production of industrial films seems to have been rather wise, as, according to Frank Kessler and Eef Masson, "between entertainment and instruction, between the picturesque and the informative, between demonstration and attraction, between the cliché and the surprising, (early) industrial films, just like any other types of non-fictional views, can serve multiple purposes."[5] Indeed, Vinzenz Hediger and Patrick Vonderau have argued that this textual indeterminacy is characteristic of the industrial film genre, which, they claim, remains more than any other "a strategically weak and parasitic form in the sense that it can assume the appearance of other, more stable genres and formats and pass as a scientific film, an educational film, or a documentary for specific strategic reasons."[6] In Canadian Films' case, these reasons were evidently commercial in nature.

Other scholars have attempted to understand the role that context and institutions play in the reception process as well as in the creation and perpetuation of genres. French theorist Roger Odin has argued that a shifting set of constraints, both textual and contextual, governs the production of meaning by spectators. A producer may consciously attempt to downplay textual constraints, but these remain inescapable: a film will necessarily be exhibited in a variety of circumstances that will either trigger or inhibit the use of certain modes of production of meaning and affect by the spectator.[7] Still, by avoiding the markers generally associated with particular genres, or more typically, by combining various markers associated with distinct genres, a producer can make it possible for its films to be more easily disseminated through different channels. Kessler and Masson have consequently argued that "genres should . . . be seen as complex and multi-layered configurations demanding to be understood in terms of historically specific, pragmatic contexts." They further suggest that "differentiation in the field of non-fiction cinema is often based upon the criterion of the *purpose* or *function* a film is supposed to serve. Denominations such as instructional, educational, scientific, ethnographic, etc. films, and also terms like newsreel or propaganda, refer to the uses these films are being put to, or to the institutional domain in which they are employed. Here, the formal characteristics are more or less irrelevant, the basic assumption being generally that form will just have to follow function."[8]

That being said, that the various labels denoting nonfictional genres generally eschew direct references to both form and content does not mean that these considerations are entirely overridden by each genre's purpose or exhibition context. French filmmaker Jean Painlevé, for example, has expounded on the often irreconcilable needs of the audiences for scientific and educational films: whereas scientific film audiences will categorically reject most types of authorial intervention (montage, commentary), educational film audiences will expect the films' content to be presented in a highly formatted way.[9] It should also be noted that industrial films with a promotional bent also frequently had a hard time finding distribution in educational institutions or commercial moving picture theaters—as Canadian Films would find out the hard way.

CANADIAN FILMS AND CANADIAN FILM HISTORY

Very little is known of John D. Tennant's life and career before and after Canadian Films. That Canadian Films significantly altered its production policy no fewer than four times over the two years it remained in operation suggests, however, that he was relatively new to the film business. Like many of his contemporaries, Tennant likely saw the booming film business first and foremost as an enticing investment opportunity. Indeed, Canadian Films was formed at the tail end of a long series of stock promotion schemes using the glamour of the burgeoning film industry to lure Canadians into investing into short-lived film companies. A typical case was that of Canadian Photo-Play Productions, a company promoted by an American expatriate, Harold J. Binney, in and around Toronto in 1918–19 (see Figure 1). In its prospectus (of which, interestingly, Canadian Films kept several copies), Canadian Photo-Play presumptuously described its coming dividends as "larger than your wildest dreams—which is saying something." The company's actual results must have been something of a letdown for its shareholders, as Canadian Photo-Play's sole film, *Polly of the Circus* (1919), failed to obtain theatrical release.[10]

Tennant's dealings with clients and investors often suggest a modus operandi in line with that of Binney's Canadian Photo-Play. Indeed, Canadian Films could be blatantly disingenuous in its reports and public statements to shareholders. Its management claimed, for instance, to control net assets totaling one million dollars[11] as the company was entering its second year of operations in February 1920—a grossly exaggerated figure, as we will see.[12] Still, it would be a mistake simply to write off Canadian Films as yet another stock-marketing scheme seeking to defraud Canadian investors. Unlike most of the other questionable film enterprises marketed to investors in the 1910s, Canadian Films managed to produce several well-received films between 1919 and 1920. This significant fact tends to show that Tennant's enterprise may have been more of a delusional scheme than a blatant scam. Actually, Canadian Films's lies and exaggerations seem to have been fed by the major difficulties that arose when the company tried to get its films exhibited. In other words, the occasional dishonesty of Canadian Films's management appears to have been more the symptom of a situation quickly spinning out of control than the essence of the enterprise.

To Tennant's credit, one had to be most cunning to survive as a film producer in Canada at the turn of the 1920s. By then, Canadian theaters had been screening U.S. films almost exclusively for nearly a decade, and filmgoers had grown to expect stars and high production values in their moving picture entertainment. Cinema had now fully entered its classical era, and Canadian Films would have had to have been most ingenious to succeed, despite its lack of access to talent and up-to-date facilities as well as its very limited capital and distribution opportunities. Canadian Films's production policies seem further to have been informed by the failure of the few legitimate attempts to launch the production of feature-length fiction films in Canada during the 1910s.[13] Tennant was no doubt aware, moreover, that the era's most successful Canadian film producer, Specialty Film Import, concentrated on newsreels and topicals and presumably remained

CANADA'S OPPORTUNITY

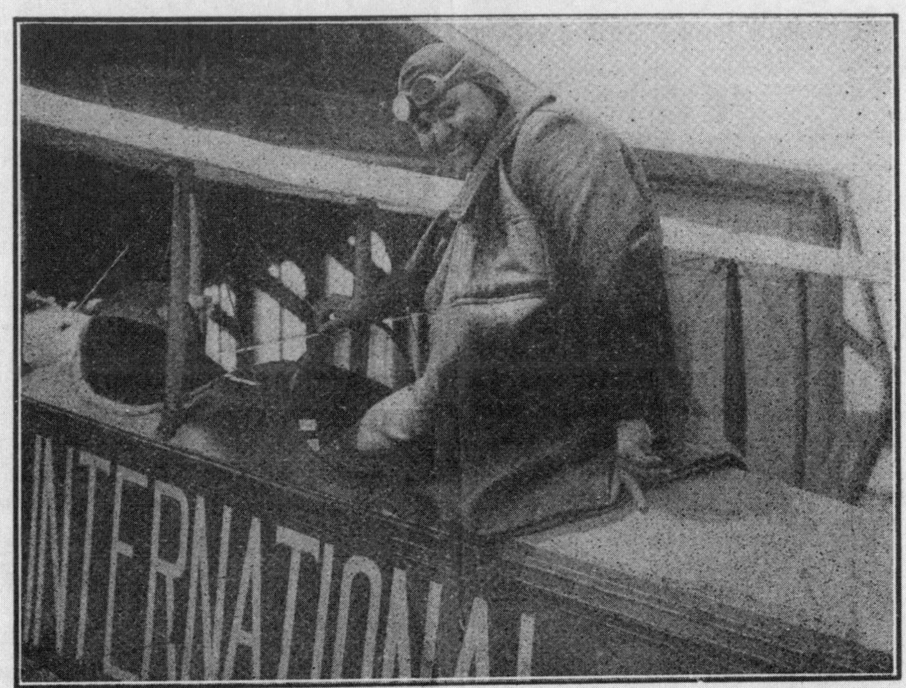

HAROLD J. BINNEY

Figure 1. Canadian Photo-Play Production's Harold J. Binney. Bibliothèque et Archives nationales du Québec, Canadian Films Limited collection, P324.

profitable through its distribution activities (it held the Pathé franchise for Canada).

Tennant obviously believed that a production policy exploiting Canadian themes and resources, yet acknowledging the dominance of imported features, could make Canadian Films profitable. The first component of Canadian Films's production program was, therefore, nationalism. The producer widely advertised that its stated purpose was "to feature Canadian scenery, Canadian subjects and boast Canadian industries whenever possible."[14] Playing on the resentment over the late entry of the United States into the Great War, a Canadian Films representative even managed to put a patriotic twist on Canada's lack of feature film production by remarking that film production had been neglected in Canada "by reason of the fact that Canadians have been so very busy in the last few years that they have had neither the time or [*sic*] inclination to even investigate [film production]."[15]

Clearly, by the late 1910s, Canadian patriotism was an issue for more than Canadian politicians and citizens. To quite a few entrepreneurs—not all of them Canadians—it was also a ripe business opportunity.[16] But patriotism does not in itself qualify as a niche market; one has to find an outlet for it. This constituted the main challenge for Canadian Films, which, from the start, seemingly had a better idea of what it would not release—feature films, which are not mentioned in any surviving correspondence—than what it would actually produce. Tennant's company's only possible course of action was to act tactically by staying attuned to the particular needs of Canadian audiences and by being ready to take advantage of changing circumstances.

At the time of Canadian Films's creation, recent developments in the field of moving images included the rise of educational and propaganda films. The Great War had prompted the Canadian government to employ moving pictures to boost and sustain its war effort. Over the war years, film had been used for recruiting and training as well as for communication between soldiers and the home front, most notably through newsreels and topicals. At home, films were also increasingly being used to educate farmers and promote healthy lifestyles. Several governmental film bureaus were created across Canada to fulfill these purposes, the most important being the Ontario Motion Picture Bureau (established in 1917) and, of course, the Canadian Government Motion Picture Bureau (also created in 1917). At the end of the hostilities, these bureaus' primary raisons d'être would become the promotion of Canadian industries and tourism.[17] It should be noted, however, that many of the provincial bureaus actually outsourced their productions to private producers, such as Filmcraft and Pathéscope of Canada, both established in Toronto.[18]

The rise of useful cinema over the war years permitted Tennant and his partner to express the belief that the production of educational, industrial, and sponsored films was about to become a commercial enterprise on par with the production of theatrical fiction films. The company's propaganda consequently hammered home the point that if Canada wanted to avoid conceding nonfiction film production to American interests, as it had done a few years before with fiction films, now was the time to act. Tennant anticipated opposition commensurate with what he perceived to be the vast commercial interests at stake:

> We know that there is an awful knock coming down from the United States as they are very loath to give up the supremacy they hold in the film business in Canada. They are taking about $9,000,000 out of Canada each year for rental of films in theaters and if they can control the Educational films, they will certainly do so, as everyone knows who is in touch with the trend of things, that within the next few years there will not be a school that will not be supplied with films.[19]

Canadian Films's propaganda consequently aimed to turn the company's project into a crusade of national interest. This line of argument did not prove entirely convincing: commentators opined that Canadian Films was deploying patriotic rhetoric to further its commercial interests. To these critics, Tennant replied, "Films can only be made on a commercial basis and nothing will ever take away from the Americans their supremacy in the film business except a well managed and properly financed film company."[20]

Ironically, Tennant's last comment brings to the fore Canadian Films's two main handicaps: its inexperienced management and its insufficient capital (by August 1919, the company had only issued $4,590 worth of shares).[21] The company's fund-raising difficulties can partly be attributed to the growing skepticism of Canadian investors toward the film business. To a proposition made early in 1919 by Canadian Films, the Halifax Board of Trade had, for example, responded that "it is only a few years ago that a Picture Film Company was organized in Halifax with rather disasterous [sic] results, owing, the writer understands, to poor management, and I am afraid the subscribing public have [sic] not yet recovered from the shock."[22] The "picture film company" referred to was most likely the Canadian Bioscope Co., whose four-reel feature adaptation of Longfellow's *Evangeline* had been very well received both in Canada and the United States on its release in 1914.

Canadian Films nevertheless benefited from a few valuable assets, the most important being its main employee, Maurice Metzger.[23] Acting as technical expert, camera operator, and lab director, Metzger was in actuality a one-man production team—and a good one at that, if he is to be judged by his other accomplishments before and after

Canadian Films. A bona fide Canadian film pioneer, Metzger had processed some of the footage shot by Joseph Rosenthal's team for the Canada: England's Premier Colony and Living Canada series sponsored by the Canadian Pacific Railway (CPR) in 1902 and 1903. He had also participated in the production of the local actualities shot in and around Montreal between 1904 and 1910 by F. Guy Bradford (who had first come to Canada with Rosenthal) and worked as a "technical expert" for the Montreal office of the General Film Co. In 1914, Metzger had been employed by the Premier Film Manufacturing Co. of Canada, a Montreal outfit that managed to release only one topical. After his stint at Canadian Films, Metzger would work for more than three decades for Associated Screen News, where he was most notably employed as a laboratory superintendent and sound engineer.[24] In short, all signs point to the fact that Canadian Films could rely on one employee, at least, who could tackle all kinds of production and postproduction tasks and produce quality work.

THE FILMS OF CANADIAN FILMS

In winter 1919, Canadian Films first attempted to launch the production of a series of travelogues that, it was hoped, could also function as promotional films for the various localities and industries featured therein. In early February, the company mailed a first round of promotional letters to the boards of trade of several cities located across Canada, from Charlottetown to Vancouver. This not-so-subtle attempt to recruit investors was almost universally turned down. Still, the board representatives who replied generally agreed that "Made in Canada" films could greatly benefit the nation and its industries.[25]

By spring 1919, Canadian Films had a clear plan. It now planned to send a camera operator—presumably Metzger—on a trip from Halifax to Victoria (and "then possibly up the Coast to Alaska"), during which he would be responsible for the production of a series of fifteen "comic-travelogue" one-reelers. The resulting films were to be subsequently released nationwide on a weekly basis.[26] To promote the project, Canadian Films sent a second round of letters to more than sixty municipal boards of trade in mid-April. These explained that cities and towns visited by Canadian Films's camera operator would be expected to cover some of the production costs of the series through the acquisition of Canadian Films stock, as commercial film exhibitors did not tolerate any paid-for advertising in the films they booked. Canadian Films made sure to outline the films' benefits for the participating cities, noting that "each city that gives us sufficient support will receive gratis their local film, the only requirement being that they do not exhibit it for pay. [If the city has] a publicity agent, he can show the film any place he happens to be, to prospective customers in the forenoon by arrangement with a Moving Picture House, as they very seldom use their theaters in the forenoon."[27] The producer thus hoped to circumvent one of the main problems it faced, the absence of a national network of nontheatrical screens, through the assignation of a double function to the extant network: theatrical screens would now be noncommercial in the morning and commercial in the afternoon and evening. This would prove to be a lackluster solution.

Canadian Films's communication to local boards of trade further explained how its projected "comic-travelogues" would take advantage of this dual network: "so that the travelogue will not be dry and uninteresting to children, we propose to introduce just enough comedy to make it attractive, taking it out of the class of dry travelogue."[28] The idea was that whereas prospective tourists and industrialists would be awed by the spectacle of Canada's scenery, resources, and industries, others would be entertained by the comedy. Interestingly, it is not too clear, by referring to a "child" audience posited as the travelogue–industrial film audience's other, whether Canadian Films meant to denote the educational film audience or the commercial moving picture show's public.

It should be noted in passing that the fiction–travelogue combination was not exactly a new idea. Canadian Films's proposed films were more particularly reminiscent of the series of twelve films sponsored by CPR and produced by the Edison Manufacturing Co. in summer 1910. Produced to advertise Canada to foreign settlers, the series (which included the "comedy and scenic" *A Wedding Trip from Montreal through Canada to Hong Kong* and the "dramatic and descriptive" *Riders of the Plains*) had received wide theatrical distribution across Europe and North America at the turn of the 1910s.[29] The main difference between the two projects was that while the Edison Co. had dispatched a whole team of professionals to Canada (director, camera operator, actors, and actresses), Canadian Films apparently hoped, in a typical fit of wishful thinking, that its camera operator could recruit and direct local amateurs for the comedic bits. In this golden era of film comedy, where new releases by Charlie Chaplin, Harold Lloyd, Roscoe "Fatty" Arbuckle, and Buster Keaton were turning up on Canadian screens on an almost weekly basis, Canadian Films's comic-travelogues would most likely have been deemed unreleasable by commercial distributors had they actually been produced. But lack of interest in the project on the part of the boards of trade effectively killed the series before Canadian Films's camera operator could depart for Halifax.

By mid-May, the plan to release weekly comic-travelogues had morphed into a plan to release a weekly *Cameragram* showing "Canadian current events, educational, industrial and travel pictures."[30] The projected series was obviously inspired by the Canadian newsreel issued twice weekly by Léo-Ernest Ouimet's Specialty Film Import since

January 1919, the *British Canadian Pathé News.* Canadian Films's fund-raising difficulties, however, prevented it from launching the proposed series in time for the biggest news event of the year: the Canadian tour of the Prince of Wales (the future King Edward VIII), which got under way on August 15, 1919. Canadian Films did attempt to buy footage of the prince's arrival from W. G. MacLaughlan, an independent camera operator based in Halifax, only to learn that MacLaughlan had already been hired by Specialty.[31] The royal visit ended up being extensively covered by the *British Canadian Pathé News* as well as by the first issues of the weekly *Canadian National Pictorial,* released by Toronto's Pathéscope of Canada.[32]

These supply difficulties no doubt largely contributed to the failure of Canadian Films's newsreel project, as not one *Cameragram* issue appears to have ever reached theaters. The projected *Cameragram* series ultimately remains the most blatant demonstration of Tennant's lack of understanding of film production and distribution: only an absolute neophyte could imagine that an independent outfit employing a single camera operator could manage to successfully turn out one full reel of varied Canadian content for nationwide release every week. For the production of its *British Canadian Pathé News,* Specialty Film Import employed several camera operators posted across Canada as well as many independent operators known as stringers. And yet Canadian content rarely represented more than half the content of the issues of the *British Canadian Pathé News,* as Specialty made abundant use of recycled segments originating from the U.S. *Pathé News* and the British *Pathé Gazette.* Pathéscope's *Canadian National Pictorial* did feature Canadian subjects almost exclusively. It benefited, however, as historian Rosemary Bergeron has discovered, from the support of the Canadian government, which granted twenty-eight thousand dollars yearly to Pathéscope and which further permitted the company's camera operators—who were based in Halifax, Ottawa, Toronto, Winnipeg, and Vancouver—to travel free of charge on the state-owned Canadian National Railway.[33]

The "Made in Canada" segments regularly featured in the *Canadian National Pictorial* may very well have inspired the new scheme devised by Canadian Films in summer 1919. Throughout the months of August and September, Canadian Films sent yet another round of promotional letters—this time, not to towns and boards of trade but to businesses and industries active in Quebec and Ontario.[34] Though the letters still presented the *Cameragram* as Canadian Films's main product, they revealed that the projected series's formula had shifted toward industrial subjects. Tennant now claimed that Canadian Films aimed "to show about 500 feet of News, Educational and Travel pictures, and about 500 feet of Industrial each week."[35] The letters also announced that Canadian Films had signed a contract with the General Film Co. of Canada, which provided for the distribution of seven prints of each of its productions across Canada: two in Quebec, two in Ontario, one in the Maritime Provinces, and two in the Prairies and British Columbia.[36]

This new campaign targeting industries was far more successful than the previous ones aimed at local boards of trade. Several businesses proved to be at least intrigued by the promotional potential of moving pictures, and a fair number ended up signing contracts with Canadian Films.[37] For sums going from five hundred to one thousand dollars, Canadian Films agreed to produce films varying between five hundred and one thousand feet in length, which generally focused on the manufacturing process of its clients' products. The production of news films soon disappeared altogether from Canadian Films's plans. These deals cleverly instituted dual channels of revenue for Canadian Films, as the producer hoped to collect money both from sponsors and, through its contract with General Films, from exhibitors.

The new scheme forced Canadian Films to be cautious about the ways in which it negotiated the demarcation between industrial and promotional films and more particularly with regard to the ways in which it mixed markers associated with both types of productions. Its preferred strategy relied on the careful placement of signs bearing the sponsors' names in films whose purported goal was to instruct the public on Canadian industries and manufacturing processes. The rationale for this strategy was made explicit in a letter sent by Canadian Films to one of its clients:

> We are afraid that we cannot show that any part of [the picture] is produced "through the Courtesy of G.A. Holland and Son, Company," for the reason that we feel almost positive that the theaters would refuse to show that. . . . In our opinion were we to state that the picture or part of it was being shown through your courtesy it would savor too much of "Bill-board Advertising." To show your name in the manner in which we suggest we believe will be much more impressive and not subject to criticism and at the same time thoroughly dignified.[38]

According to Kathryn Fuller, films deftly concealing advertisements were, at the time, still tolerated by audiences across North America, as long as they were found to be entertaining and interesting. The industry-wide ban on paid advertising would only be introduced in the code of ethics prepared in 1922 by Will H. Hays in collaboration with exhibitors' groups.[39] Though engineered in the United States, this ban would influence the conduct of the Canadian film business in the years following Canadian Films's demise.

The multiple contracts signed with Canadian firms finally permitted Canadian Films to launch its production activities in September 1919, more than six months after the company's creation. Canadian Films's first completed production was a one-reeler sponsored by Canadian Explosives Limited and titled *The Use of Explosives in Clearing New Farms and Rejuvenating Old Ones*.[40] The film has long been considered lost, but an annotated shooting script survives. It reveals a conscious effort on the producer's part to turn this filmed advertisement aimed at a narrow audience of farm owners into something more palatable to a wider audience, most notably through the injection of a strong streak of misogynistic lowbrow comedy. The script thus opens with the following exchange between the protagonist, a farmer, and his friend:

> **Scene 1.** *Farmer leaning over fence looking blue and discouraged. Friend strolls along.*
>
> **Friend.** Pretty tough looking farm you have, Tom. Is it all like this?
>
> **Farmer with a snort.** Worse: I'll show you, it's as bad as a mother-in-law with the mumps.
>
> *They walk over the fields. Farmer pointing out the stumps. Rocks. Etc.*
>
> **Farmer despairingly.** The rocky road to Dublin was a feather bed compared to this farm, all I can raise on it is malaria, chilblains and profanity.
>
> **Friend.** Huh, that's easy. Let Dinah do the work.
>
> **Farmer.** Dinah who?
>
> **Friend.** Dinamite [*sic*].
>
> *Pulls out a booklet explaining the great advantages of clearing land with C.X.L. Farmer listens dubiously at first, then becomes interested by degrees.*
>
> **Farmer.** Well Dinah might, but isn't it dangerous?
>
> **Friend.** No. Easy as making love to an old maid. Order C.X.L. dynamite before your wife asks for another new dress. I'll show how it works.
>
> **Farmer brightening up.** Thanks old man. I'll do it right away.[41]

So much for "dignified" product placement. The rest of the script concerns itself with the demonstration of various possible uses of dynamite in agriculture.

In addition to the scene breakdown and dialogues, the extant script for *The Use of Explosives* features some instructions obviously aimed at the film's camera operator (and de facto director), which provide us with a fascinating glimpse of Canadian Films's filmmaking process. The script's author, for instance, explains that

none of the operators should be looking at the camera. J.B.M. [J. B. Moriarty,
manager of Canadian Explosives's agricultural division] to be the only demon-
strator. Mr. Godfrey to appear as farmer and others as spectators. Be careful
that all photographs before and after show the same background. Be careful
to place the box of explosives, detonators, E.B. Caps and fuse in such a position throughout the picture so that the labels will distinctly show name and
trademark.[42]

The resulting film seems to have been competently made. It was, in any case, declared
to be "an A1 production" by Canadian Explosives's sales executives and directors, to
whom it had been submitted for review.[43] Canadian Explosives acquired from Canadian
Films one copy of the film printed on nonflammable film stock ($65) and one portable
projector ($225) so that its sales agents could show it to prospective customers.[44] This
proved to be a wise decision, as the film's exhibition in commercial theaters was delayed
for a full year: *The Use of Explosives* was only released by the Famous Lasky Film Service
in fall 1920, after the General Film deal fell through.[45] Even then, there is no way to tell
if it was ever exhibited in more than a handful of Canadian theaters.

Starting with its second completed production, *The Cream Industry,* Canadian
Films tried to make it easier for commercial firms to sponsor films by devising projects that
would feature the products and services of more than one firm, thus permitting multiple
sponsors to split the bill. Funding for *The Cream Industry* came from the DeLaval Separator Co., of Peterborough, Ontario (a subsidiary of the Sweden-based multinational), and
from the Montreal Dairy Co. The film showed a variety of DeLaval apparatus, including
specimens of the company's famed milk separators, in use on a farm and at the installations of the Montreal Dairy Co. Though it was not framed as a paid-for advertisement, the
film did make sure to identify various apparatus depicted as "DeLavals."[46] On completion, *The Cream Industry* was submitted to its sponsors, who declared themselves very
pleased with the results, and was exhibited between December 1919 and April 1920 in a
few Montreal theaters.[47] This minor success must, however, be weighed against the time
and energy spent in the making of *The Cream Industry.* Between Canadian Films's first
exchanges with the DeLaval Separator Co. in early June 1919 and the film's first screening
in early December, no less than half a year had elapsed. Part of this unseemly delay can
be explained by the fact that Canadian Films had found itself stuck in a position where
it had to cajole and coordinate multiple participants and sponsors. DeLaval's general
manager had, for instance, made it clear that his company would only agree to sponsor
the film if DeLaval apparatus could be showcased on J. B. Hanmer's farm, home of a

famous prize-winning cow. But at the time, Hanmer was in the process of overhauling his installations and only half-heartedly agreed to get involved after receiving several increasingly desperate letters from Tennant.[48]

The situation was even worse for *The Construction of Canada's Largest Apartment Building,* produced concurrently with *The Cream Industry* in fall 1919 and showing the rise of the ten-story Drummond building, one of Montreal's first skyscrapers.[49] This particular project was financed by no fewer than eight sponsors contributing sums ranging from $50 to $250, including Sherbrooke's McKinnon Steel Co. (structural work), Mott Co. ("sanitary earthenware of all kinds"), and G. A. Holland and Son Co. (furniture). The film's completion was eventually delayed by several months when one of the sponsors refused to pay, even after Canadian Films had agreed to make its trademark more prominent by retaking certain shots. This unseemly delay angered the other sponsors, who soon were threatening legal action.[50]

The delays encountered by Canadian Films in the production of its films proved even more critical in the case of the film it produced for the renowned furrier Holt, Renfrew, and Co. Titled *The Fur Industry of Canada,* this production was yet another advertisement masquerading as an educational–industrial film: according to the extant synopsis, it opened with an extended documentary sequence showing the breeding of silver foxes and the manufacture of cloaks and coats and closed with images of models wearing the latest Holt Renfrew creations.[51] When the film was finally completed in mid-January 1920, some four months after production began in fall 1919, timing was, in the opinion of its sponsor, less than optimal for a fur-marketing campaign. Canadian Films and Holt Renfrew consequently agreed to push the film's release to late summer 1920.[52] This forced Canadian Films to do some retakes on the film's final sequence to bring it up to date with the latest fashion trends for the 1920–21 season and to charge Holt Renfrew extra for the new footage.[53]

Holt Renfrew arranged for the revised version of *The Fur Industry of Canada* to be shown on a vessel of the Canadian Steamship Line.[54] To that purpose, Canadian Films sent the film's original negative to New York so that a 28mm safety film print could be produced by Pathéscope of America.[55] The negative, however, went missing for over a month at customs on its way back from New York (or so claimed Tennant), which thwarted Canadian Films's efforts to have the film released in theaters.[56] Relations between the film's producer and sponsor steadily deteriorated as the former systematically failed to make good on its promises: by October 1920, Holt Renfrew was sending a steady flow of threatening letters to Canadian Films.[57] Indeed, *The Fur Industry of Canada* may have been publicly exhibited only once, before retakes of the final sequence had been inserted, at the Fur Industry and Wild Life Conference held at Montreal's Windsor Hotel on February 19, 1920. The film's description published on that occasion in the Montreal *Gazette* reveals some curious editorial choices, as the reporter first remarks with a hint of relief that "what happened before [the foxes'] pelts were removed was mercifully omitted" but then goes on to explain that much footage painstakingly depicts the grisly fleshing and tanning process to which the raw skins were submitted.[58] Interestingly, the *Gazette* reporter also observed that "the pictures were calculated to show especially the male-part of the gathering the infinite pains that had to be taken before an expensive fur robe was turned out, and explain to them why such luxuries made severe demands upon the bank account."[59] Beyond its implicit celebration of the movie's educational potential, the *Gazette*'s piece thus signaled a certain degree of awareness that different groups—in this particular case, men and women—would likely read the film differently.

The last production completed by Canadian Films in its first year of operation, another industrial–promotional sponsored film titled *One of Canada's Leading Hotels,* might have been saved from some other questionable editorial choices on Canadian Films's part through exchanges between producer and sponsor. Available documents show a definite shift of emphasis between the project first presented by Canadian Films to the Windsor Hotel and the completed film. Here's how Canadian Films first pitched the project:

> Many people, not knowing the whys and wherefores, are amazed at the present day prices charged in hotels for rooms and food. They are not aware of the sanitary precautions taken at large expense, the theft and destruction by certain patrons of linen and equipment, the loss of silver and many other such things that occur; and they would be interested to know how goods are received for the kitchen, how distributed and what disposition is made of the garbage and grease. . . . One or two meetings of employees shown receiving instructions and exchanging ideas would be astonishing news to multitudes.[60]

A list of titles prepared for the completed film, however, reveals that, in all probability heeding the hotel management's good advice, Canadian Films shifted the film's emphasis over the course of production from theft and grease disposal to some more glamorous sights such as the chef's "fancy granulated sugar work" and the establishment's celebrated "Peacock Alley and Dining Halls."[61] This still did not help Canadian Films secure theatrical distribution for this production, which, for once, had been completed within a month of the contract's signature on November 26, 1919.[62] *One of Canada's Leading*

Hotels seems to have been exhibited just once, in June 1920, to the employees of the Windsor Hotel.[63] In this manner, this film, which had been conceived as a promotional sponsored film and then produced as an industrial film, finally found a limited audience by being made to function more like a home movie.

Canadian Films's continued failure to get its films the wide release it had contractually bound itself to provide meant that it could not go on producing industrial sponsored films for very long.[64] Lack of distribution not only deprived Canadian Films of a much-needed stream of revenue (the producer's representatives often claimed that the sponsors' contributions did not even cover production costs); it also put the company in a difficult position vis-à-vis prospective sponsors.[65]

So why did Canadian Films's seemingly well-crafted productions have so much trouble getting distributed? Part of the answer may lie in Canadian Films's lack of connections in the distribution and exhibition fields, in an era marked by a strong push toward vertical integration—though it must be noted that the same lack of formal connections to distributors and exhibitors did not prevent Associated Screen News from having its films widely exhibited in commercial theaters in the 1920s.[66] It is also rather obvious that Canadian Films's management had grossly overestimated widespread popular demand for industrial films. By the turn of the 1920s, theatrical audiences had long developed a taste for more glamorous and entertaining fare. It is true that, as Fuller has demonstrated, some exhibitors (mostly in small-town theaters and nontheatrical venues) still booked short films dealing with agriculture and food processing or depicting the manufacturing process of various consumer goods. We do know, for instance, that the *Ford Educational Weekly* circulated regularly in the province of Quebec in the late 1910s.[67] A central feature of the appeal of these advertising–industrial films for exhibitors, however, lay in their extremely low rental costs (the *Ford Educational Weekly* could be booked for the nominal rental fee of one dollar per week) and regular release schedules.[68] Canadian Films could offer neither.

CANADIAN FILMS'S EDUCATIONAL TURN

Canadian Films's distribution issues prompted Tennant to halt the company's filmmaking activities in December 1919. Very few efforts seem to have been undertaken to obtain distribution for Canadian Films's already completed films as Tennant pondered the company's production policy over late fall and winter 1920. Canadian Films's management eventually chose to investigate the educational market, which also seemed to permit the production of films that could be exploited in various noneducational markets. In a letter sent to a Lennoxville school commissioner as production work on the Windsor Hotel film was still going on, Canadian Films's Dickson, for instance, explained that "even a hotel properly filmed should be of value in schools."[69] This statement suggests that the company's new policy did not proceed from a change of strategy but from a mere change of primary outlet: Canadian Films would now seek new venues where different meanings would be wrung out of its modest factual films, not new ways to make films.

That being said, the company's management also seems to have been aware of some of the pitfalls associated with the production of films with dual educational and promotional purposes. A letter sent by Tennant to Toronto's chief inspector of schools, for instance, reveals that Canadian Films's manager knew perfectly well that such films were likely to be perceived as educational by some viewers and as propaganda by others. The letter addressed to the inspector further demonstrates that Tennant was fully aware that propaganda charges could also be motivated by the ideological content of the company's films. Tennant consequently guaranteed that Canadian Films's educational productions would only deal with a limited list of subjects considered safe: "Our films will be largely for the teaching of Geography, Natural History, Agriculture, Horticulture, Domestic Science and other subjects of like nature. In school work proper we will eliminate all semblance of propaganda religious, political or otherwise, as there are so many shades of opinion on these subjects that to attempt to please one would offend others. The only propaganda that we will spread will be good morals and patriotism to the flag and country."[70]

Canadian history, interestingly, which had been the very first field mined by many pioneer Canadian film producers, such as Montreal's British-American Film Manufacturing Co. (*The Battle of the Long Sault,* 1912) and Halifax's Canadian Bioscope (*Evangeline,* 1914), was not part of the abbreviated list of subjects approved by Tennant. Though this omission may very well have been a direct consequence of Canadian Films's tight production budgets, it is also quite probable that the company's management was aware of the contentious nature of much of Canadian history. The Quebec City Tercentenary of 1908 and the Great War had more particularly exposed significant rifts between the views held by many French Canadians and English Canadians, to say nothing of aboriginal peoples, on the delicate matter of Canada's colonial history.[71] As a commercial enterprise, Canadian Films had nothing to gain by getting mixed up in these quarrels.

Ironically, Canadian Films's educational turn seems to have been spurred by some of the discussions held at the National Conference on Character Education in Relation to Canadian Citizenship, held in October 1919 in Winnipeg, which, according to historians Tom Mitchell and Rosa Bruno-Jofre, had been anything but a politically neutral affair. Most participants at this conference, organized to find solutions to the perceived crisis surrounding postwar Canadian identity, had promoted a particular strand of "Canadianism rooted in Anglo-conformity and a citizenship framed in notions of service, obedience, obligation and fidelity to the state."[72] According to Bruno-Jofre,

> those who left room to accommodate diversity received little or no attention at the Conference. . . . Winnipeg labour organizations decided not to send delegates but there were participants willing to voice the workers' view without, however, making an impact on the audience. . . . Delegates from Quebec, especially the Francophones, politely dissented from the national enthusiasm of the Conference. They tried, with little obvious success, to make participants aware that there was another view of Canada. Most participants perceived teachers as playing a powerful role in transmitting an ideology of Anglo-conformity, assimilation, service, social stability, and hostility towards radical change.[73]

But these lofty debates on the subject of Canadian identity and ideals most likely were not responsible for getting Canadian Films interested in the Conference's project; rather, the producer seems to have been enticed by one particular resolution voted at the conference, which it reproduced in its entirety in a prospectus outlining its educational project:

> WHEREAS the effect of the Moving Picture on school children is incalculably powerful for good or evil, and whereas much of what is now offered as entertainment is based upon suggestions that tend to familiarize the minds of children with situations that are sensational and frequently immoral and vulgar.
>
> THEREFORE be it resolved that this Conference direct attention to the vital necessity of developing an active public opinion, demonstrated by attendance at theaters, for the support of good pictures—which can only be hoped for when it becomes good business to exhibit such pictures and also for the strengthening of the hands of the various boards of censorship in their efforts to raise the standard of the Moving Picture industry; and that every effort be made to secure film depicting Canadian and British life and sentiment.[74]

The National Conference on Character Education thus followed the lead of many reformist organizations across North America, which were then coming to realize that film was there to stay and that its appeal to groups perceived to be at risk—immigrants, workers, women, children—might as well be made to serve their causes.[75]

Canadian Films soon got in touch with members of the National Council of the

Conference on Character Education from all provinces to promote and legitimate its new business plan centering on the production of patriotically minded educational pictures. Tennant's letters explain that Canadian Films was in the process of forming an advisory board whose mandate would be to review and approve the pictures it would soon release on the educational market.[76] The invitation was also extended to several ecclesiastics and education professionals across Canada.[77] The list of advisory board members published by Canadian Film Underwriters, Canadian Films's fiscal agents, eventually listed nineteen members (mostly educators) coming from all Canadian provinces, with the exception of Manitoba.[78]

Canadian Films's partnership with the National Conference on Character Education was, however, destined to be short-lived. Irked to have seen their names printed in a Canadian Films prospectus, members of the Council of the National Conference discussed the project at a follow-up meeting held in Ottawa in February 1920. One of them eventually reported to Canadian Films that "the consensus of opinion of the meeting was that the Council was being used to further the interests of a commercial enterprise in the way of assisting it to dispose of stock."[79] As a result, most council members notified Canadian Films that they no longer wished to be associated with its advisory board. Tennant protested that the list of members of the board had been published "for the only purpose of inspiring confidence" and that this smear campaign was but part of "the American Film interests' . . . concerted fight against this Company."[80] Still, he had no choice but to grant council members their wish.

Gaining the educational community's confidence was not the only hurdle that Canadian Films would have to clear to develop and gainfully exploit the educational market. Another major difficulty was that despite nascent interest for audiovisual educational methods, the vast majority of Canadian educational institutions were still not equipped for moving pictures. Canadian Films would therefore have to sell projectors to schools before it could hope to sell films. Over fall 1919 and winter 1920, Tennant approached several manufacturers of portable film projectors, seeking to obtain a large quantity of easy-to-operate, inexpensive devices. There seems to have been very little discussion around the format preferred by Canadian Films: the safety base 28mm format, then the only viable alternative to 35mm, was quickly dismissed after a Pathéscope projector was tested and rejected, its portability having been deemed "unsatisfactory."[81] Of course, it remains entirely possible that by rejecting the 28mm Pathéscope format, Canadian Films was simply trying not to expand the market of the firm that would have been its main competitor in the Canadian educational film market, Toronto's Pathéscope of Canada. Original production in the 28mm format would furthermore have ruled out the theatrical

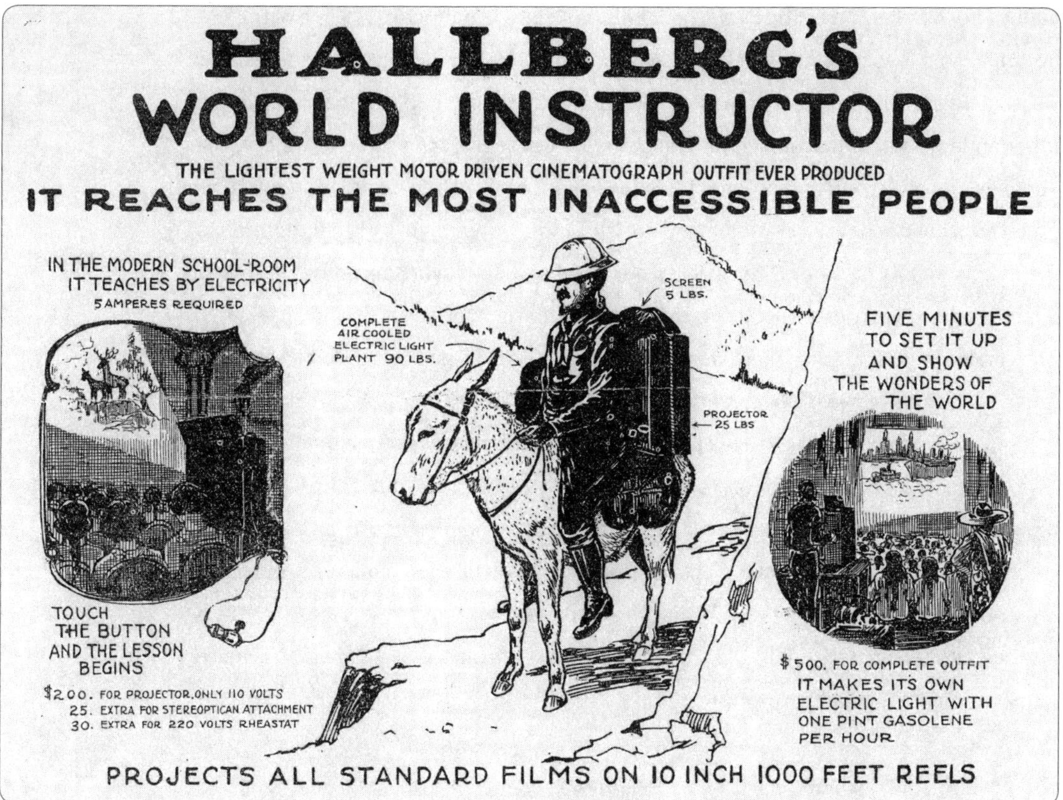

Figure 2. Hallberg promotional leaflet. Bibliothèque et Archives nationales du Québec, Canadian Films Limited collection, P324.

exhibition of its future films and thus contradicted the company's policy of producing films meant to be released through multiple screen networks.

Canadian Films's educational project would therefore have to rely on 35mm film. Tennant seems to have had no qualms about peddling 35mm projectors that could be used in any location (i.e., that would not be permanently installed inside regulation fireproof projection booths). That Canadian Films planned to print its educational films on nonflammable film was evidently considered sufficient; no thought was given to the possibility that some of these portable projectors might be used to screen nitrate prints obtained from other sources.[82] Canadian Films's technical expert examined many portable 35mm projectors and, for a variety of reasons, rejected machines manufactured by DeVry, the American Projecting Co., Educational Films, Acme, and Hallberg (the latter claiming to have perfected "the ideal outfit for lecturers, tourists, explorers and missionaries") (see Figure 2).[83]

The machine that came nearest to being adopted by Canadian Films was the portable projector manufactured by the Replogle Projector Co. of Chicago. Tennant seems to have been mainly attracted by the fact that the Replogle projector was one of the few portable machines not under the exclusive control of another agent in Canada. Its low price might also have endeared the Replogle projector to Tennant: whereas most of the other portable machines retailed for sums varying between $150 and $225 apiece, the Replogle projector could be obtained for $90. Tennant entered into negotiations with the projector's maker, Hartley L. Replogle, who, as it turns out, had just been appointed to the Illinois State's Attorney Office (where he would end up playing a leading role in the infamous 1920 Black Sox scandal) and consequently was looking to sell his firm.[84] Negotiations broke down, however, when Canadian Films received its first Replogle projectors and found them to be somewhat temperamental and thus ill fitted to the educational market.[85]

Canadian Films's change of mind over the Replogle projector should nevertheless be situated within the context of the producer's wider problems, of which it might have been more of a consequence than a cause. Tennant and his associates soon realized that their educational film project was, like their sponsored film pursuits, not going anywhere. Canadian Films's evolving discourse on the subject of schools and projectors is indeed revealing. Here is how the producer described its plan to turn Canadian schools into a new market in fall 1919:

> We propose now to make a systematic effort to place in every town throughout the Dominion a portable projecting machine. With each machine we sell we will give five reels of non-inflammable film. When we have sold machines to forty towns we will form it into a circuit and will exchange reels weekly between the different schools.
>
> We propose to teach one person in each town to operate the machine; preferably a lady teacher. She can then go from school to school in the City and exhibit the pictures on certain days in the same manner as the music teacher goes from school to school and teaches music. This field is absolutely unlimited as to educational as well as moral results.[86]

At the time of its first exchange of letters with Replogle in November 1919, Canadian Films expected to place "not less than two hundred machines" in Canadian schools during the coming twelve months.[87] For a while, Canadian Films kept up the pretense that a market for educational films was about to be formed: by March 1920, Tennant was still claiming to have Canada's one thousand schools (his figure) "well lined up" for the coming fall term.[88]

An uncharacteristically frank letter sent by Tennant to an enthusiastic educator in October 1920, however, reveals the ever-widening gap between Canadian Films's public statements and its internal assessment of the educational market's commercial potential:

> We made a thorough canvass by mail of all schools in Ontario and Manitoba where the population was more than 500. Everyone agreed with us that it was a fine thing to use films in schools, but out of the two Provinces we only received seven replies in which they stated positively that they would install educational films as part of the course. We did not receive one reply condemning film, but none of them seemed willing to invest the requisite amount of money. . . . We could not install an exchange with less than forty schools, and for that reason we dropped the matter, temporily [*sic*] at least.
>
> We have quite a number of educational films, but the films are of no value without a projector and any reliable Portable Projecting Machine would cost laid down in Canada about $250. That is very little compared to the benefits derived from the use of same, still it seems to take a personal interview to convince them.
>
> We are now producing for the Theater Exchange, and while we will be glad at any time to go into the question of educational work, we believe that the school boards are not yet ready.[89]

Unsurprisingly, Canadian Films could not accomplish what even the mighty Edison Manufacturing Co. had failed to achieve with its Edison Home Kinetoscope and its impressive catalog of reduction prints in the first half of the 1910s.[90] Though Canadian Films's failure may seem to have been predicated on its choice of a film format too expensive for schools, too bulky for "lady teachers," and presenting serious safety issues, one should remember that the appearance of 16mm film in 1923 did not result in the sudden spread of audiovisual technologies in schools, colleges, and universities. Canadian Films's own inexperience as well as the educational world's lingering mistrust of film—and sheer inertia—also contributed to the project's hasty demise.

BACK TO SPONSORED FILMS

At the conclusion of its educational episode, Canadian Films had not engaged in film production in months. To help turn things around, the company was reorganized in

March 1920, a little over a year after its creation. John D. Tennant retained his position as manager, but Ernest F. Würtele, an accountant and estate agent, replaced J. M. Tresidder as president. H. S. Couper, E. W. Dawson, and J. S. Stanford (of Stanford's Limited, butchers) were either appointed or renewed in their position as directors. A limited amount of money was raised by the sale of stock to small-time investors.[91]

The new board first tackled the issue of the company's current quarters, which were both too small and ill suited for winter work. The manager and directors resolved to look into the construction of a new building to be used as a film studio and laboratory. Soon, a lot had been located in Montreal West, an architect hired, and plans drafted.[92] The latter described an ambitious three-level structure containing offices, developing rooms, vaults, a projection booth, dressing rooms, makeup rooms and stars' rooms, a scenic studio, and a vast "six set" studio. Some of the plans' features, such as the stars' rooms and the "directors and orchestra balcony" overlooking the studio, either indicated a forthcoming turn to fiction film production or were simply put there to impress investors (see Figures 3 and 4). Ever the optimist, Tennant hoped that the new building could be completed for less than thirty-five hundred dollars.[93] Somewhat unsurprisingly, the building project stalled before construction got under way.

The films produced in 1920 by Canadian Films were generally less ambitious than the first group of films produced by the company over summer and fall 1919. In most cases, they were simple jobs contracted and supervised by outside organizations. Canadian Films first produced a series of medical films and lantern slides for Dr. Edward Archibald of McGill University, who was then seeking a cure to pancreatitis. The films and views documented two vivisection operations conducted on a dog and a cat.[94] Archibald was charged $855 for 855 feet of positive film and $26 for 26 lantern slides—not a bad deal for Canadian Films, which had received commensurate sums for the much more ambitious sponsored films it had produced the preceding year.[95] Tennant subsequently tried to get Archibald interested in a bigger project involving the making of "a complete film library of different operations." Despite Tennant's claims regarding the film library's likely "immense benefit to science as well as . . . to McGill University and ourselves," the project remained unrealized.[96]

The vivisection films were followed in June 1920 by the filming of a fire-extinguishing liquid demonstration held on Montreal's Champ-de-Mars by the Canadian Foamite Firefoam Limited. The resulting film was shown privately to the officials of the sponsoring organization but was never exhibited in commercial theaters. Canadian Foamite Firefoam declined to have the footage included (at the rate of one dollar per

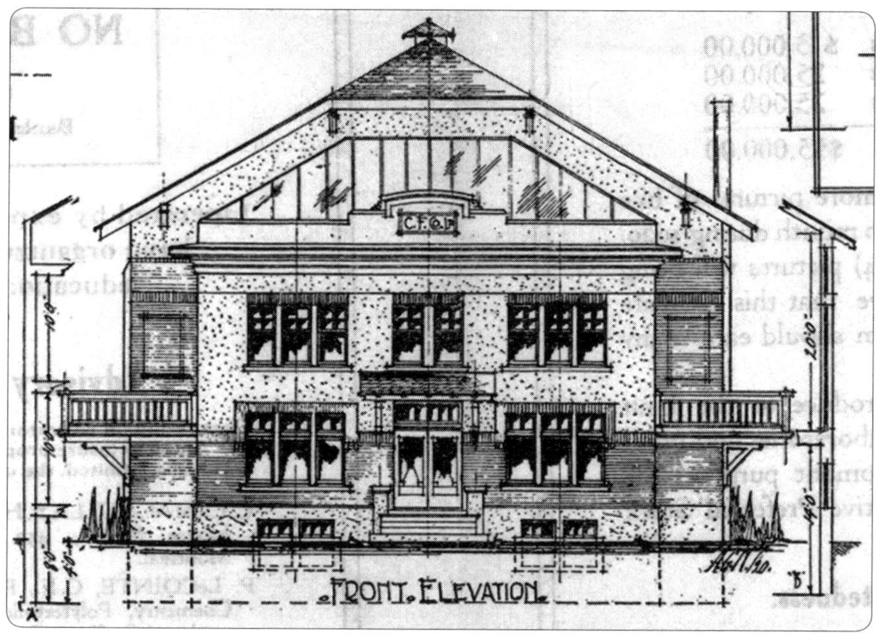

Figure 3. Proposed studio, Canadian Films, front elevation. Bibliothèque et Archives nationales du Québec, Canadian Films Limited collection, P324,D1.

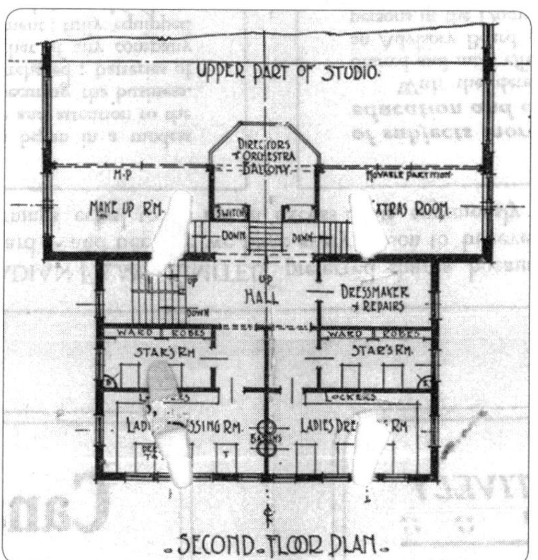

Figure 4. Proposed studio, Canadian Films, second floor. Bibliothèque et Archives nationales du Québec, Canadian Films Limited collection, P324,D1.

foot) in the sole issue of Canadian Films's screen magazine *Here and There,* which was eventually released in September.[97]

In July, at the request of the Bell Telephone Co. of Canada, Canadian Films completed a Canadian version of *Speeding the Spoken Word,* a two-reel sponsored film produced in the United States some time before 1918. The film was recut and retitled to include such gems as "when we go behind the scene in the telephone world, we enter a realm that is full of interest."[98] New interior and exterior shots of Bell's Montreal plant were also photographed and inserted. A distribution deal for the Canadian version of *Speeding the Spoken Word* was signed with the New Era Film Co. in September, but it remains impossible to ascertain if the film was ever exhibited in theaters. A Canadian version of the U.S. production *Wonders of Wireless* prepared by Canadian Films for the Marconi Wireless Telegraph Co. of Canada in August 1920 also seems to have failed to reach theaters.[99]

The last film completed by Canadian Films was also one of the first ones for which a contract had been signed, back in September 1919.[100] Variously referred to as *The Story of a Blouse* or *Your Blouse: From Factory to Home,* the film was sponsored by the D'Allaird Manufacturing Co. Work on this final Canadian Films production was completed sometime around October 1920. According to a surviving script, *The Story of a Blouse* deployed a fictional premise—a tour of the D'Allaird factory by a mother–daughter duo—to painstakingly describe the thirty-nine steps involved in the making of D'Allaird blouses. The tour guide, Miss Choquette (played by an actual D'Allaird employee), treats the duo to various remarks dealing with fabrics, manufacturing, and D'Allaird's sizeable contribution to the Canadian economy. Miss Choquette, for instance, proudly remarks that "Canadian buttons are used exclusively on all our output. . . . The establishment of D'Allaird factories has given a wonderful impetus to button making, which is gaining by leaps and bounds in our country." The inconsistent tone of many of the intertitles drafted in the script hints at the writer's struggle with the film's prosaic subject matter. Miss Choquette's comments at times refer to the book of Genesis ("You see our work is divided up more than Joseph's coat among all his brethren") or strive for a poetic view of the manufacturing process ("The eyes are the windows of the soul and button holes are the soul of a blouse"). Some of her lines express a naive view of working conditions and class relations ("The one great interest in life for this girl is tucks—that is all she does"), while others contain wisecracks that might just as well have come out of the mouth of the Canadian Explosives salesman featured in Canadian Films's first production ("The cloth is cut quicker than a profiteer guts a poor acquaintance").[101] Despite the time and effort that went into its making, *The Story of a Blouse* failed, just like the Bell and Marconi films before it, to circulate in commercial venues.[102]

A COMEDY OF ERRORS

Seemingly distraught by its difficulties in getting its films into theaters, Canadian Films announced in May 1920 that it would launch a series of twelve one-reel comedies to be produced concurrently with its industrial sponsored films.[103] The new project was much more straightforward than the company's previous schemes in that it did not involve the corralling of sponsors or the selling of projectors. Only the first title of the planned series ended up being produced, and it may very well be that the most comical thing about it was not the comedy it featured but—as film historian Germain Lacasse has discovered—an incident that occurred during its production. In the afternoon of July 6, the Canadian Films crew traveled by car to a rural area located north of Montreal to shoot a scene involving five masked bandits. The crew's day in the country was cut short, however, when the costumed actors surprised farmer Adélard Cardinal, who thought that his family was about to be attacked. Unable to explain the situation to the French-speaking farmer, the crew members were quickly forced to flee when Cardinal called his neighbors to the rescue. Emboldened by their numbers, the locals climbed in an automobile and gave pursuit to Canadian Films's team. The latter fortunately rode in a faster machine and thus managed to escape unharmed. In its report on the incident, *La Presse*—Montreal's leading French daily newspaper—noted that though the mysterious bandits had thankfully been put to rout before they could commit their horrible crimes, the inhabitants of Sainte-Dorothée were bracing themselves for their return.[104] Canadian Films's employees eventually had to meet with police detectives to explain that they were not fearsome criminals but simple "film artists."[105]

Distributed under the title *Hicks and Vamps,* this sole comedy completed by Canadian Films was privately exhibited to journalists on August 5, 1920. It then premiered on September 12 at Montreal's Imperial Theater, a prestigious movie palace operated by the Keith-Albee chain. Subsequent bookings in a few minor Montreal theaters netted Canadian Films a grand total of seventy-five dollars.[106] Published reviews were at best lukewarm. *La Presse*'s reviewer did show some leniency toward this local production, commending the film's clear photography and use of local scenery. The acting was described as being a little rough but nevertheless showing promise.[107] *La Presse* incidentally emphasized that *Hicks and Vamps* had been produced by Canadian actors and technicians. This statement, however, remains impossible to corroborate, as most of the actors and technicians involved in the production of the film are not identified in period sources. Theater advertisements only credit one actor, "Fatty Kanuck," and Canadian Films's papers name only the film's director, Fred Bezerril.[108]

Interestingly, Bezerril's sole other known film credit is for an acting turn in *The Lonely Trail,* a five-reel feature that has—mistakenly, it would seem—been credited to Canadian Films by Peter Morris in his seminal history of Canadian cinema before 1940. According to period sources, *The Lonely Trail* was shot in 1921 "in the timbered districts close by to Trois-Rivières, Quebec," as well as in the Kahnawake Mohawk reserve located on the outskirts of Montreal.[109] Its backers clearly intended to profit from the notoriety of the film's lead player, Indian guide Fred K. Beauvais, who had just been involved in the infamous Stillman divorce case.[110] Somewhat predictably, the film was rejected by the Quebec Board of Censors and widely condemned by the press in the United States, where it was briefly exhibited in early 1922.[111] The film's eventual failure to make much of an impression at the box office, however, appears to have been largely attributable not to its scandalous subtext but to its more prosaic lack of storytelling skill and entertainment value. Indeed, *Moving Picture World*'s review accused it of "[committing] the crime of killing moving picture entertainment," while *Variety* called it "the saddest bit of screen production shown anywhere near Broadway in a long time." Both reviews singled out the "awful" acting, with *Moving Picture World* noting that the man playing the "heavy" (most likely Bezerril himself) was "about the poorest excuse for an actor ever."[112]

The Lonely Trail was attributed by Morris to Canadian Films on the basis of a later comment made by its director, one Julian Rivero.[113] Period documents corroborating Rivero's assertion, however, have failed to turn up. On the contrary, the Canadian Films collection held by Bibliothèque et Archives nationales du Québec and the Municipal Archives of Montreal suggests that Canadian Films had ceased all activities by winter 1921—at least half a year before the start of *The Lonely Trail*'s production. The company's correspondence more particularly reveals that founder John D. Tennant had severed his connection to the company on or about November 1, 1920. Canadian Films was officially declared insolvent a few weeks later, in early December.[114] A company representative finally announced in February 1921 that Lieutenant Colonel H. A. S. Würtele, brother of President Ernest F. Würtele, who had replaced Tennant as manager, had also resigned and that the company had closed its plant "pending reorganization."[115] This appears to have been the end of Canadian Films.

THE RISE OF ASSOCIATED SCREEN NEWS

In summer 1920, just as Canadian Films was shooting what would turn out to be its last few productions, a new film production outfit, Associated Screen News, was established in Montreal. It would quickly become the leading Canadian private film producer. Associated Screen News's enduring success (it remained active until 1957) rested on the production of theatrical shorts (*Canadian Cameos, Kinogram Travelogues, Camera Rambles*); the production of nontheatrical educational, industrial, and sponsored films; and its laboratory services, which were used by many U.S. studios for the preparation of Canadian release prints (see Figure 5).[116] It also operated film rental libraries in Montreal, Toronto, Winnipeg, and Vancouver and—through its Benograph branch—sold 16mm projectors and other film apparatus.[117] In short, Associated Screen News did many of the things that Canadian Films had first proposed doing, and thrived.

So why did Canadian Films fail? The collected evidence suggests that insufficient capital and inexperienced management vastly contributed to making Tennant's firm a nonstarter. Associated Screen News was supported by Canada's largest company, CPR, which was its majority shareholder. It moreover benefited from the skilled management of Bernard E. Norrish, who had first launched and supervised the federal government's film bureau.[118] Norrish hired skilled technicians, such as Canadian Films's Maurice Metzger (who would remain in Associated Screen News's employ until the 1950s), but also recruited talented filmmakers such as Gordon Sparling, who had learned his trade at the Canadian Government Motion Picture Bureau and at Paramount's New York studio (see Figure 6).[119]

But Associated Screen News's success was not entirely predicated on its internal organization. Unlike Canadian Films, Associated Screen News also benefited for most of its life span from a more fully developed nontheatrical market. Though it is true that some of its productions were hits in both theatrical and nontheatrical markets (such as its shorts featuring Archibald "Grey Owl" Belaney: *Grey Owl's Little Brother* [Gordon Sparling, 1932] and *Grey Owl's Strange Guests* [Gordon Sparling, 1934]), Associated Screen News did not have to compromise by producing films that were meant to be successively disseminated through several screen networks; in other words, the profitability of most Associated Screen News productions was not dependent on their crossover potential. Unlike Tennant's firm, Associated Screen News could tailor its production to the needs of a specific market and hope to get a wide release in the screen network serving it. Indeed, in a 1932 article on "commercial movies," Gordon Sparling hammers home that "a study

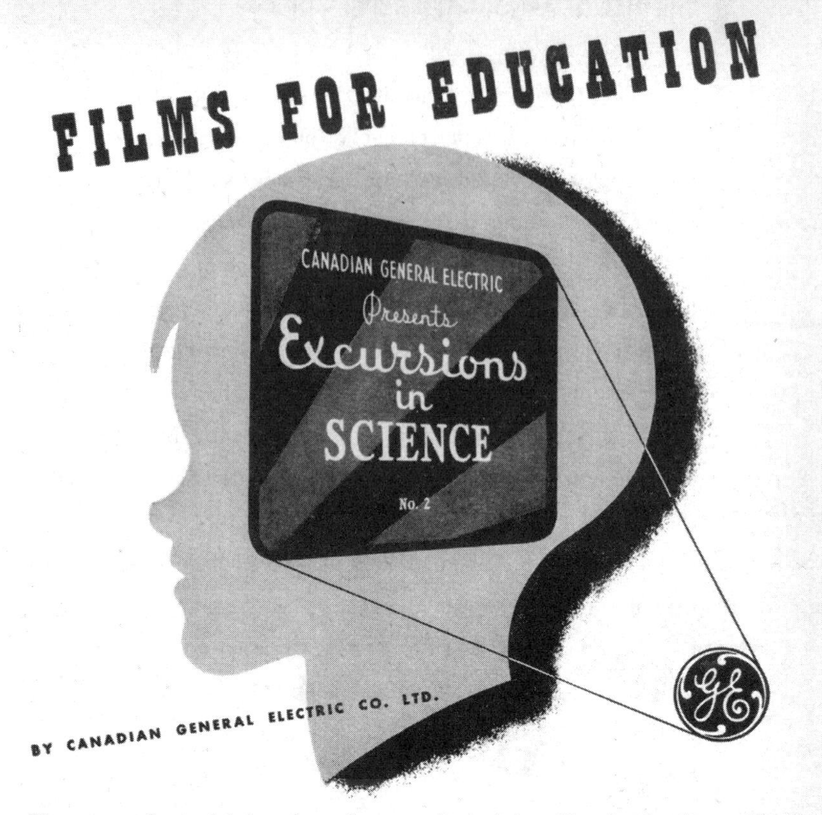

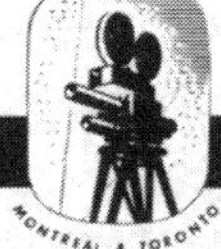

Figure 5. Print advertisement for a series of sponsored educational films distributed by Associated Screen News. *Canadian Business* 21, no. 10 (1948): 105.

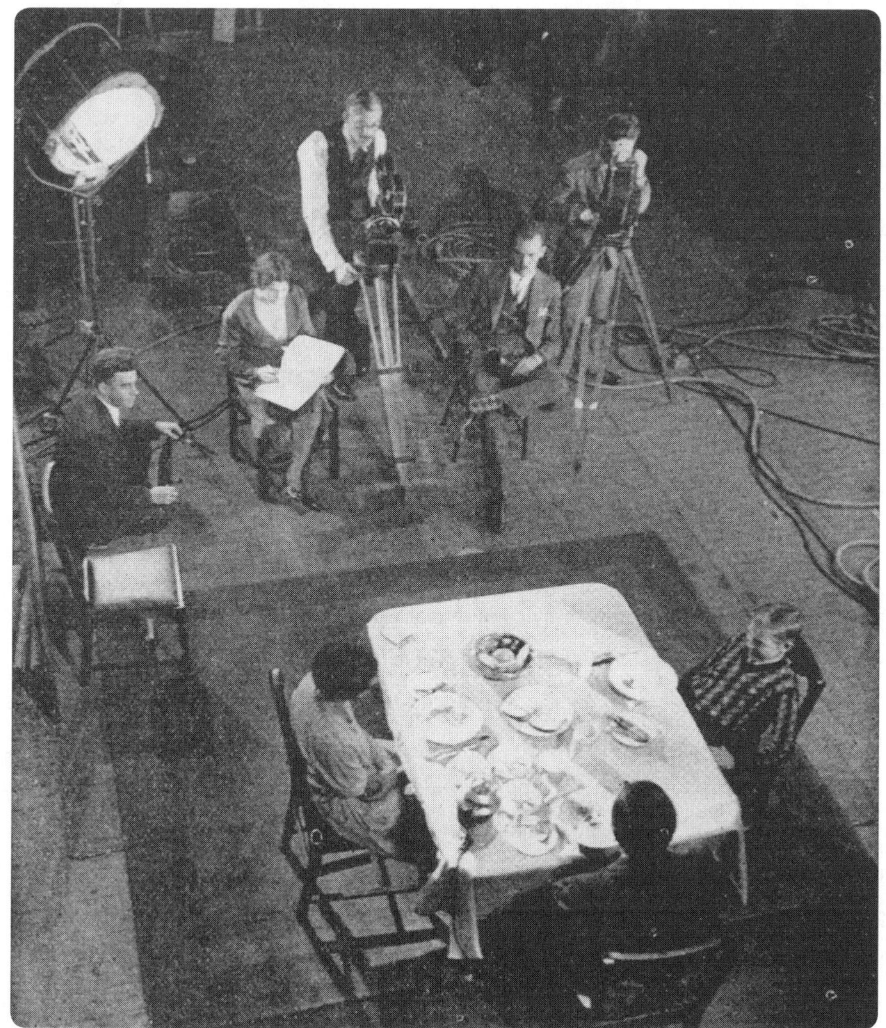

Figure 6. Gordon Sparling at work on a sponsored film. Sparling, "Movies Tell the Story," *Commerce of the Nation* 5, no. 8 (1932): 13.

of the most suitable outlets is of as great importance as the construction of the scenario."[120]

A comparison of Canadian Films's *The Story of a Blouse* (1920) and Associated Screen News's *The Miracle of a Locomotive* (1928)—both process films—is quite telling. As we have seen, the *Story of a Blouse* script suggests that the completed film's lack of a commercial career might have been partly caused by its makers' insistence on showing the full thirty-nine steps involved in the making of a D'Allaird

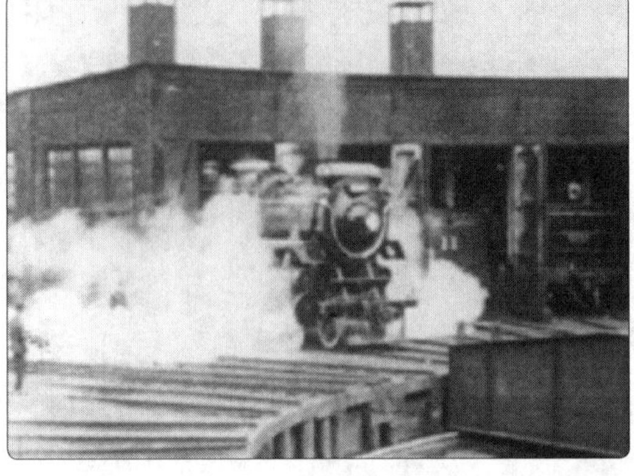

Figure 7. Frame from *The Miracle of a Locomotive* (Associated Screen News, 1928). Cinémathèque québécoise.

blouse. As a result, this film, too brief to function as a training tool, was too tedious to be bothered with by commercial exhibitors and was thus prevented from performing its advertising function. *The Miracle of a Locomotive,* on the other hand, still remains an engaging production. Produced for theatrical release by Associated Screen News, the film deals with an exciting subject: the making of the Commonwealth's largest locomotive, "from pattern shop to the rails." It was skillfully edited by none other than Terry Ramsaye and is full of images of gigantic molds and presses and glowing molten metal. The film's final sequence is particularly spectacular: it shows the majestic locomotive coming out of the shops, letting out a cloud of steam and then darting on the rails for a trial run (see Figure 7). The locomotive runs over the camera, concealed in a pit dug between the tracks, for the film's grand finale.

It is only through these spectacular—and at times somewhat hammy—scenes that the two main functions of the process film identified by Hediger and Vonderau become operative. First, by framing *The Miracle of a Locomotive* as a piece of entertainment, Associated Screen News enabled it to reach the mass audience that it needed to fulfill its mercantile function, which was to give testimony to the quality of the CPR's fleet. Second, these visual records situated the film in an educational tradition going back, once again according to Hediger and Vonderau, to Diderot's and Alembert's eighteenth-century *Encyclopédie.* Just like that of the *Encyclopédie,* the film's profuse visual documentation of the production process of a locomotive was (quite obviously) tailored to the needs of an audience having no intention of participating in the process. In other words, it was not intended for practical purposes.[121]

Through its skillful uses of photography and editing, *The Miracle of a Locomotive* manages to create drama from an industrial subject. In doing so, it brings forth one of the main reasons why "useful cinema" has largely been written out of film history: the very limited use of cinema's expressive tools by many educational, industrial, and sponsored films. Quite a few of the films falling under these categories were conceived as simple visual records or didactic tools and consequently did not rely on mise-en-scène or editing to guide the reception process and generate meaning. They depended, instead, on external elements, be they a printed manual or the explanations of a lecturer or instructor. Taken out of their intended reception contexts, that is, devoid of these adjuncts, they can become quite opaque (which partly explains the repeated uses of educational, industrial, and sponsored films' images and tropes by avant-garde filmmakers and, more particularly, by artists working with found footage). Though these practices constituted an entirely legitimate use of film, they have resulted in a tendency to situate this particular strand of filmmaking outside the field of inquiry of film studies, which has long primarily been interested in film as a narrative form of expression and in the filmmaker as an auteur. The situation of educational, industrial, and sponsored films can thus be likened to that of early fiction films, which also depended on external agents (a lecturer, the viewer's previous knowledge of the story) and have consequently been dismissed as "primitive" and thus have been glossed over in film histories for many years.

Canadian Films did intend to produce films that would stand on their own, that is, that would rely on their formal properties rather than on external agents to guide the reception process. The company lacked a clear idea, however, of whom its films were intended for. This indecision prevented it from devising the right mixture of genres for each of its productions. Evidence tends to demonstrate that though film genres and categories can indeed be combined, various reception contexts will require some genres to be subordinated to others. The educational side of the process film *The Miracle of a Locomotive,* for instance, was most likely accepted by theatrical audiences because the spectacle offered by the film was deemed entertaining. Similarly, the slight comedic side of *Grey Owl's Little Brother* was tolerated by the educators who frequently presented it because it was made to serve the film's educational content. It should also be noted that in every reception context, some genres would routinely be rejected. Promotional films, for example, were frowned on in most theatrical and educational contexts. Associated Screen News did manage to get an advertisement for CPR past theatrical audiences with *The Miracle of a Locomotive,* but only by framing it as a routine process film and by making the film's few explicit references to CPR appear incidental. Canadian Films, with its blatant advertisements for dynamite, blouses, and apartment buildings, did not stand much of a chance to get its films exhibited in theaters.

The Miracle of a Locomotive's success, finally, points to yet another possible cause of Canadian Films's failure. Associated Screen News could get sponsored films shown in schools and commercial theaters because it preferred the soft-sell approach, but also, more importantly, because it employed creative individuals who knew how to effectively sugarcoat the films' messages. The few extant Canadian Films scripts as well as the failure of the producer's sole title framed as pure entertainment, *Hicks and Vamps,* suggest that Canadian Films's personnel were somewhat less gifted at humor and storytelling. Canadian Films's story thus serves as a useful reminder that though educational, industrial, and sponsored films must be treated on their own terms (most notably by paying attention to the networks and uses to which they were destined) if they are to be given a fair shake by film history, issues of narration and aesthetics are not always irrelevant when dealing with them. Political economy and market studies can only explain so much.

NOTES

I am most grateful to Carolina Lucchesi Lavoie and JoAnne Stober for helping me gain access to some of the documents used in my research. Many thanks also go to Charles Acland and the two anonymous readers who provided much constructive criticism of this article and to Timothy Barnard, who helped revise it for publication. This project was funded by research grants from the Social Sciences and Humanities Research Council of Canada and Bibliothèque et Archives nationales du Québec.

1. Canadian Films was incorporated on March 17, 1919. It had actively been seeking out customers since at least early February of that year, however. Fact sheet, Bibliothèque et Archives nationales du Québec, Canadian Films Limited collection, P324 (hereinafter BAnQ); Halifax Board of Trade to Canadian Films, February 7, 1919, BAnQ.
2. Peter Morris, *Embattled Shadows: A History of Canadian Cinema, 1895–1939* (Montreal, QC: McGill/Queen's University Press, 1978); Germain Lacasse, *Histoires de scopes: le cinéma muet au Québec* (Montreal, QC: Cinémathèque québécoise, 1988). André Gaudreault, Germain Lacasse, and Pierre Véronneau have collaborated on the Silent Era Quebec Filmography Project (http://cri.histart.umontreal.ca/grafics/fr/filmo/default.asp), while Charles Acland has initiated the Canadian Educational, Sponsored, and Industrial Film Project, whose database will be made available online in 2011.
3. On the category of useful cinema, see Charles Acland and Haidee Wasson, eds., *Useful Cinema* (Durham, NC: Duke University Press, forthcoming).
4. Rick Altman, "Reusable Packaging: Generic Products and the Recycling Process," in *Refiguring American Film Genres,* ed. Nick Browne (Berkeley: University of California Press, 1998), 7.
5. Frank Kessler and Eef Masson, "Layers of Cheese: Generic Overlap in Early

Non-fiction Films on Production Processes," in *Films That Work: Industrial Film and the Productivity of Media*, ed. Vinzenz Hediger and Patrick Vonderau (Amsterdam: Amsterdam University Press, 2009), 83.

6. Vinzenz Hediger and Patrick Vonderau, "Record, Rhetoric, Rationalization: Industrial Organization and Film," in Hediger and Vonderau, *Films That Work*, 46.

7. Roger Odin, "Sémio-pragmatique du cinéma et de l'audiovisuel: Modes et institutions," in *Towards a Pragmatics of the Audiovisual: Theory and History*, ed. Jürgen E. Müller (Münster, Germany: Nodus Publikationen, 1994), 39.

8. Kessler and Masson, "Layers of Cheese," 75–76.

9. *Jean Painlevé au fil de ses films* (La Sept/GMT Productions, 1988).

10. Canadian Photo-Play Productions prospectus, BAnQ; Morris, *Embattled Shadows*, 83–84.

11. Throughout, dollars are Canadian dollars.

12. Statement of Canadian Films Limited, February 20, 1920, BAnQ.

13. The long list of Canadian film producers missing in action includes Montreal's British American Manufacturing Co. (1912–13), Halifax's Canadian Bioscope (1913–14), Windsor's All-Red Feature Film Co. (1914), and Toronto's Conness Till Film Co. (1914–15). Morris, *Embattled Shadows*, 47–54.

14. A. A. Dickson to the Secretary of the Board of Education, Victoria Harbour, Ontario, December 2, 1919, BAnQ.

15. Canadian Films to H. A. Wilson, Montreal Cottons Ltd., May 2, 1919, BAnQ.

16. Evidence suggests that John D. Tennant might have been a U.S. citizen. A letter to the Beta Theta Pi Club of New York (December 18, 1919) indicates that somebody at Canadian Films, most likely Tennant, had graduated in 1905 from Knox College (Galesburg, Illinois) (BAnQ). Moreover, Tennant is not listed in pre-1919 editions of Lovell's Montreal directory.

17. Morris, *Embattled Shadows*, 131–37, 149–52.

18. Ibid., 143–49; Anke Mebold and Charles Tepperman, "Resurrecting the Lost History of 28mm in North America," *Film History* 15, no. 2 (2003): 146.

19. J. D. Tennant to Prof. H. T. J. Coleman (Queen's University), February 23, 1920, BAnQ.

20. J. D. Tennant to Rev. J. A. Richardson, March 1, 1920, BAnQ.

21. J. D. Tennant to W. A. Wilson, August 27, 1919, Montreal Municipal Archives, Canadian Films Limited collection (hereinafter MMA), BM54,D2.

22. E. A. Saunders, Secretary, Halifax Board of Trade, to Canadian Films, February 7, 1919, BAnQ. See also Wallace L. Higgins, Charlottetown Board of Trade, to Canadian Films, February 13, 1919, BAnQ.

23. Canadian Films, income tax return for the year 1919, BAnQ. Maurice Metzger received $1,680 for the twenty-eight weeks he spent working for Canadian Films in 1919.

24. *Filmographie des "vues" tournées au Québec au temps du muet*, http:// cri.histart.umontreal.ca/grafics/fr/filmo/viewrec.asp?lang=fr&id=324; prospectus, Premier Film Manufacturing Co. of Canada, BAnQ; H. H. McArthur to Hye Bossin, March 31, 1951, Library and Archives Canada,

2000–0012, Container 4, Hye Bossin File; Gordon Sparling, "The Great Canadian Movie," lecture presented at the University of Toronto, December 11, 1951, Canadian Film Institute collection, 2000–0012, Container 7, General Histories File; Gerald G. Graham, *The Birth of Canadian Film Technology* (London: Associated University Presses, 1989), 71–72.

25. See the following replies to Canadian Films's inquiry: A. P. Simard, Industrial Commissioner, City of Vancouver, to Canadian Films, February 24, 1919, BAnQ; E. A. Saunders, Secretary, Halifax Board of Trade, to Canadian Films, February 7, 1919, BAnQ; Wallace L. Higgins, Charlottetown Board of Trade, to Canadian Films, February 13, 1919, BAnQ.

26. J. D. Tennant to D. K. Walker, May 21, 1919, BAnQ.

27. Canadian Films, copy of the letter sent to the boards of trade in the Canadian West, April 11, 1919, BAnQ.

28. Ibid.

29. *Edison Kinetogram* 2, no. 5 (1910): 4; 2, no. 4 (1910): 4.

30. J. D. Tennant to the J. L. Mathieu Syrup Co., undated, BAnQ. The earliest mention of the Cameragram series in Canadian Films's papers appears in a letter from J. D. Tennant to A. W. Wilson dated May 16, 1919 (BAnQ).

31. Canadian Films, telegram to W. G. McLaughlan, August 5, 1919, BAnQ; W. G. McLaughlan, telegram to Canadian Films, August 11, 1919, BAnQ.

32. Morris, *Embattled Shadows*, 61.

33. Rosemary Bergeron, "A History of the Newsreel in Canada," *The Moving Image* 7, no. 2 (2007): 27–31.

34. A partial list of companies contacted in August and September of 1919 can be consulted in BAnQ.

35. J. D. Tennant to McKinnon Steel Co., Sherbrooke, September 1919, BAnQ.

36. J. D. Tennant to Geo. Phillips and Co., August 28, 1919, BAnQ.

37. For a list of companies interested by Canadian Films's proposal, see J. D. Tennant to W. A. Wilson, August 27, 1919, MMA, BM54,D2.

38. Canadian Films to G. A. Holland and Son Co., September 26, 1919, BAnQ.

39. Kathryn H. Fuller, *At the Picture Show: Small-town Audiences and the Creation of Movie-fan Culture* (Washington, DC: Smithsonian Institution Press, 1996), 84–85, 94.

40. Canadian Films Questionnaire, undated, BAnQ. The film's shooting script bears the title *Farming with Dynamite*, which, interestingly enough, was also the title of a film distributed by du Pont de Nemours and Co. in the early 1920s (*Wid's Year Book*, 1920–21, 169). There is no way to tell if this is a coincidence or an indication that Canadian Films's first production actually circulated outside Canada, or if this situation points to a possible case of plagiarism.

41. *Farming with Dynamite*, dramatis personae, MMA, BM54,D2.

42. Ibid.

43. J. B. Moriarty to Canadian Films, October 20, 1919, BAnQ.

44. Canadian Films, invoices sent to Canadian Explosives, November 26, 1919, and February 18, 1920, BAnQ.

45. J. D. Tennant to Ed. English, Famous Lasky Film Service Ltd., October 12, 1920, BAnQ.

46. William F. Breyfogle to J. D. Tennant, August 21, 1919, MMA, BM54,D1.

47. Montreal Dairy Co. to Canadian Films, December 9, 1919, BAnQ; J. D. Tennant to DeLaval Separator Co., April 13, 1920, MMA, BM54,D1; W. R. Breyfogle to J. D. Tennant, May 20, 1920, MMA, BM54,D1; *Montreal Daily Star*, December 20, 1919, 24; *Moving Picture World* 43, no. 2 (1920): 243.

48. W. R. Breyfogle to Canadian Films, August 15, 1919, MMA, BM54,D1.

49. A detailed list of shots and titles, identifying sponsors, is included in BAnQ's Canadian Films Limited collection.

50. J. D. Tennant to Mott Co., December 10, 1919, BAnQ; J. D. Tennant to McKinnon Steel Co., May 17, 1920, BAnQ.

51. *The Fur Industry of Canada*, synopsis, BAnQ.

52. Canadian Films, contract with Holt, Renfrew, and Co., September 10, 1919, BAnQ; J. D. Tennant to Holt, Renfrew, and Co., January 13, 1920, BAnQ; Canadian Films to Holt, Renfrew, and Co., June 21, 1920, BAnQ.

53. Canadian Films to Holt, Renfrew, and Co., June 21, 1920, BAnQ; Canadian Films, invoice sent to Holt, Renfrew, and Co., August 10, 1920, BAnQ.

54. Holt, Renfrew, and Co. to Canadian Films, May 22, 1920, BAnQ.

55. Canadian Films paid US $61.13 to have the 960' 35mm negative copied unto 768' Pathéscope positive. Pathéscope of America, invoice sent to Canadian Films, August 4, 1920, BAnQ. Toronto's Pathéscope of Canada treated Canadian Films as a competitor and consequently declined to prepare the 28mm print of *The Fur Industry of Canada*. Pathéscope of Canada to J. D. Tennant, June 25, 1920, BAnQ.

56. J. D. Tennant to Holt, Renfrew, and Co., October 2, 1920, BAnQ.

57. Holt, Renfrew, and Co. to Canadian Films, October 23, 1920, BAnQ.

58. "Pictured Making of Fur Garment," *The Gazette*, February 20, 1920, 6.

59. Ibid.

60. A. A. Dickson to Windsor Hotel, November 21, 1919, MMA, BM54,D2.

61. *One of Canada's Leading Hotels*, list of titles, MMA, BM54,D2.

62. Canadian Films, contract with the Windsor Hotel Co., November 26, 1919, MMA, BM54,D2; Canadian Films to *Keeler's Hotel Weekly*, December 27, 1919, MMA, BM54,D2.

63. John D. Davidson to Canadian Films, September 7, 1920, MMA, BM54,D2.

64. Canadian Films, contract with the Windsor Hotel Co., November 26, 1919, MMA, BM54,D2.

65. See, e.g., J. D. Tennant to Mott Co., December 10, 1919, BAnQ.

66. The epoch-making agreement between Adolph Zukor's Famous Players–Lasky and Nathan L. Nathanson's Famous Players Canadian Corp. was signed on February 5, 1920. See Manjunath Pendakur, *Canadian Dreams and American Control: The Political Economy of the Canadian Film Industry* (Toronto, ON: Garamond Press, 1990), 57–58.

67. Files of the Bureau de censure des vues animées de la Province de Québec, Bibliothèque et Archives nationales du Québec, Régie du Cinéma collection, E188.

68. Fuller, *At the Picture Show*, 83–85.

69. A. A. Dickson to W. H. Abbott, School Commissioner, Lennoxville, Quebec, December 12, 1919, BAnQ.

70. J. D. Tennant to the chief inspector of schools, Toronto, Ontario, January 13, 1920, BAnQ.

71. See, e.g., H. V. Nelles, *The Art of Nation-building: Pageantry and Spectacle at Quebec's Tercentenary* (Toronto, ON: University of Toronto Press, 1999).

72. Tom Mitchell, "The Manufacture of Souls of Good Quality: Winnipeg's 1919 National Conference on Canadian Citizenship, English–Canadian Nationalism, and the New Order after the Great War," *Journal of Canadian Studies* 31, no. 4 (1996–97): 21, quoted in Rosa Bruno-Jofre, "Citizenship and Schooling in Manitoba, 1918–1945," *Manitoba History* 36 (1998): 26–28.

73. Bruno-Jofre, "Citizenship and Schooling," 26–28.

74. The resolution contains another section on the censoring of film posters and advertisements. Quoted in undated Canadian Films Prospectus, BAnQ.

75. Lee Grieveson, *Policing Cinema: Movies and Censorship in Early-twentieth-century America* (Berkeley: University Press of California, 2004), 12–14; Ronald Walter Greene, "Y Movies: Films and the Modernization of Pastoral Power," *Communication and Critical/Cultural Studies* 2, no. 1 (2005): 21.

76. J. D. Tennant to Tom Moore, President, Trades and Labour Congress of Canada, January 3, 1920, BAnQ.

77. J. T. M. Anderson to Canadian Films, January 7, 1920, BAnQ; Louis Bourgoin to J. D. Tennant, January 19, 1920, BAnQ; Margaret Boyle to J. D. Tennant, December 29, 1919, BAnQ; Jean E. Brown to J. D. Tennant, December 29, 1919, BAnQ; Austin Ireland, letter to Canadian Films, February 20, 1920, BAnQ.

78. Canadian Film Underwriters, Advisory Board of Canadian Films Limited, undated, BAnQ.

79. W. G. Carpenter, Superintendent of Schools, Edmonton Public School Board, to J. D. Tennant, March 15, 1920, BAnQ.

80. J. D. Tennant to P. LeCointe, École Polytechnique de Montréal, March 5, 1920, BAnQ.

81. J. D. Tennant to the Replogle Projector Co., November 6, 1919, BAnQ; Pathéscope Co. of America to Canadian Films, December 5, 1919, BAnQ.

82. J. D. Tennant to the Protestant Board of School Commissioners, December 11, 1919, BAnQ.

83. Ray Film Co. to Canadian Films, October 28, 1919, BAnQ; J. D. Tennant to the Replogle Projector Co., November 6, 1919, BAnQ; Educational Films, temporary prospectus for the new Rotary projection machine, BAnQ; J. D. Tennant to United Theatre Equipment, January 9, 1920, BAnQ; J. D. Tennant to United Theatre Equipment, March 2, 1920, BAnQ; American Projecting Co. to J. D. Tennant, February 19, 1920, BAnQ.

84. In fall 1920, several members of the Chicago team were found guilty of having thrown the 1919 World Series. See Lewis Thompson and Charles Boswell, "Say It Ain't So, Joe!" *American Heritage* 11, no. 4 (1960), http://

www.americanheritage.com/articles/magazine/ah/1960/4/1960_4_24.shtml;
Hartley L. Replogle to J. D. Tennant, January 5, 1920, BAnQ.

85. J. D. Tennant to Hartley L. Replogle, January 20, 1920, BAnQ.

86. Canadian Films, undated prospectus (most likely November or December 1919), BAnQ.

87. J. D. Tennant to the Replogle Projector Co., November 6, 1919, BAnQ.

88. J. D. Tennant to United Theatre Equipment Corp., March 2, 1920, BAnQ.

89. J. D. Tennant to J. M. Shuttleworth, October 9, 1920, BAnQ.

90. The 22mm Edison Home Kinetoscope had been introduced in 1912 and discontinued when a fire destroyed much of Edison's plant in December 1914. Most of the rhetoric deployed by its marketing campaign had focused on its educational potential. See "Edison and the New Education," *Talking Machine World* 8, no. 2 (1912): 42; Ben Singer, "Early Home Cinema and the Edison Home Projecting Kinetoscope," *Film History* 2, no. 1 (1988): 37–69.

91. Minutes of a meeting of the directors of Canadian Films, March 1, 1920, BAnQ; Canadian Films to D. S. Perrin and Co., March 22, 1920, BAnQ; Ernest W. Würtele to J. D. Tennant, November 30, 1920, BAnQ; Canadian Films, sale of stock certificates, BAnQ; *Lovell's.*

92. Minutes of a meeting of the directors of Canadian Films, April 14, 1920, BAnQ; Canadian Films to V. W. Dawson, July 14, 1920, BAnQ.

93. Minutes of a meeting of the directors of Canadian Films, June 15, 1920, BAnQ; Alfred G. Nosworthy to Canadian Films, September 29, 1920, BAnQ.

94. J. D. Tennant to Dr. Edward Archibald, March 25, 1920; descriptive list of films and slides, MMA, BM54,D1.

95. Invoices sent by Canadian Films to Dr. Edward Archibald, November 4 and 19, 1920, MMA, BM54,D1.

96. J. D. Tennant to Dr. Edward Archibald, March 25, 1920, MMA, BM54,D1.

97. Canadian Foamite Firefoam to Canadian Films, June 23, 1920; July 22, 1920, MMA, BM54,D3; Canadian Films to Canadian Foamite and Firefoam, June 25, 1920, MMA, BM54,D3; Ronald Press and Advertising Agency, invoice for twenty-one titles for *Here and There*, BAnQ; Files of the Board of Censors of Moving Pictures of the Province of Quebec, September 11, 1920, Bibliothèque et Archives nationales du Québec, Régie du cinéma collection, E188.

98. Canadian Films to V. W. Dawson, July 14, 1920, BAnQ. The contract between Canadian Films and the Bell Telephone Co. of Canada had been signed on January 16, 1920 (see copy in MMA, BM54,D1). *Speeding the Spoken Word* was mentioned in *The Rotarian* 10, no. 6 (1917): 674. The intertitle is from Bell Telephone Co. of Canada to Canadian Films, April 22, 1920, MMA, BM54,D1.

99. J. D. Tennant to the Marconi Wireless Telegraph Co. of Canada, August 19, 1920; October 9, 1920, BAnQ. Files of the Board of Censors of Moving Pictures of the Province of Quebec, August 5, 1920, Bibliothèque et Archives nationales du Québec, Régie du cinéma collection, E188.

100. Canadian Films, contract with D'Allaird Manufacturing Co., September 2, 1919, MMA, BM54,D1.

101. Script, *Your Blouse: From Factory to Home*, MMA, BM54,D1.

102. D'Allaird Manufacturing Co. to Canadian Films, January 26, 1921, MMA, BM54,D1.

103. J. D. Tennant to Estelle Cuffe, May 12, 1920, MMA, BM54,D1.

104. "Cinq bandits masqués causent un vif émoi dans Sainte-Dorothée," *La Presse*, July 8, 1920, 13, quoted in Lacasse, *Histoires de scopes*, 63–64.

105. "Des artistes de cinéma et non de terribles bandits," *La Presse*, July 9, 1920, 9.

106. "Une représentation d'un film canadien," *La Presse*, August 6, 1920, 3; Imperial Theater advertisement, *La Patrie*, September 11, 1920, 21; Canadian Films, invoice sent to the Imperial Theater, October 7, 1920, BAnQ; Arthur St-Germain to Canadian Films, October 9, 1920, BAnQ; Canadian Films, invoice sent to Passe-temps Theater, November 17, 1920, BAnQ.

107. "Une représentation d'un film canadien."

108. Canadian Films's papers nevertheless reveal that five persons were hired for the production of *Hicks and Vamps*. Imperial Theater advertisement, *La Patrie*, September 11, 1920, 21; minutes of a meeting of the directors of Canadian Films, July 15, 1920, BAnQ.

109. "Beauvais to Star in Broadway Movie—'The Lonely Trail,' Written by the Indian Guide, Will Be Presented Here Soon," *New York Times*, December 22, 1921, 18; "Producers Reject Beauvais Picture," *New York Times*, December 23, 1921, 18; Morris, *Embattled Shadows*, 295.

110. In 1921, James A. Stillman, chairman of National City Bank, accused his wife, Anne Urquhart Stillman, of having had an affair with Fred K. Beauvais, an Indian guide she had met while summering in Quebec. The sensational Stillman divorce case made headlines for months. See, e.g., "Asks Medium's Aid for Mrs. Stillman," *New York Times*, May 16, 1921, 10; "Beauvais Confers with Mrs. Stillman," *New York Times*, January 6, 1922, 10.

111. The film had been submitted to the Board of Censors by Specialty Film Import. The reason given for the rejection was that the main character was involved in a scandalous affair. Files of the Board of Censors of Moving Pictures of the Province of Quebec, August 5, 1920, Bibliothèque et Archives nationales du Québec, Régie du cinéma collection, E188; Files of the Board of Censors of Moving Pictures of the Province of Quebec, August 5, 1920, Bibliothèque et Archives nationales du Québec, Régie du cinéma collection, E188.

112. "'Indian Guide' Feature 'Will Die If Let Alone,'" *Variety*, January 6, 1922; Fritz Tidden, "'The Lonely Trail' Has the Distinction of Being the Worst Picture That Has Screened Itself This Way in Years," *Moving Picture World* 54, no. 2 (1922): 205, quoted in Morris, *Embattled Shadows*, 295.

113. Morris, *Embattled Shadows*, 295.

114. Canadian Films to Ernest F. Würtele, December 15, 1920, BAnQ.

115. WCS to D'Allaird Manufacturing Co., February 5, 1921, MMA.

116. "Screen News of Canada Made by Newly Organized Company," *Moving Picture World* 45, no. 4 (1920): 475, quoted in Morris, *Embattled Shadows*, 223.

117. "To Discontinue Film Rentals," *The Shawinigan Standard*, March 31, 1954, 4.

118. "Canadian Pacific Owns Control of Screen News," *New York Times,* January 29, 1937, 27; Morris, *Embattled Shadows,* 132–33, 222.

119. *Business Screen* 14, no. 1 (1953): 90; "With Associated Screen News: Gordon Sparling to Direct and Edit Commercial Films," *The Gazette,* July 23, 1931, 27.

120. Gordon Sparling, "Movies Tell the Story," *Commerce of the Nation* 5, no. 8 (1932): 13.

121. Hediger and Vonderau, "Record, Rhetoric, Rationalization," 44–45.

FORUM

FORU

Present at the Creation

A Memoir

WENDY ANN SHAY

There are facts and there are memories. One thing is certain: everyone involved with the creation of the Association of Moving Image Archivists (AMIA) was focused on establishing an organization. That we would ever celebrate the organization's twentieth anniversary never entered our minds.

AMIA was certainly not created in a day. There was never a Mickey Rooney–Judy Garland moment when we all thought, "Let's have a professional organization," and there it was. Creating AMIA was a multiyear, multistep process to which many people contributed and about which even more people had a say.

The growth of the field was one of the most important factors leading to the creation of a formal North American group interested in moving image archiving. Beginning as a trickle in the early 1980s, the mid-1980s saw a huge increase in the number of individuals and institutions caring for moving image materials. Suddenly people trained as archivists, librarians, and museum specialists found themselves responsible for film and video collections. Published information about caring for these formats was limited. Consequently, newly minted film and television archivists cast about looking for guidance. The lucky ones found out about the Film Archives Advisory Committee and the Television Archives Advisory Committee (F/TAAC), the informal but significant group described by William T. Murphy in his contribution to this issue. As Murphy points out, during its early years, F/TAAC participants all sat around a single table to share information and discuss common concerns. By the late 1980s, there were just too many people to sit around a single table and talk.

Murphy discusses the evolution in F/TAAC meetings as a growing roster of participants necessitated holding the meetings in larger venues as well as organizing panels with presenters and guided discussions. However, throughout its growth, F/TAAC retained its essential roundtable discussion quality. Meetings always provided the opportunity for updates, conversation about matters of concern, and information sharing. In addition, F/TAAC provided new and veteran film and television archivists—many of whom were considered seriously out of the mainstream in their home institutions—with a sense of community as moving image archivists. Attending F/TAAC meetings reaffirmed that moving images were primary historical and cultural documents that deserved archival attention. Despite its lack of formal structure, or maybe because of it, F/TAAC was a unique professional group in which everyone was equal.

By 1989, however, it was clear to many of us that we needed to consider how F/TAAC should move forward. There was the issue of pure numbers. Could the group continue to function as it had as more and more people became involved? There was also the issue of representing the field. Without any formal structure, it was impossible for the group to speak in support of film and television preservation. In fact, the group had no mechanism for voting on where to hold the next gathering, let alone for taking public stands on issues of concern.

The first Future of F/TAAC Committee was constituted in 1988 during a gathering in Ottawa. With Gregory Lukow of the National Center for Film and Video Preservation volunteering to coordinate the effort, the committee was asked to prepare a questionnaire to survey the field regarding the various options. Committee

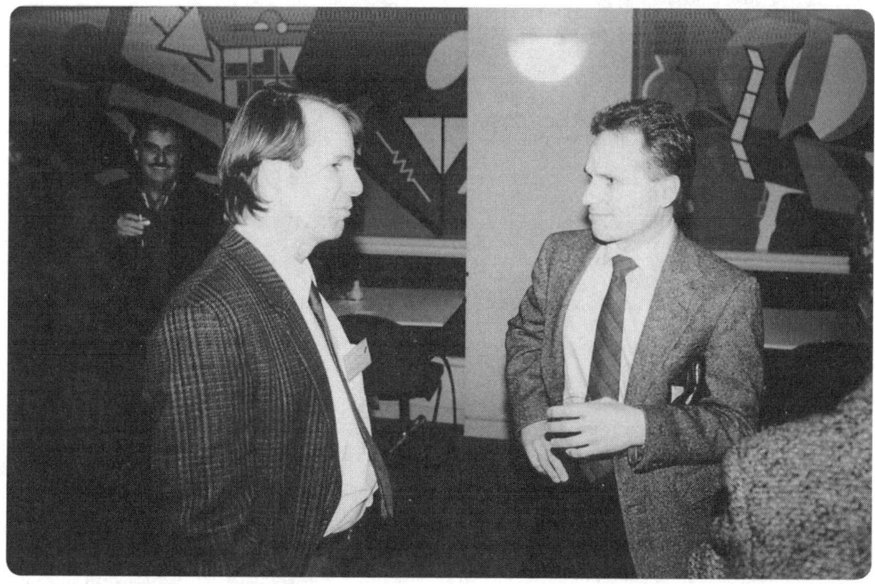

Michael Friend and Grover Crisp at the first AMIA conference in New York City, 1991, three years before they organized the first The Reel Thing Technical Symposium at the 1994 Boston conference. Photo courtesy Gregory Lukow.

volunteers included Murphy (National Archives and Records Administration), Sara Meyerson (ABC News Library), Fay Schreibman (Museum of Jewish Heritage), Maxine Fleckner Ducey (Wisconsin Center for Film and Theater Research), Sam Kula (National Archive of Canada), Barbara Humphrys (Archives Center, National Museum of American History), Steve Davidson (Louis Wolfson II Media History Center), William Reader (U.S. Department of Defense), Sarah Richards (National Library of Medicine), and me (Human Studies Film Archive, Smithsonian Institution).

I have no memory of the meetings we held to develop the questionnaire. According to the summary of the survey results, basic questions regarding the size and type of the respondents' archives were followed by the all-critical F/TAAC-specific questions: what do you want from F/TAAC? Exchanging information? Expressing positions on archival matters? Organizing work-shops and seminars? Establishing standards? Publishing? Lobbying? Unified fund-raising?

The survey then posed the questions that got to the crux of the matter of how F/TAAC could best carry out these functions. Nineteen respondents voted in favor of becoming a formal organization, and seven wanted to remain an informally organized group. Seventeen felt that if F/TAAC were to become formal, it should be both institutional and individual, whereas seven felt it should be institutional only, and three felt it should be individual only.

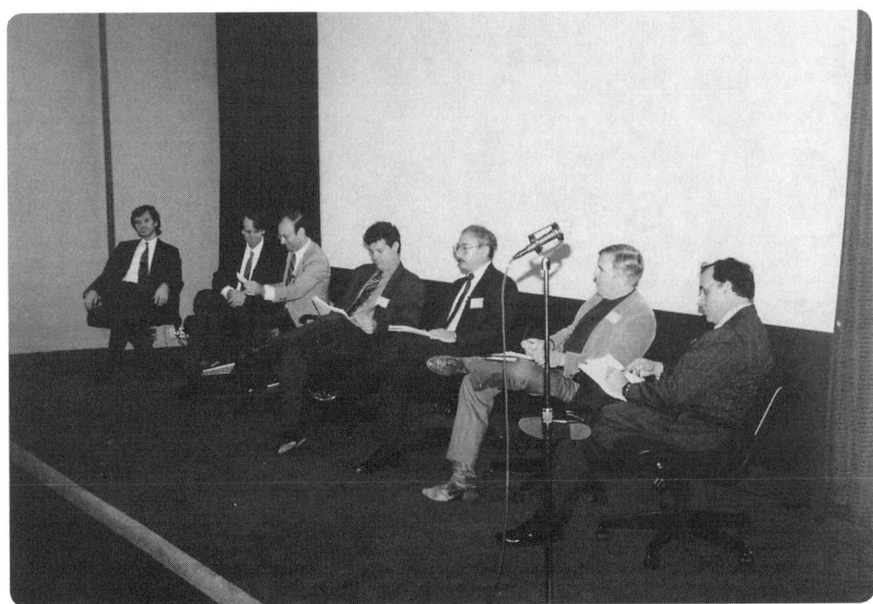

A special session on archival storage was held at the Museum of Television and Radio (as it was then known) during the inaugural AMIA conference in 1991. Left to right: Ron Simon, Michael Friend, Eddie Richmond, William Humphrey, Bill Murphy, G. William Jones, and Alan Lewis. Photo courtesy Gregory Lukow.

In response to interest from the community, the Future of F/TAAC Committee explored the option of becoming part of the Society of American Archivists (SAA). Consequently, the final question asked, "Would you favor joining the SAA provided that we can remain together as a film and video group and that we can continue to conduct our annual meetings?" Sixteen voted no and nine voted yes.

Though I do not remember developing the questionnaire, I do recall extensive discussion about who should be eligible to complete it. Should it be everyone who ever attended a F/TAAC meeting? Should there be only one survey per institution? Ultimately, according to the minutes of the 1989 Miami F/TAAC meeting, "the survey was sent to institutions with moving image collections who attended at least two of the seven F/TAAC conferences held during the five years prior to the Miami meeting."

I should note that throughout this process, Gregory Lukow did the lion's share of the committee work. He developed the list of attendees so we could determine who would complete the survey. He coordinated mailing the surveys and receiving the completed ones. He compiled the results and wrote the report. Most important, he kept the committee on track by providing secretariat support as well as offering his extensive knowledge of the field and individual archivists.

The survey results were reported at the 1989 Miami meeting. It was clear that the community wanted some sort of formalization, but what would it look like? The second Future of F/TAAC Committee was appointed to do the following:

1. study the feasibility of various formalization options and develop a draft mission statement
2. determine the financial implications of formalization
3. address the impact of formalization on the relationship between F/TAAC and the National Center for Film and Video Preservation

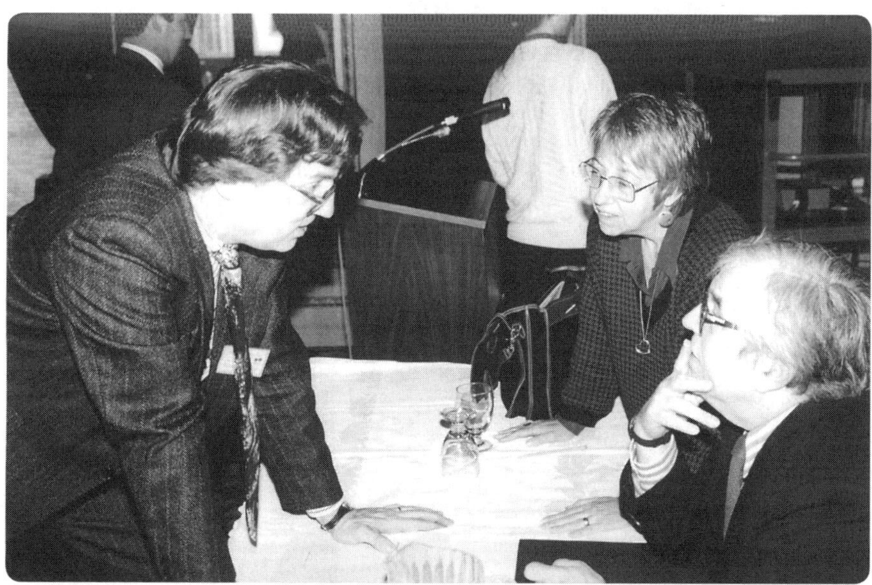

Jan-Christopher Horak (then at George Eastman House), Sharon Pucker Rivo (National Center for Jewish Film), and historian-author Thomas Cripps at the 1991 AMIA conference. Photo courtesy Gregory Lukow.

4. address the issue of institutional versus individual membership and create an ad hoc voting procedure to assist the field in making decisions on the future of the organization

5. prepare a "run-off" election among the names for the association that had been suggested in the recent survey

Once again, Gregory Lukow was the coordinating force behind the work of the committee. Eddie Richmond (UCLA Film & Television Archive) and Alan Lewis (independent audiovisual preservation consultant) were added to the roster and became important voices in the decisions that were made. I do not remember the details of the deliberations. I do remember another survey vote that resulted in the new formal organization being named the Association of Moving Image Archivists. I remember tears and arguments, but I cannot recall the specific issues. I remember Barbara Humphrys encouraging us to look to the Association of Recorded Sound Collections as a model of an association that was both institutional and individual. I remember Eddie Richmond and others spending hours crafting a preliminary set of bylaws that would satisfy those of us, including me, most concerned that the new organization retain the simple democracy of F/TAAC.

F/TAAC was officially renamed the Association of Moving Image Archivists in fall 1990. By January 1991, the committee had a final adopted version of "Bylaws for the Association of Moving Image Archivists." At fourteen pages, the original bylaws were amazingly succinct. They included the objectives and purposes of the organization, resolved the membership issue by providing for both individual and institutional members, provided the option for requiring dues, outlined required meetings, outlined the officer positions and their roles, and dealt with how elections would be conducted. It is difficult to imagine that with these relatively brief bylaws, we were able to establish AMIA. Nevertheless, the first election was held during the late summer–early fall of 1991, and the association was a full-fledged formal organization by the November 1991 conference in New York.

In the end, AMIA was formed by all the individuals who served on the Future of F/TAAC committees, completed surveys, expressed opinions in open discussion, ran for office, and joined as charter members. Together we managed to create a formal organization able to serve a large and diverse membership while retaining the qualities that made F/TAAC so important.

I thought it would be easy to write about AMIA's beginnings—after all, I was present at its creation—but I have come to understand that there are facts and there are memories, and for me, they are intertwined. Though it is important to remember our beginnings, it is more important to celebrate AMIA's success and ensure its future.

NOTE
Although many people deserve thanks and recognition for their contribution to the association, I could not have written this historical memoir without Gregory Lukow, who wrote many of the Future of F/TAAC Committee documents I consulted, and Barbara Humphrys, who kept them for me to discover in her files at the Archives Center of the National Museum of American History.

Genesis of a Profession

*Origins of the Film and
Television Archives Advisory
Committees*

WILLIAM T. MURPHY

On November 1, 1990, in a small but crowded meeting room at the Oregon Historical Society, the assembled archivists, librarians, curators, preservationists, and other interested persons formally resolved to establish the Association of Moving Image Archivists (AMIA). They had come to Portland to attend what would be the last annual conference of the joint Film Archives Advisory Committee and the Television Archives Advisory Committee, more familiarly known as FAAC/TAAC (also, in writing, as F/TAAC). The Future of F/TAAC Committee had moved the formalization process forward by working on a mission statement and drafting bylaws, subsequently approved by the membership, and the rest, as they say, is history. Today, after some twenty years since its founding, the successor to F/TACC has become the premier professional organization for individuals, institutions, and enterprises that share an appreciation of moving images as an essential part of our cultural heritage and a desire to safeguard and preserve them well into the future.[1]

Many current AMIA members who participated in F/TAAC no doubt recall the modest steps that were taken to address the informational needs of an ever-growing number of archives, libraries, and museums that had custody of large film and videotape collections. Since the late 1960s and throughout the 1970s, the field had grown dramatically, a growth reflected in today's AMIA membership numbers and in the services the organization offers to the archival community, ranging from basic training workshops to demonstrations of the latest digital applications.

EARLY YEARS

Several precedents mark the beginning of professionalization in moving image preservation and access, an audiovisual field that, in reality, encompasses many disciplines in the humanities, sciences, and technology. A reasonable place to start is with the idea that cultural institutions should take responsibility for collecting film and television materials along with traditional archival formats. Accepting large rolls of paper prints beginning in 1894 as copyright deposit copies for motion pictures was a landmark acquisition for the Library of Congress (LOC). So, too, was its acceptance of the first television program for copyright in 1949. Other institutions, such as the National Archives and MoMA, started collecting motion pictures in the 1930s, and on a broader level, the International Federation of Film Archives (FIAF), established in 1938, served the needs of its member archives, which, after the intrusion of World War II, contributed to professionalization on an international scale. As will be discussed, it was the American FIAF-affiliated archives that, in effect, formed the initial archives advisory committee or Film Archives Advisory Committee group.

FAAC traces its origins primarily to the National Endowment for the Arts (NEA) and the American Film Institute (AFI), established in 1965 and 1967, respectively, whose relationship required participation of the major nitrate motion picture film archives. This select group included the AFI, which acted as the secretariat, the George Eastman House (GEH), MoMA, and the LOC. Subsequently, the University of California, Los Angeles (UCLA), became a participant, and the National Archives and Records Service (NARS; National Archives and Records Administration [NARA] after 1985) became an observer because, as an agency of the executive branch, it could not accept NEA funding. To minimize competition and avoid duplication of effort, this core group of advisers initially convened to rationalize acquisition and collections policies among their own institutions. During most of the 1970s, the committee advised NEA on funding levels for film preservation for their own institutions, until the process was changed to allow peer review. NEA later funded other major AFI projects that were administered by its National Center for Film and Video Preservation, established in 1983. As the former center director, Gregory Lukow described it as follows: "By the late 1970s, when NEA grants advisory rules changed, FAAC changed from a group advising the NEA to a group whose expanding membership 'advised' and shared information among themselves."[2]

NEA's crucial role is incontestable in the context of motion picture film, first in nitrate film preservation and second in cinema education, and arguably much less so in television and video preservation. Leading a media campaign promoting American cinema as a major art form, AFI's first director, George Stevens Jr., and others brought public attention to huge losses of American movies, in particular of silent films, and successfully persuaded the NEA to establish annual funding for film preservation. Film preservation was defined as copying nitrocellulose reels to safety cellulose triacetate negatives, master positives, and prints. As carried out by the nitrate film archives, silent entertainment or fiction films became the national preservation priority almost to the exclusion of other film genres, not to mention television. In sum, it is fair to say that the first FAAC group formed a relatively narrow base, as measured by its lion's share of NEA funding and by its specialized priorities and interests.

Even so, within the committee, this could have been a fairly competitive or contentious process because of overlapping collections policies with respect to silent films. More difficult to resolve were preservation needs always much greater than available funding, a situation that still remains sadly familiar. Nonetheless, with help from AFI's good offices, during the early 1970s, grant recipients met informally to discuss their priorities and advise NEA on funding they could effectively expend. Printing capacities were a constant constraint, exacerbated by film lab closings. Having to match NEA preservation grants effectively served as another constraint. Owing to a subsequent change in federal rules, LOC stopped accepting NEA funding but, joined by NARA, continued to participate in the archives advisory committee meetings as an observer. Among the archives, only LOC and NARA were fortunate enough not only to receive annual appropriations from Congress but to operate their own motion picture labs.

Facilitated by the AFI, representatives of the nitrate film archives then formed the initial basis of FAAC. Dr. Sam Kula, hired from the BFI, who, along with Stevens, traveled around the country promoting the newly established AFI, initially managed its preservation portfolio. He was succeeded by Dr. Lawrence Karr, who then acted as the committee's secretary. Eileen Bowser and Mary Lea Bandy from MoMA, James Card and John Kuiper from GEH, and Paul Spehr from LOC provided continuity from meeting to meeting. Karr's diplomacy in managing the roundtable discussions helped minimize potential institutional conflicts as well as mollify differences that would surface from time to time. After all, as a rather select group of film scholars and aficionados, they were like pioneers very accustomed to thinking independently, searching to find solutions and best practices for the films in their care and establishing ground rules for a nascent profession.

Based on a roundtable format, a typical FAAC session followed a loosely assembled agenda, often adjusted even on meeting days. Whoever suggested an agenda topic took responsibility for introducing it, while others added what they knew or made recommendations for follow-up. Agendas included important topics such as reports of diacetate (low-acetyl) film deterioration, color dye fading, inadequacy of videotape as a surrogate for film, and archives administrative matters. Given the restrictive discussion format, few topics could be presented in depth, and occasionally, there was a sense of finality about views and opinions, as though nothing more remained to be said.

By the late 1970s, FAAC came into usage as a familiar acronym that described a group of potential grant recipients because NEA began to recognize that additional institutions had meritorious film preservation needs. The AFI therefore invited other archives and libraries to participate in the meetings as representatives of their institutions. Individual professionals who just represented themselves—for example, film collectors or commercial service or product suppliers—were purposely excluded. This restriction on participation became a significant issue for discussion in planning the new AMIA as a professional association, which, in the end, was opened for membership to everyone who subscribed to its goals, whether interested members were individual or institutional, commercial or nonprofit.

Accordingly, FAAC agendas were expanded

to include not only recent acquisitions and nitrate film conversion projects, which dominated in the beginning, but a range of subjects broadly applicable to the field. The agenda for the March 1980 annual conference included a report from the past FIAF Congress and the seminal UNESCO Resolution for Safeguarding and Preserving the Moving Image Heritage. Other topics included restoration projects, an increase in lab prices, silver recovery, and an "update on the lab situation," an oblique reference to numerous motion picture lab closings in the wake of videotape inroads. Collecting strategies, principles of selection, and internal administrative practices were also discussed. In addition to customary social events, evening screenings of newly preserved films became a regular part of the program.

By 1980, FAAC included several new member archives: the Anthology Film Archives, the American Archives of the Factual Film (at Iowa State University), Cinematheque Quebecoise, the National Archives of Canada, and the University of Wisconsin Center for Film and Theater Research. The NEA sent representatives, as did the National Historical Publications and Records Commission (NHPRC), which became the major funding organization for the preservation of local television news. The welcome participation of Canadian archives became a permanent feature of FAAC, TAAC, and later, AMIA.

TAAC EVOLVES

The television and video archives movement sprouted up all over North America as a much-needed response to the general use of videotape for education and documentation as well as entertainment. In 1957, Ampex introduced commercial videotape as primarily a studio format, but it was not until the introduction of affordable Electronic Industries Association of Japan open reels and U-matic cassettes in the 1970s that videotape libraries became ubiquitous outside network television. In addition, a major revision of American copyright law in 1976 encouraged off-air taping of hard news broadcasts and established within the LOC the American Television and Radio Archives. Media scholar Erik Barnouw, the library's new chief of the Motion Picture, Broadcasting, and Recorded Sound Division, organized a television archives

conference in 1978. LOC and the AFI sponsored a moving image cataloging conference the same year. Also during this period, UCLA formed an alliance with the Academy of Television Arts and Sciences (ATAS), and the Museum of Broadcasting was founded in New York with a little help from William Paley. Finally, it is worth noting that the network television news off-air video project at Vanderbilt University, started amid the tumultuous presidential election campaign of 1968, preceded all these activities.[3]

The first TAAC conference took place in Washington, D.C., in January 1979 under the auspices of the AFI, which still acted as secretariat and facilitator, but in contrast to earlier FAAC meetings, there was no money to recommend to needful television and video archives. The core institutions consisted of ATAS, AFI, Canadian Broadcasting Corporation, CBS News, International Museum of Photography-GEH, LOC, the Museum of Broadcasting, MoMA, NARS and its NHPRC, the National Film Archives of Canada, NBC News, PBS, UCLA, the University of Georgia Peabody Collection, and the University of Wisconsin. In attendance were forty-five participants, observers, and guests.

Presenting institutional profiles took up a good part of the first day. This was probably a good idea at first because few people had any idea of the variety of efforts that were undertaken among repositories across the country. In the interest of saving time for more substantive discussions, these presentations were soon eliminated from future programs but distributed as briefing papers in conference handouts. Regardless of presentation format, these profiles helped members appreciate the breadth and diversity of collections nationwide and the sincerity of interests in learning more about the archiving of television and related materials. Discussion focused on such subjects as cataloging and network and local television news archives. A lawyer from the Copyright Office spoke about the provision for fair use in the new copyright law. Sam Kula, representing the National Film Archives of Canada, described ramifications of the draft UNESCO resolution that were applicable to film and television materials. Larry Hackman first announced that local television materials fell within the funding interests of NHPRC. Kula and Robert Rosen (UCLA) submitted a draft statement that, after its acceptance, more or less outlined the philosophical and operating guidelines for TAAC, which would last until the founding of AMIA. Essentially, it described TAAC as a forum for a consortium of institutions, advisory in nature, that avoided taking stands on issues. No formal leadership was intended as such—there was only a two-year assignment as secretary or facilitator—and host institutions would act as chairs of the conferences. All proposed agenda items were categorically acceptable. The requirement for institutional membership was very deliberate, in part a veiled reference to a television collector who had published a newsletter that unfortunately gave the appearance of speaking for TAAC members.

Throughout the 1980s, FAAC and TAAC met jointly, and as word spread, attendance increased, more or less, year after year. Thus, as the program became an increasingly complex endeavor, agenda responsibility gradually shifted from the AFI and the conference host institution to a formal program committee. An effective program, for example, had to address interests in motion picture film and in television and video. Fortunately, some panel topics, such as appraisal, cataloging, and reference services, applied across the board. As a concession to the FIAF-member nitrate archives (LOC, MoMA, GEH, UCLA, and the AFI), blocks of conference time were always set aside for their use. Other FIAF associate members (not full members) also participated in these meetings, including the Wisconsin Center, the Smithsonian Human Studies Film Archive, and NARA. So, too, did the two Canadian full members: the National Archives of Canada and the Cinematheque Quebecois.

The F/TAAC conference of 1981 used two locations: one day devoted to television and video topics at the LOC and two days for crossover and film-related issues at the National Archives. As an indication of growing complexity, there was an unwieldy agenda consisting of thirty-five items. The LOC again hosted a joint meeting in May 1986, which more than 125 persons attended.

Even more complicated were conference logistics, which fell solely on the shoulders of the poor soul who volunteered an institution as a conference host. In reality, the conferences were becoming too large to fit conveniently within a host institution, where meeting room capacities, audiovisual services, 35mm theaters, and other amenities, such as food and refreshments, along with requirements for special diets, were problematic. Screenings were also becoming a problem because of their accumulative running time and the increasing quantity of submissions. Finally, bus transportation and travel time to venues added to the complexity of preparations.

Hosting and planning for a F/TAAC conference became almost a full-time occupation in the last few weeks before the event. For reasons that seem too obvious to mention, these arrangements had many drawbacks and could not conceivably remain commensurate with the phenomenal growth of institutional and professional interest in F/TAAC's work.

By the mid-1980s, FAAC and TAAC were inextricably intertwined. Presentations, papers, and panel discussions became much more substantial than the earlier roundtable discussions. Participants delivered presentations on archival subjects that still have application today such as film and tape enclosures, storage surveys, and cold storage standards. Outside experts were invited as guest speakers. To further its objectives, F/TAAC established working groups based around natural affinities such as cataloging and documentation, local television archives, subject-oriented collections, and independent collections. As an accommodation to the nitrate film archives, a working group was established for FIAF member institutions. In 1983, under its new incarnation, the National Center for Film and Video Preservation (NCFVP), the AFI preservation office continued to provide invaluable administrative assistance to F/TAAC and also to the field, enlarging the National Moving Image Database and preparing for publication the new volumes of the monumental AFI Catalog. The center also solicited input for and edited, published, and distributed the quarterly *F/TAAC Newsletter,* beginning with the summer 1988 issue. None too fancy, the newsletters always contained interesting announcements of acquisitions and archival projects, grant awards, job opportunities, and conference information, and they provided an addi-

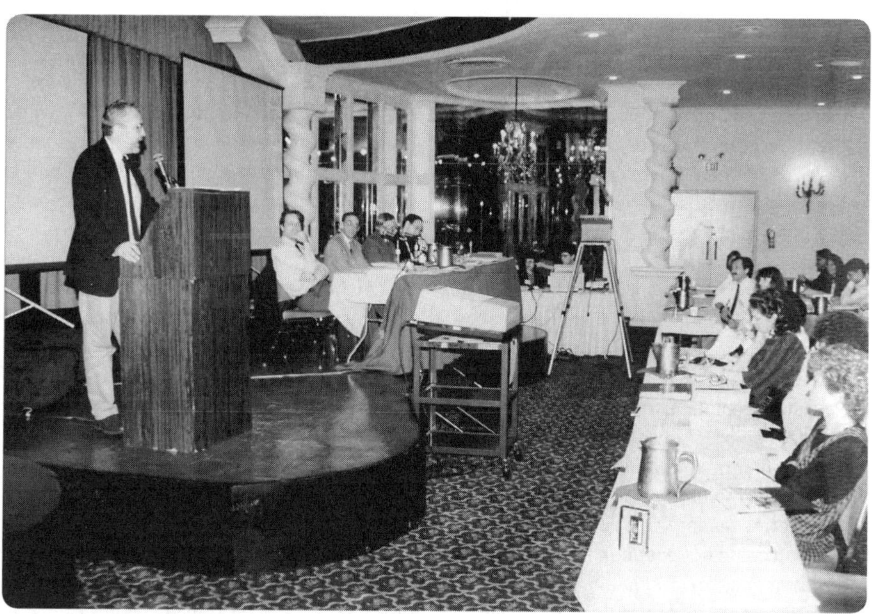

Figure 1. Larry Viskochil
of the Chicago Historical
Society, speaking amid the
deco splendor of the Eden Roc
Hotel at the 1989 F/TAAC
conference in Miami. Photo
courtesy Gregory Lukow.

tional forum for discussion of F/TAAC's future.

At the same time, important events took place outside of or perhaps despite F/TAAC that helped to galvanize the television and video archives movement, if not film archives, toward some kind of formalization. Funded by an NHPRC grant to the NCFVP, in October 1989, the State Historical Society of Wisconsin hosted the Local Television News Conference, attended by about seventy persons, most representing different organizations. The National Film Preservation Act of 1988 established the National Film Preservation Board within the LOC. In May 1989, the Annenberg Roundtable on Television Preservation, coordinated by Fay Schreibman (Museum of Jewish Heritage) and Dr. Sam Surratt (CBS News Archives), in response to a justifiably perceived crisis in television preservation, "brought together key decision makers from government, the television and motion picture industry, the video technology industry, academia, and the philanthropic community."[4]

The penultimate F/TAAC conference, held in Miami in 1989 and chaired and hosted by Steve Davidson, director of the Louis Wolfson II Media History Center, was by all accounts a very successful meeting, owing to the program's substance and Miami Beach's pleasant amenities. Robert Gitt's presentation about the history of color film was a memorable highlight. But it was in Miami that F/TAAC planted the seeds of its own demise. In a manner of speaking, the informal group became a victim of its own success. It was introduced by the question of formalization. The Future of F/TACC Committee was assigned the task of developing a questionnaire to gauge views in the field. At this point, lacking a consensus about F/TAAC's future, opinions and sentiments seemed to be divided along two general lines. Briefly summarized, on one side were those who felt well served by F/TAAC's informality and remained opposed to the bureaucracies, committees, and bylaws that would inexorably follow with formalization. After all, they argued, the informal meetings still generated timely and valuable information and facilitated archives networking. Some representatives of the nitrate film archives leaned in this direction based on their specialty and their fallback to

FIAF, which always remained a source of professional information, developing standards, and best practices.

Yet on the other side of the line were those (this writer included) who felt that the profession had dramatically grown based on collections or acquisition policies that recognized moving images as a legitimate part of our cultural heritage to be preserved and that, owing to inherent vulnerabilities of film and videotape, there was a genuine need to exchange and disseminate professional information on a wider, more effective, and permanent basis. A consistent complaint at conferences pointed to the rehashing of introductory material for new participants who would have been better served by orientation workshops. By and large, for budgetary reasons and other constraints, this group could not count on participating in international associations like FIAF or in the International Federation of Television Archives, both of which only rarely convened in North America.

Although many F/TAAC participants, such as professional librarians or archivists, were also Society of American Archivists (SAA) members, it was felt that SAA did not offer substantial resources or program time for moving image archival issues. Don Neal, SAA's executive director, correctly emphasized that "archival work is archival work, what ever the medium, although there may be some special considerations that the medium imposes. Appraisal, description, reference—the knowledge and skills from these and other archival functions cut across differences of medium."[5] He then described the benefits of SAA membership and raised the possibility of a roundtable for film and television archives. Nonetheless, although negotiations with SAA about the possibility of bringing F/TAAC under its umbrella were not unfriendly, no material cooperation ever took place.

The formalization issue also left criteria for membership unresolved, that is to say, institutional or individual, for profit or nonprofit. As helpful as the AFI center had been in nurturing F/TAAC's growth, its future role as an ad hoc secretariat was also left uncertain.

As encouraged by the Future of F/TACC Committee, a few members expressed their opinions in the *F/TAAC Newsletter*. With due modesty, I quote some of my own words:

> [F/TAAC] served a useful purpose when meetings were small and archives were few in number. Over the last few years, however, several important changes have taken place. Meetings have grown into large scale conferences. Moving image archives have grown by leaps and bounds, becoming at the same time more diverse and specialized than ever before. Numerous archivists have entered the field, creating a huge demand for information and training brought on by the challenge of changing technologies.

I went on to describe the advantages of a formal organizational structure, including national recognition as an authoritative source of information regarding preservation of moving images, nationwide coordination, specialized committee work, fund-raising, training venues, and awards recognition.[6] (See Figure 2 for additional positions on the future of F/TAAC excerpted from the 1989 newsletter.)

The Future of F/TACC Committee conducted several meetings in 1989 and 1990 in preparation for the annual conference in Portland, and it reported its progress in the newsletter. It looked into many practical aspects of establishing a new professional association, including a preliminary mission statement, bylaws on organizational structure and functions, membership criteria, dues, voting eligibility, incorporation or tax exemption, working groups, and the continuing relationship with the AFI, a relationship that, in one form or another, lasted more than twenty years.

Beginning in the late 1960s, these events set the stage for the 1990 meeting in Portland, which led to the steps that established AMIA. In Portland, the attendees voted to change the group's name from F/TAAC to AMIA and launched a series of formalization steps that would lead to the first official AMIA conference, which took place in New York City in 1991, as described by Jan-Christopher Horak in his contribution to this issue. So the Portland conference began as an F/TAAC meeting and ended as an AMIA meeting, paving the way

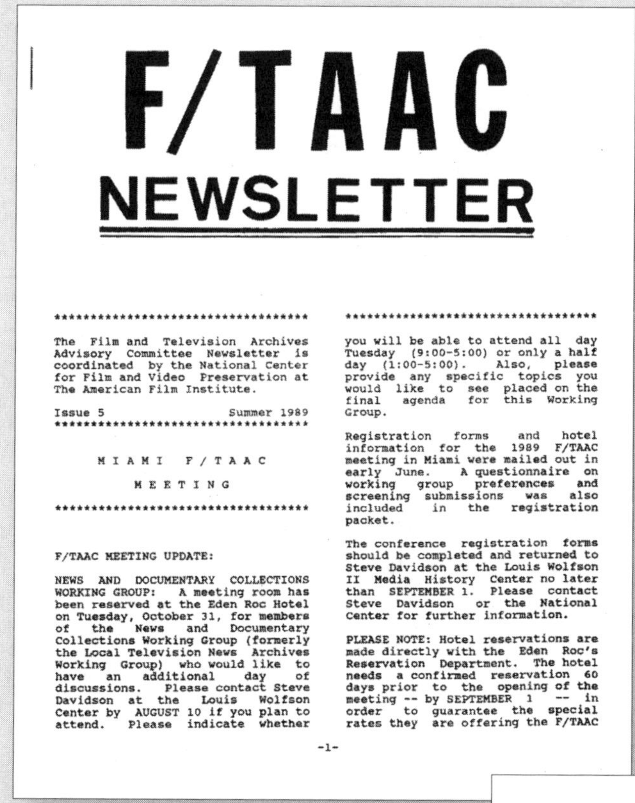

F/TAAC NEWSLETTER

****

The Film and Television Archives Advisory Committee Newsletter is coordinated by the National Center for Film and Video Preservation at The American Film Institute.

Issue 5   Summer 1989
****

M I A M I   F / T A A C

M E E T I N G

****

F/TAAC MEETING UPDATE:

NEWS AND DOCUMENTARY COLLECTIONS WORKING GROUP: A meeting room has been reserved at the Eden Roc Hotel on Tuesday, October 31, for members of the News and Documentary Collections Working Group (formerly the Local Television News Archives Working Group) who would like to have an additional day of discussions. Please contact Steve Davidson at the Louis Wolfson Center by AUGUST 10 if you plan to attend. Please indicate whether you will be able to attend all day Tuesday (9:00-5:00) or only a half day (1:00-5:00). Also, please provide any specific topics you would like to see placed on the final agenda for this Working Group.

Registration forms and hotel information for the 1989 F/TAAC meeting in Miami were mailed out in early June. A questionnaire on working group preferences and screening submissions was also included in the registration packet.

The conference registration forms should be completed and returned to Steve Davidson at the Louis Wolfson II Media History Center no later than SEPTEMBER 1. Please contact Steve Davidson or the National Center for further information.

PLEASE NOTE: Hotel reservations are made directly with the Eden Roc's Reservation Department. The hotel needs a confirmed reservation 60 days prior to the opening of the meeting -- by SEPTEMBER 1 -- in order to guarantee the special rates they are offering the F/TAAC

-1-

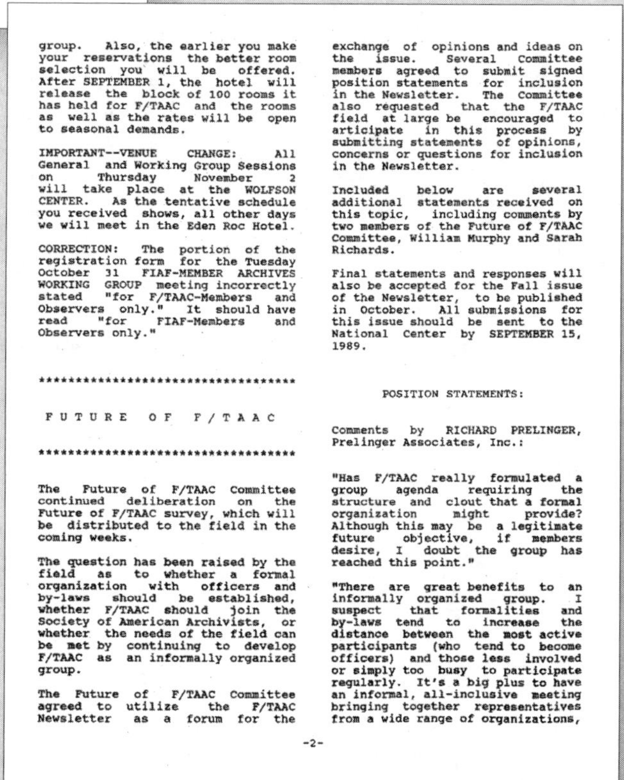

---

group. Also, the earlier you make your reservations the better room selection you will be offered. After SEPTEMBER 1, the hotel will release the block of 100 rooms it has held for F/TAAC and the rooms as well as the rates will be open to seasonal demands.

IMPORTANT--VENUE CHANGE: All General and Working Group Sessions on Thursday November 2 will take place at the WOLFSON CENTER. As the tentative schedule you received shows, all other days we will meet in the Eden Roc Hotel.

CORRECTION: The portion of the registration form for the Tuesday October 31 FIAF-MEMBER ARCHIVES WORKING GROUP meeting incorrectly stated "for F/TAAC-Members and Observers only." It should have read "for FIAF-Members and Observers only."

****

F U T U R E   O F   F / T A A C

****

The Future of F/TAAC Committee continued deliberation on the Future of F/TAAC survey, which will be distributed to the field in the coming weeks.

The question has been raised by the field as to whether a formal organization with officers and by-laws should be established, whether F/TAAC should join the Society of American Archivists, or whether the needs of the field can be met by continuing to develop F/TAAC as an informally organized group.

The Future of F/TAAC Committee agreed to utilize the F/TAAC Newsletter as a forum for the exchange of opinions and ideas on the issue. Several Committee members agreed to submit signed position statements for inclusion in the Newsletter. The Committee also requested that the F/TAAC field at large be encouraged to articipate in this process by submitting statements of opinions, concerns or questions for inclusion in the Newsletter.

Included below are several additional statements received on this topic, including comments by two members of the Future of F/TAAC Committee, William Murphy and Sarah Richards.

Final statements and responses will also be accepted for the Fall issue of the Newsletter, to be published in October. All submissions for this issue should be sent to the National Center by SEPTEMBER 15, 1989.

POSITION STATEMENTS:

Comments by RICHARD PRELINGER, Prelinger Associates, Inc.:

"Has F/TAAC really formulated a group agenda requiring the structure and clout that a formal organization might provide? Although this may be a legitimate future objective, if members desire, I doubt the group has reached this point."

"There are great benefits to an informally organized group. I suspect that formalities and by-laws tend to increase the distance between the most active participants (who tend to become officers) and those less involved or simply too busy to participate regularly. It's a big plus to have an informal, all-inclusive meeting bringing together representatives from a wide range of organizations,

-2-

Figure 2. Excerpts from issue 5 (summer 1989) of the *F/TAAC Newsletter*, featuring Richard Prelinger, William Murphy, and Sarah Richards expressing a variety of positions on the future of F/TAAC. Courtesy Newsfilm Collections, Moving Image Research Collections, University of South Carolina.

and once a year is an appropriate frequency."

"Informality has its difficulties, too. I've noticed that meetings often tend to cover the same ground, in part because of the recent membership increase (of which I am a part) and the consequent interest in basic concepts of moving image archival practice. Would there be any interest in instituting some sort of orientation program directed at newer members, especially those representing smaller archives and collections? Such a program might attempt to impart the best available information on practices, procedures and technology, and aim to develop a body of knowledge for all to share. In this way, the information overhead that now clogs many sessions (and is, no doubt, repetitious to some) could be diminished."

Comments by WILLIAM T. MURPHY, National Archives and Records Administration:

"F/TAAC emerged from the genuine needs of film and television archives. It served a useful purpose when meetings were small and archives were few in number. Over the last few years, however, several important changes have taken place. Meetings have grown into large scale conferences. Moving image archives have grown by leaps and bounds, becoming at the same time more diverse and specialized than ever before. Numerous archivists have entered the field, creating a huge demand for information and training brought on by the challenge of changing technologies. There is more competition for scarce funding; film and television preservation priorities are in conflict."

"In view of these changes F/TAAC as presently constituted faces the real danger of becoming irrelevant. The establishment of the National Film Preservation Board and the recently held Annenberg Roundtable on Television Preservation have already underscored its irrelevancy at the national level."

"F/TAAC needs a formal structure to accommodate the growing number of moving image archives and the professionals that service them. The principal advantages of a formal structure can only be outlined in the limited space available here."

1. National recognition as an umbrella organization for moving image archives and as a collective source for responsible and authoritative views and policies concerning the preservation of moving images.

2. Coordination of moving image preservation on a nationwide basis.

3. The ability, based on the work of specialized committees, to produce standards, manuals, bibliographies, and other useful publications in order to encourage the application of safe and effective techniques for the preservation of moving images.

4. The ability, based on non-profit status, to apply for, solicit, or raise funds for preservation, training, exhibition, travel support, and other worthwhile activities.

5. The ability to foster professionalism among moving image archivists through meetings, training workshops, exchange of information, and other appropriate means.

6. Recognition of achievement by moving image archives or by individual archivists, recognition that will serve a purpose within

each of our institutions as well as within the profession at large.

7. Enhanced understanding by the heads of our institutions and by the public of the importance and priority of safeguarding and preserving the moving image heritage.

8. Better justification for travel support in order to attend meetings.

"These advantages deliberately emphasize preservation over other aspects of moving image archives, because preservation remains the most compelling objective that unites our interests, regardless of the variety of collections held by F/TAAC affiliates. A formal structure will help make these advantages a reality. Accepting F/TAAC's relative inertia unhappily impedes nationwide progress toward preserving our moving image culture and heritage."

See comments by Sarah L. Richards, National Library of Medicine, on following two pages.

Comments by:
Sarah L. Richards

DID YOU KNOW?

. . . that F/TAAC did not defend
one of our most esteemed archivists
and his archival practices from a
reckless, offensive article in the
New York Times, because we had no
official representative to write a
letter to the editor?

. . . that meeting organizers have
trouble acquiring meeting and hotel
rooms for F/TAAC, because we have
no one to accept financial
responsibility and no mechanism for
accepting or spending money?

. . . that F/TAAC has so little
prestige and visibility that we are
not even listed in the
Encyclopedia of Associations and
were not consulted or appointed
when the government created the
National Film Preservation Board?

Big problems! How can we solve
them? Electing a president,
vice-president, treasurer, and
secretary and using
Robert's Rules of Order for the
business part of the meetings would
help.

Organizing formally will provide
officials who could quickly respond
to the media and who could receive
correspondence. It will also allow
us admittance to the
Encyclopedia of Associations--a
start on the road to recognition.
Organizing formally gives us a
mechanism for accepting and
spending money and a structure for
approving and distributing
standards and information on
preservation, etc. In time, we
might even have a journal.

Yes, other methods may also solve
some of these problems, but they
would not give us A VOICE.

WE NEED A STRONG VOICE.

If you speak as the officer of a
national organization, your voice
carries more weight than it does as
as the representative of a single
institution. If you are speaking
as a representative of your own
institution, the institute may
silence or greatly restrict the
action you may want to take on
tough issues. It may not overtly
tell you not to take action, you,
yourself, may feel it is
politically unwise to do so, unless
you do it under the banner of an
unaffiliated national organization.
Even the employees of the National
Center for Film and Video
Preservation must be careful not to
offend their director and board
members, administrators and board
of the American Film Institute, and
potential donors or supporters.
However, as a national officer, you
may tackle any issue.

Also important to remember--NO ONE
CAN SPEAK FOR F/TAAC UNLESS THEY
ARE CHOSEN BY AND ACCOUNTABLE TO
THE MEMBERS OF F/TAAC. In other
words, a representative must be
elected or hired. That way we can
monitor their behavior, and if they
no longer represent us, we may fire
them or elect a new official.

F/TAAC needs a strong voice--it
needs officers who can speak and be
monitored by the field, officers
who can review and approve staff
activities like newsletters, etc.
F/TAAC needs to be a formal
organization.

HOW DO YOU ORGANIZE?
BY INSTITUTE OR INDIVIDUAL?

If we organize by institute, it
means that:

. . we are no longer free to
speak for ourselves. Whenever we
make a statement at the meetings,

we speak officially for our
institutes.

. . that the majority of
attendees at the meetings may not
vote for officers, approval of
standards, meeting locations, or
the focus and direction the
organization will take.

If we organize by individual, it
means that:

. . each person represents
himself when he wants to and
represents his institution when he
and his institution so desires.

. . each person has a voice
and votes for officers, etc., and
will have a hand in the direction
the organization takes.

. . as there are more
individuals than institutes, if the
organization votes for dues, the
treasury will be larger with more
people to donate to it.

. . the current structure is
duplicated in the newly formed
organization, thus allowing the
continuation of free-flowing
information and
communication--F/TAAC's greatest
asset.

NOTES:

Council of Institutions. If enough
people believe there is a need for
the heads of institutions to meet
separately from the general
sessions, a council of
institutional heads could be
created within F/TAAC. Meeting
prior to the general F/TAAC
sessions, the council would provide
a forum for formal institutional
communication while the general
sessions would remain individually
based.

Block Voting. There are those who
believe that a large institute's
members will gather together and
vote in a block, thereby taking
control of the organization.
However, with secret ballots, no
supervisor can see how their staff
has voted. Coercion would be
difficult, if not impossible.
Additionally, there are enough
individual members at large to
outnumber any large institute who
would even try to do this.

Undesirables. Some believe that if
we are a group of individuals, a
few undesirable people may wish to
join. However, the archivists are,
by far, the largest majority of the
members and will outnumber any
undesirables on votes. John
Fleckner, President of the Society
of American Archivists, says that
product salesmen, etc. have never
been a problem in the SAA. It will
not be one for us either.

Goals. Regardless of whether we
organize by institute or
individual, our goals may be:
establishing standards, publishing,
lobbying, fund raising, organizing
workshops and seminars, and
expressing official positions. The
Society for Motion Picture
Television Engineers (SMPTE) and
the Society of American Archivists
(SAA) are individual-based
associations and do pursue these
goals.

HELP KEEP THE BEST F/TAAC HAS TO
OFFER while making it a _stronger
organization_. PLEASE mark your
ballot to _ORGANIZE FORMALLY_ into an
association of INDIVIDUALS.

Sarah L. Richards, Curator
Historical Audiovisuals Coll.
History of Medicine Division
National Library of Medicine

for the birth of AMIA in the months to come. Even though the only vote that took place there was to change the organization's name, it was clear in Portland that critical mass had been reached to establish AMIA as a stand-alone formal organization.

Notes

1. The history described in this article is based on the author's recollections since he participated in many of the meetings described here. Gregory Lukow, surely one of the key participants for F/TAAC, the AFI Center, and AMIA, has kindly provided me with copies of the *F/TAAC Newsletter,* issues 1–10, now on file at the AMIA offices. Donna Ross, Library of Congress Motion Picture, Broadcasting, and Recorded Sound Division, and Sara Meyerson, director of the ABC News Library (now retired), also supplied copies of agendas and other meeting materials. For a detailed history of the development of national policies toward the funding of moving image preservation, which frequently touches on the development of F/TAAC, see an excellent thesis by Sarah Ziebell Mann, "American Moving Preservation, 1967–1987," MA thesis, University of Texas at Austin, 2000.

2. Gregory Lukow, e-mail correspondence with the author, April 26, 2010.

3. The Vanderbilt Television News Archive began off-air taping onto videocassettes of the three major network nightly newscasts beginning in September 1968. They continue this activity to this day (having later added PBS, Fox News, and CNN) and make the tapes available on- and off-site to interested researchers.

4. Fay Schreibman and Sam Surratt, "Roundtable on Television Preservation: Rapporteur Summary," May 19, 1989. From her days at the George Washington University Media Study Center, Schreibman was one of the leading advocates of television preservation. See her article "Searching for Television's History," in *Broadcast Research Methods,* ed. J. R. Dominick and J. E. Fletcher, 16–45 (Boston: Allyn and Bacon, 1985).

5. Neal's letter was published in *F/TAAC Newsletter,* no. 6 (Fall 1989): 3–4.

6. *F/TAAC Newsletter,* no. 5 (Summer 1989): 3–4.

Surveying AMIA's First Twenty Years

JAN-CHRISTOPHER HORAK

In February 1991, film and television archivists who had been meeting as the Film/Television Archives Advisory Committee (F/TAAC) for over fifteen years voted to formalize as an individual-based professional organization, the Association of Moving Image Archivists (AMIA). In the late 1980s, the ad hoc organization's mailing list had grown dramatically from fewer than one hundred persons and organizations to more than seven hundred. Ballots were sent out to every individual who had attended at least two F/TAAC conferences since 1984. Of the sixty-eight ballots returned, sixty (88 percent) voted for formalization.[1] By the time AMIA met for its first official conference in New York in November 1991, an "executive committee" consisting of William Murphy (president), me (vice president), Gregory Lukow (secretary), and Karan Sheldon (treasurer) had been elected and now presided over the fall conference, which was held between November 5 and 9, 1991, at the fabulous St. Moritz Hotel on Central Park South.

President Bill Murphy called the first official meeting of the new association to order on November 8. One of the first orders of business was to establish a dues structure, which, after some debate, was approved at the level of fifty dollars per year. According to the minutes, "a number of attendees immediately gave personal checks to the Treasurer of charter memberships in the association." The first five members were Steve Davidson, D. J. Turner, Richard Costellano, Ruth Tamura, and me.[2] Unfortunately, dues-paying membership would grow much less quickly than the free mailing list had. In the first several years of AMIA's existence, membership hovered around two hundred, with approximately thirty to forty nonprofit and for-profit institutional members. Given the initial slow growth, the executive board established an ad hoc Membership Development Committee in March 1995. That committee published its report in summer 1996 and was simultaneously transitioned to a per-manent committee of the board. Among the committee's recommendations were to develop membership among the production and broadcast communities, students, and faculty in moving image archive programs; among archivists whose mandate encompassed materials other than moving images; and among commercial and nonprofit institutions connected to moving image preservation. It also called for a Web site, an AMIA logo, a brochure, and alliances with similar archival organizations.[3] By 1997, AMIA membership had grown to 419 from 266 in 1995, inching up to 576 in the year 2000. Not until 2008 would membership peak at 1,033 members. Analyzing just who was signing up year for year, one can see that membership not only grew relatively slowly but that there was a 43 percent attrition rate between 2001 and 2003 and a 35 percent attrition rate between 2003 and 2005, which meant that even though overall membership increased slightly from 633 (2001) members to 672 (2003) members, in fact, 312 new members had actually joined, with a concomitant loss of 273 members. Between 2003 and 2005, AMIA again gained 255 new members but lost 237 members. Indeed, for twenty years, AMIA has relied on a core of activist members, probably numbering only a couple hundred.

Even before the New York conference, the executive board had begun the process of incorporation so that AMIA could be registered as a nonprofit public benefit corporation with 501(c)(3) tax status. Lukow reported in New York that AMIA would be incorporated in the state of California, with Eddie Richmond from the UCLA Film & Television Archive as its resident agent. The process of incorporation was completed in January 1993 and was approved at the AMIA Chicago conference in October that same year. The association filed for tax-exempt status with both the federal government and the state of California in August 1993.

For the business meeting's next agenda point, I spoke about AMIA's relationship to the American Film Institute (AFI). Through its National Center for Film Preservation, AFI had been providing a whole host of secretarial and organizational services for F/TAAC, including publishing the conference programs and the *F/TAAC Newsletter*, which, with issue numbers 11–12, was renamed the *AMIA Newsletter*.

A M I A

Association of Moving Image Archivists

JOIN AMIA IN 1992!

The Association of Moving Image Archivists (AMIA) is now offering charter memberships and invites you to become a part of the community of archivists, scholars and concerned supporters of moving image preservation.

AMIA is a professional association established to provide a means for cooperation among individuals concerned with the collection, preservation, exhibition and use of moving image materials. The objectives of AMIA are to exchange information, promote archival activities and professional standards, facilitate research, and encourage public awareness of film and video preservation.

Since the late 1960s, representatives from moving image archives have recognized the value of regular meetings to exchange practical information and experiences. Over the years, this group of archivists, originally known as the Film and Television Archives Advisory Committee (F/TAAC), has evolved to include several hundred archivists from over 100 national, regional and local institutions from the United States and Canada working in film and television preservation. In 1990, the name of the group was changed to the Association of Moving Image Archivists, and in 1991, the organization voted to formalize as an individual-based professional association.

A broad cross-section of film and television media are represented. There are also a number of significant specialized collections, including independently produced film and video art, film and television programs reflecting ethnic and minority experiences, local and regional film and television programming, and anthropological films.

Membership is open to any interested individual, institution, organization or corporation. Membership dues are $50 for individuals, $150 for non-profit institutions, and $300 for for-profit institutions.

As a member of AMIA you will be entitled to receive the AMIA NEWSLETTER free of charge, invitations to all AMIA meetings and events, and the benefits of affiliation with the North American professional organization of moving image archivists. Individual members are entitled to vote, hold elective office, and participate in all AMIA activities. Any number of individuals from the same institution can join.

Join AMIA in 1992 and become a Charter Member! Please complete the enclosed membership application form and send your dues to the AMIA Secretariat at the following address:

Association of Moving Image Archivists
c/o The National Center for Film and Video Preservation
The American Film Institute
P.O. Box 27999
2021 N. Western Avenue
Los Angeles, CA 90027

For additional information please call the AMIA Secretariat at 213/856-7637.

Invitation to join AMIA as
a charter member in 1992.
Courtesy Wendy Shay.

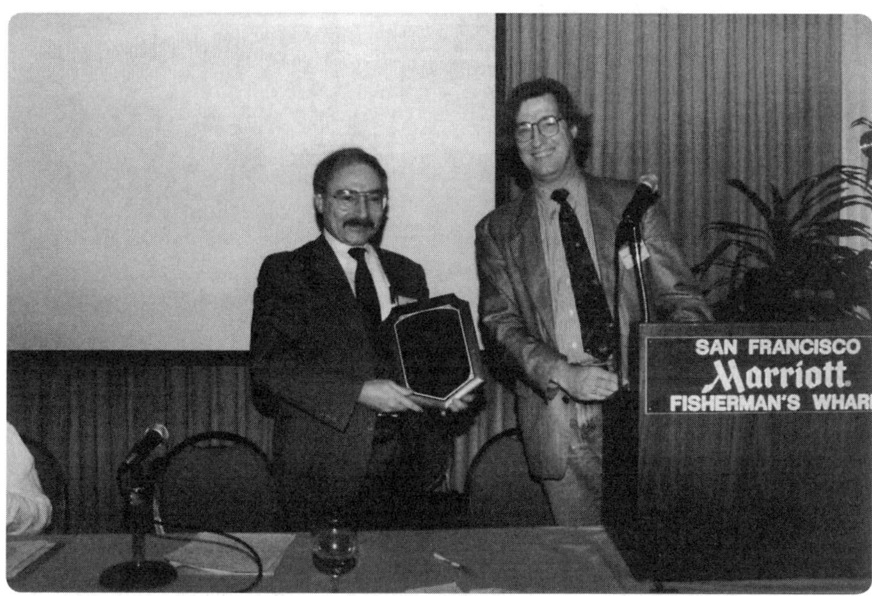

Bill Murphy, outgoing AMIA president (left), receives a commemorative plaque honoring his service as the association's first president from incoming president Jan-Christopher Horak at the 1992 annual AMIA conference in San Francisco. Photo courtesy Gregory Lukow.

Though Lukow, as AFI's representative, argued for a continued ad hoc relationship, the majority of the executive board felt that AMIA's annual budget needed to reflect not only all hard costs and operational expenses paid to the center and other vendors but also in-kind services provided by the AFI. I was charged with drawing up a draft agreement, which was subsequently ratified at the San Francisco conference, after the membership approved several changes, including a termination clause. The final signed agreement was announced at the Chicago conference, but the relationship between the two organizations would continue to be a contentious one within the executive board and AMIA because of sometimes conflicting agendas between the two organizations. Nevertheless, AMIA would probably not have developed as quickly in its formative years were it not for the hard work of secretary Gregory Lukow.

When the AFI announced that it was terminating support for the secretariat in summer 1996, the Academy of Motion Picture Arts and Sciences graciously stepped in to offer office space and financial support, which continues to this day. In April 1997, the AMIA office moved to the Academy Film Archive's office on Wilshire Boulevard (and then to North Vine Street in Hollywood in 2002), and the following autumn, the board appointed Janice Simpson as its first permanent administrative coordinator. In 1999, a part-time administrative assistant was added. Since then, the AMIA staff has expanded to three full-time staff persons, led since 2007 by Laura Rooney. The unwavering support of the Academy of Motion Picture Arts and Sciences and its administration has been invaluable to the association, not only relieving the membership of a very extensive financial burden but also providing a collegial working environment for AMIA's staff.

Given the lack of a dues structure, there was very little for the AMIA treasurer, Karan Sheldon, to report at that first AMIA meeting. That would change radically in subsequent years, and indeed, the association has done an excellent job of managing its finances. At the San Francisco conference in 1992, Sheldon

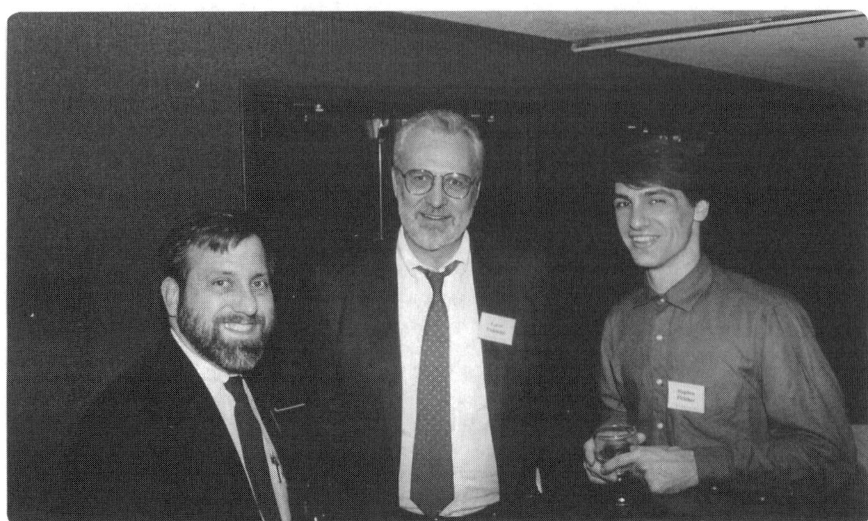

Richard Fauss (West Virginia Division of Culture and History), Larry Viskochil (Chicago Historical Society, 1993 conference local host), and Stephen Fletcher (Indiana Historical Society) at the 1992 AMIA conference. Photo courtesy Gregory Lukow.

reported that AMIA probably would carry over nine thousand dollars into the budget year 1993.[4] By the end of 1996, the organization's annual income had expanded to over one hundred thousand dollars. As AMIA headed into its tenth year in 2000, the revenue stream continued to expand, with solid financial returns. Net assets, mostly in cash and cash instruments, exceeded four hundred thousand dollars. By 2009, AMIA finances were very healthy, with net assets of over $650,000, leaving a reserve larger than the operational costs for one year.

Returning to that first business meeting, the association next established an ad hoc Publications Committee to oversee the production of the *AMIA Newsletter,* in direct response to a question from the floor. The publication had been edited by AFI staff and, it was now agreed, should be editorially controlled by AMIA; in San Francisco, the Publications Committee was then given the status of a standing committee. Published quarterly, the *Newsletter* would also continue to evolve. The fall 1992 *Newsletter,* for example, included, for the first time, a "Letter from the President" (penned by Bill Murphy), which would become a standing feature of all subsequent newsletters. With issue 19 (March 1993), the *AMIA Newsletter* received a new look and fell under the editorship of AMIA publications chair Ruth Tamura. The previous issue had already included a first membership directory, which would be distributed to the membership

annually as a separate publication beginning in July 1995 (and would go online in January 2009).

Apart from news of conferences, committees, and reports from the field, the *Newsletter* began publishing special sections on a variety of themes in 1995, including sections on amateur film, access issues, and preservation. Other regular features were a digest of AMIA-L Listserv threads (beginning with issue 23, January 1994), a section on "Publications Received and Noted" (issue 24, April 1994), and Jim Lindner and Jim Wheeler's "Video Q&A with Jim & Jim" (issue 26, October 1994). To support funding, the AMIA office began accepting advertising with issue 35 (Winter 1997) of the *Newsletter,* and soon it was sporting enough advertisements from vendors to make it almost self-sustaining. The *AMIA Newsletter* received its next design makeover with issue 76 in summer 2006 and finally went green when it transitioned into a paperless, online publication in fall 2008.

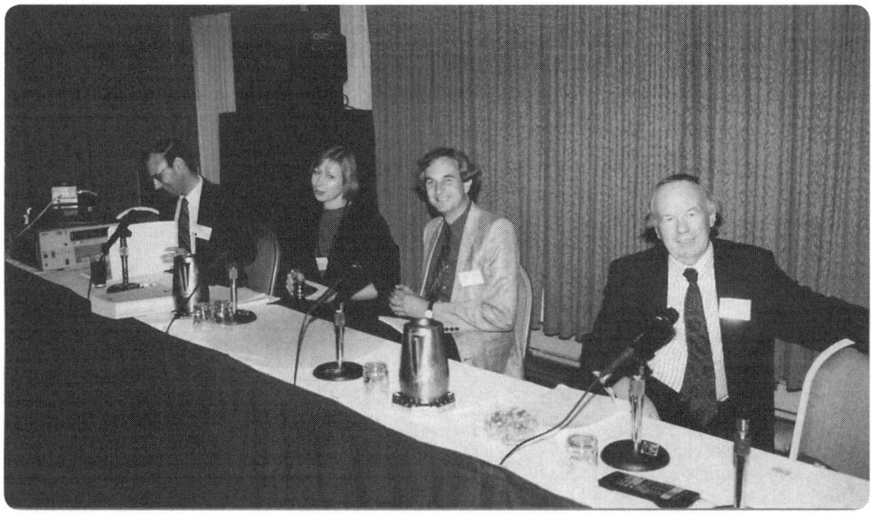

The *Newsletter*'s special sections, in particular, pointed out a need for an AMIA forum for longer and more in-depth articles on subjects of interest to the membership. A first proposal for a journal of moving image technology was proposed by Andrea Kalas in 1997 but failed to find board support, in large part because the board felt that it would be too difficult to marshal content. In spring 2001, after nearly two years of preparation and intense lobbying of the board, however, AMIA's Publications Committee was able to launch *The Moving Image: The Journal of the Association of Moving Image Archivists,* in association with University of Minnesota Press, which I edited for the journal's first twelve issues. AMIA had, after ten years, achieved the degree of maturity that warranted a peer-reviewed academic journal as a forum for the membership and all other parties interested in the field of moving image preservation and access. As I noted in my introduction, "*The Moving Image* will address issues involving all moving image materials, including historic and contemporary film, television, video, new and emerging digital technologies, as well as paper and three-dimensional collections documenting the history of moving image media."[5] Historical essays; in-depth articles on preservation projects; profiles of moving image collections; reports on new technologies; articles on access strategies; theoretical think pieces on the nature of the field; and conference, book,

Speakers for the October 20, 1993, panel "Film Preservation 1993: A Study of the Current State of American Film Preservation" at the 1993 AMIA conference in Chicago. Left to right: Eddie Richmond (UCLA Film & Television Archive and future AMIA president), Maxine Fleckner Ducey (Wisconsin Center for Film and Theater Research and future AMIA president), Scott Simmon (coauthor of the National Film Preservation Study), and David Francis (Library of Congress). Photo courtesy Gregory Lukow.

and film and video reviews would all fall under the purview of the journal. The first issue sold out almost immediately. Ten years later, *The Moving Image* is alive and well under its current editors, Marsha and Devin Orgeron. In spring 2010, the association founded the online journal *AMIA Tech Review,* "a timely technical review oriented to those things new and old which will or have already impacted our work," edited by Ralph Sargent.[6]

Bill Murphy next called for the establishment of two standing committees within AMIA, a Preservation Committee and a Cataloging and Documentation Committee, both built on

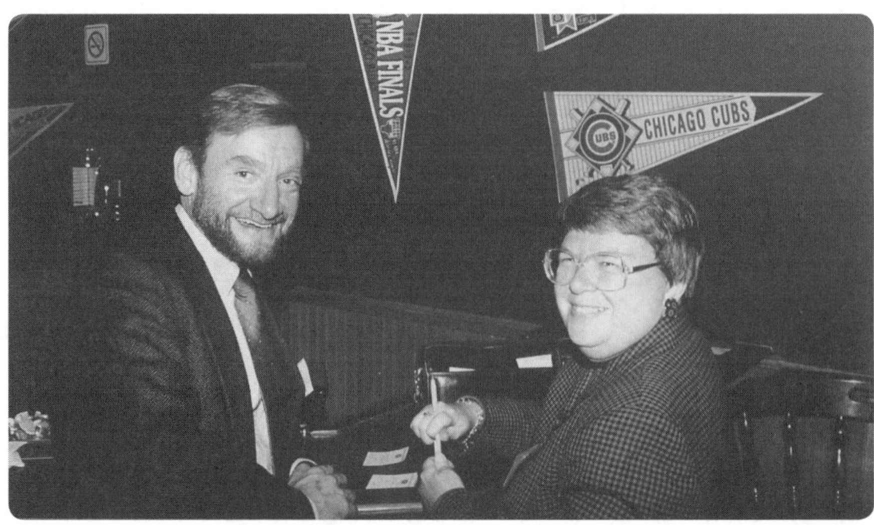

Ern Dick (National Archives of Canada and incoming AMIA president) and Lynn Farnell (WGBH) at the 1993 AMIA conference. Photo courtesy Gregory Lukow.

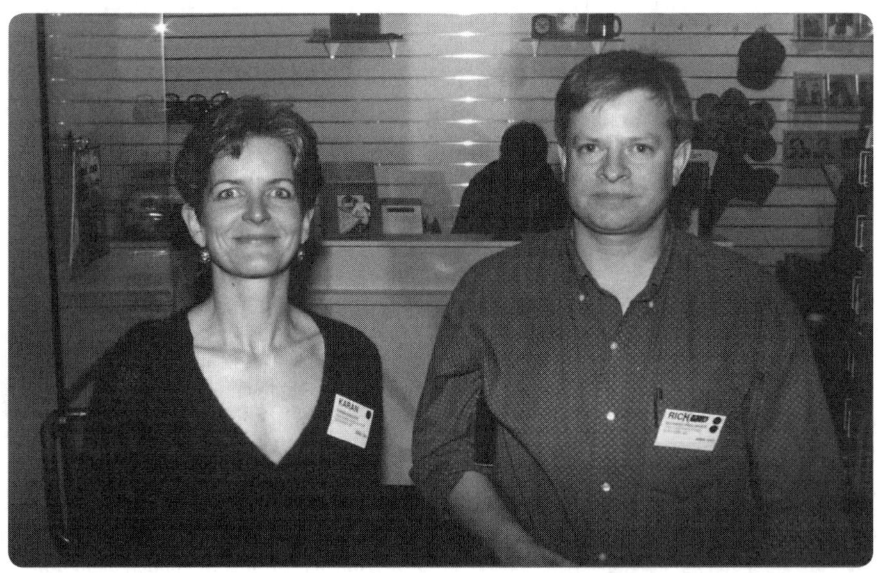

Karan Sheldon (Northeast Historic Film) and Rick Prelinger (Prelinger Archives) at the 1993 AMIA conference. Photo courtesy Gregory Lukow.

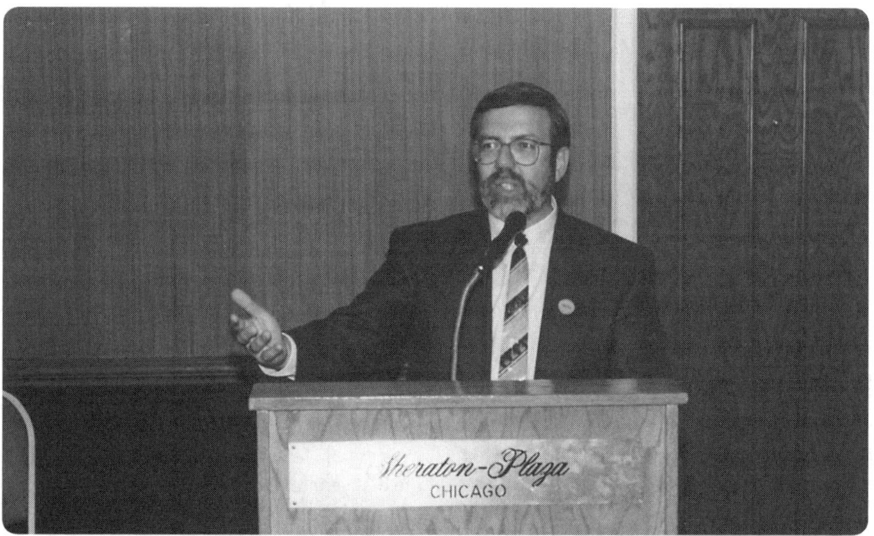

Film historian and critic
Leonard Maltin delivering the
AMIA conference keynote
address at the October 20,
1993, luncheon. Photo
courtesy Gregory Lukow.

the model of the International Federation of Film Archives (FIAF). These committees were to accomplish specific tasks for the organization and constitute part of the formal infrastructure of AMIA, in contrast to various working groups, which had been established by F/TAAC and were to remain more informal, including the Independent and Media Arts Working Group, the Inédits-Amateur Film Working Group, and the News and Documentary Working Group. In response to another question from the membership asking why the board had not established a programming and access committee, similar to FIAF's recently founded commission of the same name, the board responded that they wanted the organization's infrastructure to evolve naturally through the needs and wishes of the membership rather than being imposed from above. An Access Working Group was formed at the Boston conference in 1994, which became a standing committee as a result of the AMIA elections in 1995. The 1993 conference in Chicago constituted an Archival Training and Education Working Group, which then met officially in Boston. At the 1996 conference in Atlanta, that group was replaced by the Education Committee of the Board.

One challenge that AMIA has had to face over its entire existence is that AMIA activities rely largely on volunteer participation and support. Participation in committees has always been voluntary so that those commit-tees remained to a degree ad hoc, depending on who attended the annual conference. The productivity of most of the committees has always been highly variable, depending on the energy and commitment of the committee chair and its members. Various AMIA presidents have focused on increasing volunteerism. However, like most other professional membership organizations, the activist core of AMIA has increased over the years, but its proportion to overall membership has remained constant, with a handful of committed individuals consistently shouldering the bulk of the work.

In point of fact, the committee structure of AMIA would continue to grow and evolve over the next twenty years, as AMIA established its own unique identity. While the chairs of the original standing committees were automatically members of the executive board, the rapid development of new committees soon made the board unwieldy. As a result, the membership was asked to vote in October 1995, at the Toronto conference, on a major revision to the organization's bylaws, which called for an executive board consisting of the president, treasurer, secretary, and four elected members at large.

The committee structure was revised to include committees of the board (AMIA functions), committees of the membership (archival functions), and interest groups of the association. The vote passed, and the final version of the new by-laws was approved by the board in April 1996.

One of the committees of the board that was already hard at work was the Elections Committee, which took annual nominations, carried out the elections, and put together an *Elections Manual*. In 1996, a Development Committee of the Board was established to oversee the creation of a five-year plan for the association as well as a Conference Committee to organize the yearly conference, which continued to be AMIA's most important annual event. By the time of Miami's 1998 conference, AMIA had also established further working groups for Academic–Archival Interests, Digital Archives, and Regional Archives as well as an Internationalization Task Force to look at questions related to AMIA's growing international membership and a Diversity Task Force to look at the field's and AMIA's efforts to diversify the organization's membership. At the Montreal conference in 1999, Lesbian, Gay, Bisexual, and Transgender (LGBT) and Moving Image–Related Material and Documentation interest groups were added to the roster of committees.

In 2008–9, in an effort to improve committee operations, the board proposed a new committee structure: (1) committees of the board included Awards and Scholarships; Conference; Development; Future Directions; Governance; Membership Services; Nominations and Elections; Publications; and Web Site, and (2) committees of the membership included Academic Archival; Access, Advocacy, Cataloging, and Metadata; Copyright; Digital Initiatives; Diversity; Education; Independent Media; International Outreach; LGBT; Moving Image–Related Materials and Documentation; Nitrate; Preservation; Regional Audiovisual Archives; Small Gauge–Amateur Film; and TV, News, and Documentary. This diversity of committees attests not only to the range and breadth of AMIA activity but also to the overall increase in the range of members' interests.

By the late 1990s, the annual AMIA conference had increased in size and complexity, attracting both AMIA members and many industry vendors and supporters. Indeed, conference sponsors and vendor fees soon earned enough revenue to begin expanding activities. Among the most consistent sponsor-vendors at the conference have been Consolidated Film Industries, Chace Productions, Cineric Inc., Fotokem Film and Video, Vidfilm, Iron Mountain, Hollywood Vaults, Monaco Film/Video/Digital, YCM Data Automation Group, Sony Pictures, Tuscan Corporation, Colorlab, and NT Audio Video Film Labs. The annual AMIA conference was not only the association's biggest revenue-generating event but a consistent motor for drawing new members, as can be seen by the fact that conference attendance continued to increase year by year from fewer than two hundred attendees the first year to almost five hundred at the 1997 in Bethesda, Maryland, conference. At the annual conference in 2002 (Boston), attendance peaked at over 650. In 2010, on its twentieth anniversary, AMIA partnered with the International Association of Sound and Audiovisual Archives on a joint annual conference—a testament to the event's expansion and diversification.

The annual AMIA conference constitutes one of the most valuable contributions of AMIA to the field. In membership surveys, the conference consistently scores highest as a benefit of membership. For working professionals, students, and interested parties, the conference affords an opportunity for interpersonal communication within the archival community and the profession. Within the context of the conference, AMIA provides continuing education, information sharing, stimulating research, the promotion of standards, and intense discussions of issues relevant to the field and our culture.

One reason for the success of the AMIA conferences is that, very early on, the event's preconference program began offering basic services to the membership that went beyond thematic panels and opportunities for networking. At the 1993 Chicago conference, a basic training workshop for novice film and television archivists was instituted, taught by Alan Lewis and Wendy Shay. This workshop has continued to be an extremely popular feature of the conference, given that smaller archives, in particular, may not have trained moving image archivists on staff. The 1995 Toronto conference saw the first iteration of The Reel Thing Technical

Symposium, a mini-symposium at which the latest technical achievements for film, television, and digital preservation and storage were introduced. Conceived and curated by Sony Picture's Grover Crisp and Michael Friend, The Reel Thing has become so popular that it has been offered in encore performances outside the conference in Los Angeles and abroad. In summer 2010, AMIA hosted The Reel Thing XXV in Los Angeles. At the 1999 conference in Montreal, AMIA instituted a mentoring program for first-time conference attendees, partnering an AMIA old-timer with a newbie both to welcome new members and new conference attendees and to guarantee that they were welcomed into the association and provided with the information they needed about the conference and the association.

Almost from the moment of its founding, AMIA has endeavored to establish relations with other organizations and archival initiatives. Even before the New York conference in 1991, the Future of F/TAAC Committee had joined the Motion Picture Centennial Committee. Formed in 1989 by a core group of Los Angeles–based organizations, the committee acted as a clearinghouse for all motion picture centennial celebrations, culminating with the centennial year 1995. By the time AMIA joined, the Centennial Committee included more than sixty organizations and had its own logo, designed pro bono by Hollywood film designer and director Saul Bass. More recent initiatives have included AMIA's membership in the Coordinating Council of Audiovisual Archives Associations (CCAAA) and AMIA host-coordinating the Joint Technical Symposium in 2004 and 2007 on behalf of CCAAA.

The next major interinstitutional initiative of AMIA occurred in early 1993, when the National Film Preservation Board organized hearings in Los Angeles (February 12) and Washington, D.C. (February 26), on the National Film Preservation Act of 1992 (NFPA). A product of the NFPA, the National Film Preservation Board (NFPB) met for the first time in September 1992 and included representatives from sixteen different film industry organizations, including the Academy of Motion Picture Arts and Sciences, the Writers Guild of America, the Society for Cinema Studies, the Motion Picture Association of American, the National Association of Theater Owners, and the National Association of Broadcasters. While AMIA members Michael Friend (Academy Film Archive), Gregory Lukow (AFI), Stephan Gong (Pacific Film Archive), Robert Rosen (UCLA Film & Television Archive), Roger Bell (Fox), Phil Murphy (Paramount), Bob O'Neil (Universal), Bob Heiber (Chase Audio), and Alan Stark (Film Technology) testified for their respective organizations in Los Angeles, Washington speakers included Bob Harris (independent consultant), Jonas Mekas (Anthology), John Homiak (Smithsonian Institution), Paul Spehr (Library of Congress), Mary Lea Bandy (MoMA), and Balazs Nyari (Cineric). As AMIA president, I testified in Washington for the association, the first time AMIA was visible in a public forum other than its own.

Not surprisingly, while the Los Angeles hearings focused almost exclusively on the preservation status of Hollywood cinema, the Washington hearings focused more heavily on orphan films, reflecting AMIA's shift in membership from large nitrate holding archives to small archives holding nontheatrical film and television material. Given the extremely diverse nature of AMIA's membership, my expressed concerns in Washington also addressed the dire state of non-Hollywood film preservation:

> Yet the fact remains, that the overwhelming majority of moving image materials in need of preservation in this country are no longer or have never been covered by copyright, i.e. no private individual or corporation can be made responsible for the financing or their preservation. . . . These include:
>
> 1. Silent films, where copyright has expired
>
> 2. All films produced by major film and television companies which were never copyrighted
>
> 3. All those films produced by smaller companies, which have since gone out of business, and/or their films were not renewed for copyright
>
> 4. All newsreels, documentaries, avant-garde productions, animation, and other ephemeral films, created by a diverse array of film producers which were never copyrighted and are therefore in the public domain

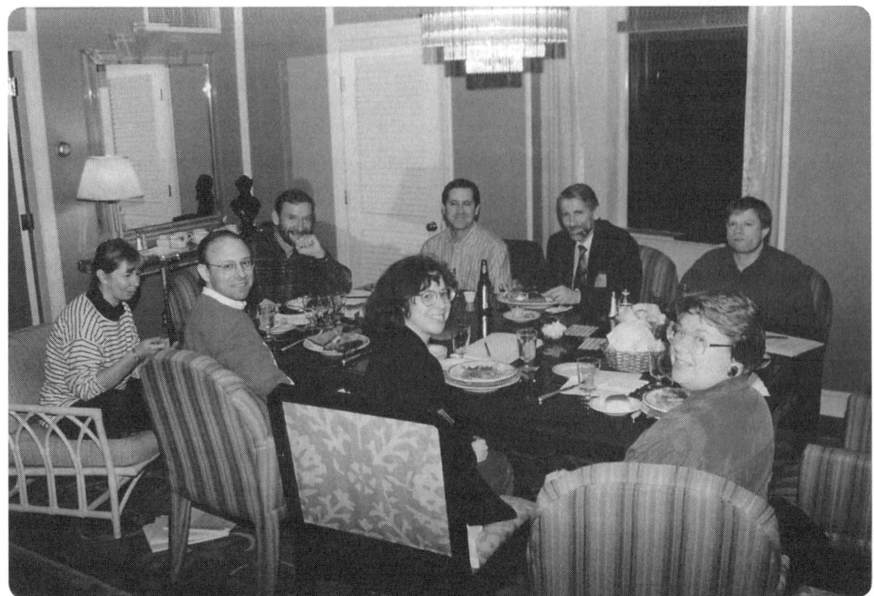

AMIA Executive Board members meeting in Boston during the 1994 conference. Clockwise from far left: Maxine Fleckner Ducey, Ern Dick, Bill O'Farrell, FIAT president Tedd Johansen (guest), Rick Prelinger, Boston Local Arrangements chair Lynn Farnell (guest), Wendy Shay, and Eddie Richmond. Photo courtesy Gregory Lukow.

5. Films/videos of living and/or dead artists who worked independently

6. Many of these films are literally in the public domain, making them a public concern and a public responsibility.[7]

In point of fact, lobbying by AMIA members and AMIA itself eventually contributed in part to the dramatic shift in government film preservation funding priorities. Indeed, after the National Endowment for the Arts (NEA) quietly announced in October 1994 that it was suspending its AFI-NEA Film Preservation Program, copyrighted films became the exclusive responsibility of copyright holders and such organizations as the Film Foundation. The studios themselves often still held copyrights and, in many cases, also still owned the physical material, stored in publicly funded nitrate film archives. AMIA president Eddie Richmond sent a letter of protest to NEA chairman Jane Alexander, noting that the cut in funding made it almost impossible for public-sector film archives to support film preservation or to seek matching funds from private sources.[8] Meanwhile, in December 1994, Dr. James Billington of the Library of Congress invited AMIA to name a representative to the NFPB. In his letter, Billington wrote, "The Association has done an excellent job in bringing together film archivists, the film industry, and the academic community."[9]

When the NFPA came up for renewal in 1995, AMIA president Eddie Richmond testified before the House Subcommittee on Courts and Intellectual Property. H.R. 1734 called not only for the reauthorization of the NFPB but also for the establishment of the National Film Preservation Foundation (NFPF). Richmond noted of the soon to be established foundation that "the foundation's role will be to help preserve those films which are held in the public trust by non-profit institutions and which simply will not survive without public intervention. These films—sometimes referred to as 'orphan' films—constitute a very large and indispensable portion of America's film heritage."[10] The

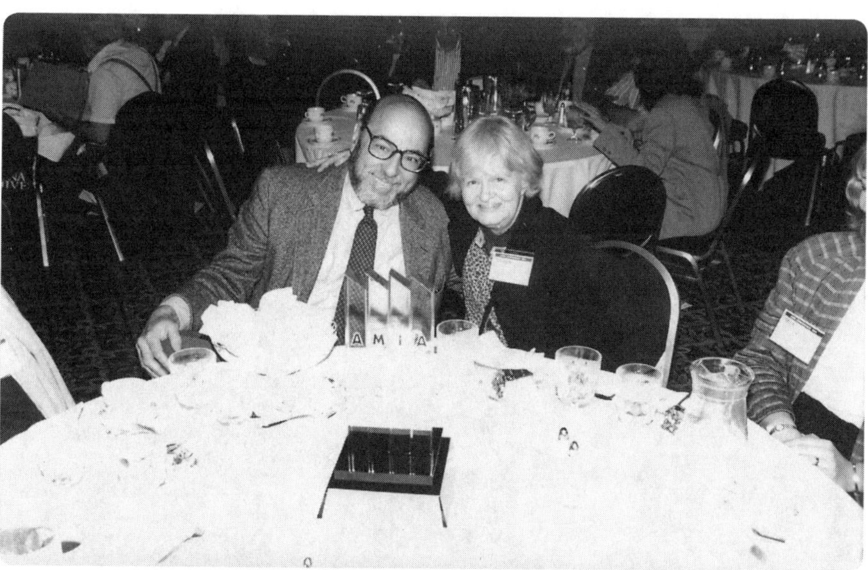

Eileen Bowser (right), recipient of the first AMIA Career Recognition Award, with Dan Leab (Seton Hall University) at the November 16, 1994, Recognition Award Luncheon held during the Boston AMIA conference. This award later became known as the AMIA Silver Light Award. Dan Leab introduced and presented Eileen and later funded AMIA's Dan and Kathy Leab Award. Photo courtesy Gregory Lukow.

NFPA of 1996 was signed into law by President Clinton on October 11, 1996. Thus, whereas NEA funding through the AFI had, for more than twenty-five years, focused almost exclusively on surviving Hollywood studio nitrate films, the NFPF would have a mandate to fund so-called orphan films exclusively.

With the NFPF established, the Library of Congress set its sights on television preservation. AMIA member and ex-president William Murphy was commissioned to write a study on the state of television preservation. In March 1996, the library held hearings on "The Current State of American Television and Video Preservation." Among AMIA members testifying were Jim Wheeler, Roger Mayer, Janet Bergstrom, David Weiss, and Sam Surrat. AMIA president Maxine Fleckner Ducey testified in Washington, D.C., on behalf of the organization. In her statement, she noted, "Increased funding for television and video preservation is the bottom line for any national plan. With it, all other elements of the plan are possible; without it, very little can be done. Here is where the plan must be creative, bold and ultimately successful."[11]

Unfortunately, despite all the work put into the hearings, the national plan, and the lobbying efforts of AMIA, the Library of Congress failed to muster the legislative will to establish a Television Preservation Founda-tion, similar to the NFPF. Indeed, it abdicated all responsibility for television preservation at a national level by recommending in its national plan that such a foundation be strictly a separate and private-sector entity rather than chartered by Congress and eligible for federal matching funds. As President Andrea Kalas noted critically in AMIA's official response to the published national television preservation plan, a single preservation funding entity for all moving images would have been preferable, given the ever rapidly accelerating convergence of all moving image media: "One unified foundation will not only lend itself to elimination of duplication, economies of scale, and the pooling of information and resources; it will

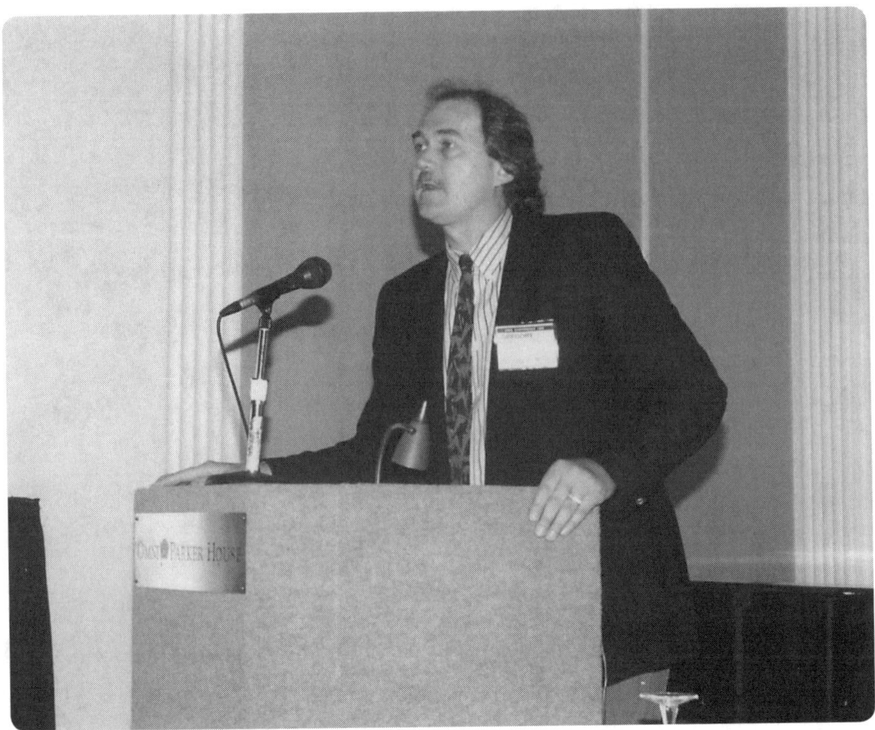

Gregory Lukow (AFI National Center for Film and Video Preservation) chairs the November 16, 1994, plenary session on "National Strategies for Moving Image Preservation" at the Boston AMIA conference. Photo courtesy Gregory Lukow.

mirror more precisely the one field it seeks to serve and the common heritage it seeks to save."[12] AMIA's ad hoc Steering Committee on U.S. National Moving Image Preservation Plans also worked for several years to establish a TV foundation, without coming to fruition. Subsequently, it remained for a group of private individuals, led by James Lindner, to found the National Film and Video Preservation Foundation in 2004. The foundation operates out of AMIA's offices in Hollywood and has funded the preservation of over thirty works through donated laboratory services.

One of the areas in which AMIA began expanding its outreach in the mid-1990s was in the establishment of various awards. Eileen Bowser, the retired curator at MoMA's Film Department, had received the first Silver Light Award at the Boston AMIA conference in 1994. The Silver Light recognizes substantial achievement over a long period of time in archival work relating to moving images. Among the recipients have been Hugh Taylor, Paul Spehr, Dan Den Bleyker, Jim Wheeler, William Murphy, Howard Walls, David Cleveland, Ray Edmondson, David Francis, Alan Katelle, Sam Kula, David Shepard, and the late Bill O'Farrell.

To manage the awards in future years, AMIA established an AMIA Awards Committee in early 1995. In January of that same year, AMIA announced the establishment of the Dan and Kathy Leab Award, funded by the longtime patrons of archives whose names the award bears. The award has been given annually to a "working archivist who has rarely been accorded recognition outside his or her own institution." Rosemary Bergeron of the National Film Archives of Canada was the first to receive the Leab Award. Other past award winners have been Michael Godwin, Edward Stratman, Doug Kirby, Michelle Kribs, Marlena Wyman, Andrew Murdoch, Todd Van Dusan, Madeline Matz, Arthur Wehrhahn, and Charles

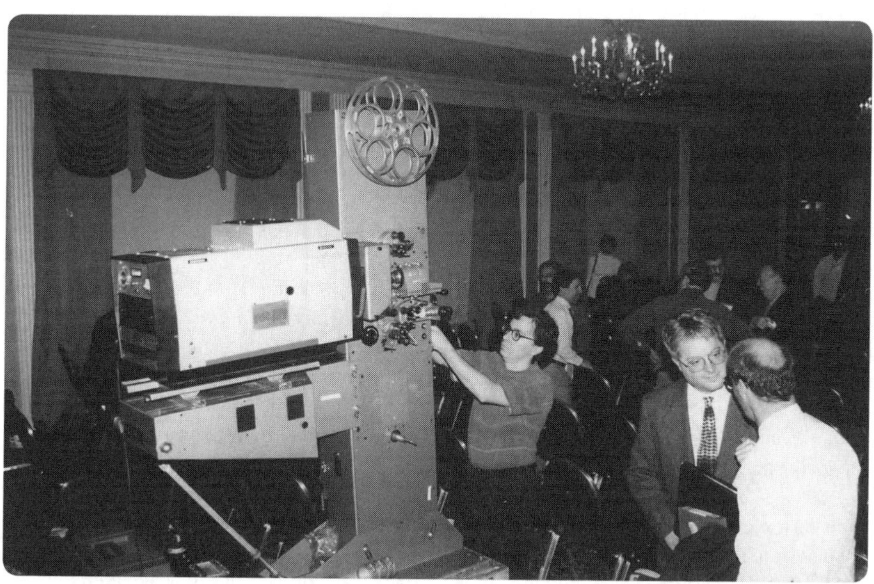

The portable 35mm projector that was set up in the main conference meeting room for the "Film–Digital–Film" session at the 1994 Boston AMIA conference. Photo courtesy Gregory Lukow.

Hopkins. In 2009, AMIA established the William S. O'Farrell Volunteer Award, created to honor the significant volunteer contributions of our dear colleague Bill O'Farrell. The inaugural recipient was Grover Crisp.

The year 1996 also saw the establishment of AMIA's first academic scholarship, funded by the Mary Pickford Foundation. As Robert Dirig discusses in detail in another contribution to this issue, AMIA and the board clearly recognized that training the next generation of moving image archivists was a paramount task of the association. As history has proven, the investment in youth through the establishment of numerous scholarship funds has paid off as many scholarship winners have become active supporters of AMIA once they entered the field professionally. With increased student activity, and the founding of moving image archive studies programs at the University of California, Los Angeles (UCLA), and New York University (NYU), as well as the Jeffrey Selznick Certificate Program at George Eastman House, it is also not surprising that an AMIA student chapter was founded at UCLA in 2000, initially organized by MLS student Olivia Solis.[13] AMIA student chapters have followed at the Selznick School and NYU.

In August 1999, the AMIA board approved its first strategic plan for the period 1999–2003. The process of writing the strategic plan involved the 1998 and 1999 boards and the chairs of several committees and was led by the AMIA administrative coordinator. Apart from defining a number of expanded activities for the organization, the plan called for hiring an administrative assistant to support the administrative coordinator. In the plan, the board outlined five core services to the field:

1. providing opportunities to exchange information about the field
2. promoting public advocacy and awareness about issues important to archivists
3. establishing and developing the profession
4. developing professional standards
5. promoting cooperation and collaboration

A second strategic plan was approved for the period 2003–7, which has since been renewed annually. The strategic plan serves the organization in multiple ways, allowing AMIA to gauge not only where it has come from but also the progress it is making in where it is going. That AMIA completed a strategic plan a mere eight years after its founding attests to the rapid maturity of the association. Not that there wouldn't still be bumps in the road, in particular concerning its short-lived executive director and the continuing struggle to define the exact nature of the board. At the same time, the strategic plan is a theoretical document about our field because it attempts, at least partially, to project trends in the future.

The growth and maturation of AMIA over a twenty-year period has been nothing short of miraculous. Certainly the growth of the field of moving image archiving, as more and more institutions have realized their need to protect their own moving image media, helped the association achieve such growth. However, the dedicated volunteers of the organization have provided a base of support that cannot be underestimated, nor can the work of the AMIA office staff. In a field that is rapidly changing, where the catchall phrase of convergence provides many challenges for the profession as well as for moving image archivists individually, the association can serve as both a safe haven and a space for advocacy. No other professional organization offers the same level of service, specifically directed toward moving image archivists. At AMIA, archivists do have more fun.

NOTES

1. "AMIA Votes to Formalize," *AMIA Newsletter,* nos. 11–12 (Winter–Spring 1991): 1.

2. "Minutes of the Business Meeting: AMIA 1991 Annual Conference," *AMIA Newsletter,* nos. 14–15 (Fall 1991–Winter 1992): 5.

3. "Membership Development Committee Report," *AMIA Newsletter,* no. 33 (Summer 1996): 6–7.

4. "AMIA Business Meeting," *AMIA Newsletter,* no. 19 (March 1993): 5.

5. Jan-Christopher Horak, "Editor's Introduction," *The Moving Image* 1, no. 1 (2001): viii.

6. http://www.amiatechreview.com/.

7. Jan-Christopher Horak, "Statement by AMIA to the National Film Preservation Board," *AMIA Newsletter,* no. 20 (May 1993): 5.

8. Eddie Richmond, "AMIA Protests Cuts in NEA Film Preservation Grant Program," *AMIA Newsletter,* no. 27 (January 1995): 1, 18.

9. James H. Billington to AMIA, December 19, 1994, reprinted in *AMIA Newsletter,* no. 28 (Spring 1995): 3.

10. "AMIA Supports Film Preservation Act at Congressional Hearings," *AMIA Newsletter,* no. 29 (Summer 1995): 17.

11. Maxine Fleckner Ducey, "AMIA Statement: LOC Study on the State of U.S. TV/Video Preservation," *AMIA Newsletter,* no. 32 (Spring 1996): 27.

12. Andrea Kalas to David Francis, regarding "Television and Video Preservation Report," *AMIA Newsletter,* no. 35 (Winter 1997): 11.

13. Andrea Leigh, "AMIA Student Chapter at UCLA," *AMIA Newsletter,* no. 51 (Winter 2001): 16.

We Are the World

AMIA Comes of Age and Discovers International Relations

SAM KULA

One can easily overhype the "we are the world" bit because there are large parts of the globe in which activity in audiovisual archives is either marginal or nonexistent, and there are many countries in which there are archives with which the Association of Moving Image Archivists (AMIA) only has contact through other federations or associations of archives. However, AMIA has come a long way in the last five years in reaching out beyond North America to anyone, anywhere, with a sincere desire to collect and protect a piece of the world's audiovisual heritage.

In a sense, AMIA has always been international. Once the Film Archives Advisory and Television Archives Advisory Committees (F/TAAC), from which AMIA emerged in 1991, had outgrown their original function of coordinating the activity on a national level and of advising the American Film Institute (AFI) on how to distribute the National Endowment for the Arts funding then available, they became effectively the body linking moving image archives in North America.

Canadian members were welcome. Certainly, when I shifted from managing the AFI's archives program and began directing the audiovisual program at the Public Archives of Canada (now Library and Archives Canada) in 1973, I assumed I could continue sharing knowledge and experience with my American friends. There may have been one or two other Canadians attending FAAC in those early days (the records are nonexistent—we used to signify agreement with a nodding of heads!), but in due course of time, more than forty other Canadian archivists joined.

It should be clear from the history statement on the organization's Web site that AMIA has always been an association open to moving image archivists from anywhere in the world.[1] They can work in national institutions with substantial budgets or in the equivalent of mom-and-pop storefront operations hanging on from day to day, hoping that some funding source will recognize the value of their work. Terminology tends to be imprecise in our field: you can't *restore* or *preserve* unless you first *protect,* and if all you can do is protect, even in substandard storage conditions, you are still carrying out a vital archival function.

Public access is not an essential characteristic in defining moving image archives. AMIA is unique in that the membership includes archivists from production companies in film and television to distributors, footage libraries, and laboratories—anyone involved with protecting, restoring, and disseminating the heritage.

In AMIA's first ten years, the membership grew steadily, until it leveled off at about seven hundred. While foreign membership (defined as residents outside North America) grew as well, developments in the moving image archives world elsewhere held the increase to modest numbers. One was the establishment of the Southeast Asia-Pacific Audiovisual Archive Association (SEAPAVAA) in 1996, which grouped moving image archives and individual archivists from the ten nations of the Association of Southeast Asian Nations, Australia and New Zealand, and the Pacific Islands into an association with a mandate very similar to that of AMIA. Another was the impact of digitization with converging recording technologies in sound and images, leading organizations such as the International Association of Sound and Audiovisual Archives (IASA; originally the International Association of Sound Archives) to expand their mandates. A third factor was the significant increase in resources available for audiovisual archives throughout the European Union. Numerous collaborative and well-funded projects in preservation and data management in the past ten years have linked archives and archivists in Europe in ways that the rest of the world can only envy.

While all this activity was taking place, AMIA faced a dilemma. With the vast majority of its members located in the United States, there was resistance to holding the annual conference outside the United States because of cost and travel restrictions. This denied AMIA the opportunity to use conferences in other regions of the globe as a means of developing the field and of attracting new members. This has been the practice of the International Federation of Film Archives (FIAF) and the International Federation of Television Archives (FIAT), as well as of IASA and SEAPAVAA, since they were founded.

The first break in the insular position AMIA adopted was the decision to hold the annual conference in Toronto in 1995. The argument was that Toronto was within easy reach of the majority of the membership, travel costs would be no greater than the average for a conference in the United States, and the conversion rate for the Canadian dollar at that time made the whole package very attractive. The conference was a great success, there were no adverse consequences, and conferences in Montreal and Vancouver were set for 1999 and 2003. AMIA had successfully crossed an international border and survived!

I happened to be president of AMIA from 1999 to 2003, and as a Canadian with service in moving image archives in three countries, I was conditioned to pursue international cooperation. In fact, finding myself on the executive committees of both FIAF and FIAT one year, I was active in promoting the first Joint Technical Symposium (IASA was asked to join), which was held in Stockholm in 1983. AMIA was not in the game then, but individual AMIA members were active participants in Berlin (1987), Ottawa (1990), London (1995), and Paris (2000).

With the proliferation of nongovernmental organizations in audiovisual archives, UNESCO decided that some coordination was needed. The first annual meeting of what was accurately if somewhat cumbersomely labeled the Coordinating Council of Audiovisual Archives Associations (CCAAA) was held in Paris in 2000. It was a measure of AMIA's growing stature in the international community that we were asked to join for the third meeting in 2002. It was my privilege to represent the organization at this first foray into international cooperation. The CCAAA is composed of FIAF, FIAT, IASA, SEAPAVAA, and the audiovisual committees of both the International Council on Archives and the International Federation of Library Associations—a formidable gathering! AMIA

still does not have a direct formal relationship with UNESCO, but negotiations are under way.

The year 2002 was a watershed year in many ways. Under the prodding of a few like-minded expansionists like Ray Edmondson, the peripatetic Australian who had been instrumental in establishing SEAPAVAA and served as its president in its formative years, AMIA's executive board established a task force to promote and coordinate AMIA's contacts with archivists outside North America. As board liaison to the International Outreach Task Force (IOTF), Ray and I cochaired the group meetings for the first two years. It was originally called the Task Force on Internationalization, but it became clear very quickly that this was a name that would not fly, and it was renamed the IOTF.

The primary task of the IOTF[2] was to develop policies and programs to enable AMIA to reach out to moving image archivists throughout the world, with the specific objective of extending AMIA's services, such as workshops, by organizing activities outside continental North America. Members of the IOTF share experiences in carrying out volunteer missions to archives in developing countries and promote best practices in rendering assistance in such missions. One way to sharpen the focus on these needs was to invite archivists from so-called third world countries to speak at AMIA conferences—Lim Ky from the National Archives of Cambodia is an example—so that the reality of working under really difficult conditions could be forcibly presented and personal contacts could be established. Consciousness raising is slow work, but in retrospect, the IOTF had and is having an impact on how AMIA's first world members, even those with perpetual resource shortfalls of their own, see themselves as members of the world community.

The "task force" label implied that outreach was a project with an end date. By 2008, it had become clear that the work of the IOTF would not end in the foreseeable future. The work being done by IOTF was too important for AMIA and the worldwide constituency it hoped to serve, and so the IOTF became a committee of the membership. In 2007, Brigitte Paulowitz and Reto Kromer, restoration specialists working in Switzerland, took over as cochairs of the committee, which now had about fifty members.

AMIA was looking outward and agreed to host the Joint Technical Symposium (JTS), which was held in Toronto in 2004. This was a huge success, largely due to the efforts of Grover Crisp and Michael Friend, who, as program chairs, utilized the expertise and international contacts they had developed organizing The Reel Thing, the technical highlight of the AMIA conferences for the past twenty years. Grover and Michael—again on behalf of AMIA as host—repeated the success as program chairs of the JTS, again in Toronto, in 2007. UNESCO enhanced the value of the JTS experience in sharing expertise on the impact of rapidly shifting technologies by financing the attendance of ten people from developing countries at the 2004 and 2007 JTS.

Organizing workshops and/or seminars in other countries is more difficult than it appears for a relatively small organization with decidedly limited resources. The Outreach Committee has identified the needs, and AMIA certainly has the will, but it has not as yet been possible to organize workshops outside the venue of the annual conference. AMIA has acquired some experience with the logistics involved in working offshore by responding to invitations from the EYE Film Institute Netherlands in Amsterdam to participate in the Biennale. In 2007, and again in 2010, AMIA organized a half-day seminar on current issues in media archives, with the other half-day given over to a truncated version of The Reel Thing. This has allowed hundreds of moving image archivists who would not have been able to travel to North America to taste what AMIA has to offer.

Another approach to reaching out to a wider community is to organize joint conferences. These, too, have proven very difficult to arrange, but some success was achieved in 2003 when SEAPAVAA offered sessions at the Vancouver conference. In 2010, a joint conference was fully realized when AMIA and IASA met in Philadelphia. The conference featured not only joint sessions but a joint plenary, receptions, and cross-registration to provide more choices for participants from both organizations.

As AMIA approaches its twenty-first year, it can honestly declare that it has opened its doors to the world. But with only nineteen countries represented among the 864 individual members in 2009, there is obviously a very long way to go. The links that AMIA has forged with other international associations and with UNESCO should lead to greater growth in the ever-expanding universe of audiovisual archives, but the locations for future annual conferences remain a debatable issue. We are not yet the world, but the welcome mat is out for anyone who shares our objectives.

NOTES

1. Online at http://www.amianet.org/.
2. See http://www.amianet.org/groups/committees/outreach/outreach.php.

Antipodean Reflections on AMIA

RAY EDMONDSON

In browsing through back issues of the *AMIA Newsletter,* I came across, with some pleasure, issue 31 (Winter 1996), where I am not only listed as a new member and a participant at the Toronto conference (my first) but am also included in Greg Lukow's compilation of "Publications Received and Noted" as follows:

> Edmondson, Ray, and the members of AVAPIN. *A Philosophy of Audiovisual (AV) Archiving: Draft Two.* Audiovisual Archiving Philosophy Interest Network (AVAPIN), August 1995. 38 pages plus appendices. Prepared for discussion at the Toronto AMIA conference, October 1995, and the UNESCO Round Table on AV Archiving, March 1996.

The present successor to that document, the eighty-page *Audiovisual Archiving: Philosophy and Principles,* was published by UNESCO in 2004. Available, to date, in nine languages, it might be fairly said that it has become part of the furniture of our profession. Back in 1995, however, it was far from obvious that there was any need for a manual that delved into the values and philosophical fundamentals underlying our work. The Association of Moving Image Archivists (AMIA) conference forum and the resulting discussion were instrumental in shaping the then embryonic text, and it has always seemed to me significant that AMIA found space for what may have seemed at the time a rather esoteric topic.

I think this says something about the style of AMIA conferences. Unlike other associations that take a disciplined, thematic approach to conference papers and symposia, AMIA offers unrestricted scope: it seeks (to quote the call for the 2010 conference) "papers, panels and posters on all issues to do with sound and audiovisual archives." Nothing is off the table or under the radar, and invariably, the result is a rich and challenging, if sometimes unconventional, diet. The parallel streaming of sessions, which means that one is always conflicted for choice, reflects the real world in which AMIA members live.

That brings me to the nature of AMIA itself. My wife vividly recalls my coming home from the Toronto conference in 1995, enthused about AMIA. "I can *talk* to these people. They understand me," she remembers me saying. Although I had known about AMIA for some time, it was the first time I had actually encountered it in the flesh. I have rarely missed a conference since, and I have never failed to be energized by the experience. It may be a function of the size of the gathering—it is easily the largest annual conference in the audiovisual archiving field—or the diversity of the participants, or the quality and range of the sessions. It might be that so much is compressed into an intensive four or five days.

But there is also an intangible quality to the event that derives from a specific source. I have always felt *welcome.* That does not mean faux camaraderie, nor does it mean organized mentoring, important as that is; it simply speaks to the character of the membership and the reason people join AMIA and come to the conference at all. We are there because we are engaged in a mission that matters, and anyone who shares that motivation is automatically welcome. We are energized and encouraged by each other.

AMIA's great strength is that it is based on individual rather than corporate or institutional membership. It is inclusive rather than exclusive. Wherever its members sit in their respective organizational hierarchies, they participate in AMIA as individuals. This makes AMIA a great leveler. It encourages a democratic approach in its activities and its committees. It's expressed in the liveliest Listserv in the profession. Potentially, it allows AMIA to take public stances on professional issues without fear or favor, and it is what appeals to people outside North America, for whom AMIA membership is a relatively expensive affair—particularly when the cost of conference attendance (always at a North American venue) is taken into account.

A case in point is the unique influence AMIA members had on the fortunes of Australia's National Film and Sound Archive (NFSA). Some readers will remember the long, troubled saga of the archive's puzzling, if short-lived, name change (to ScreenSound Australia) in 1999 and its subsequent ill-advised takeover by the Australian Film Commission—an event that threatened its continued existence. Periodic updates on the saga were carried by the *AMIA Newsletter* and more in-depth pieces in *The Moving Image.* What is not generally known is that many individual AMIA members—from outside Australia—rallied to the NFSA's defense by writing to its minister. The happy, cumulative result was that the NFSA is now finally an autonomous statutory authority, secured by its own act of parliament. I hope it will never be forgotten that AMIA played a special part in the NFSA's story.

So perhaps it is no coincidence that my principal committee activities in AMIA have been associated with international outreach and advocacy. In his separate article in this issue, Sam Kula has related our joint involvement in convening the International Outreach Task Force (IOTF)—now the International Outreach Committee. The setting up of this task force arose from an e-mail discussion group that the board invited me to convene in 1998. The group's report urged its establishment with a view to growing AMIA's vision of itself as an international rather than regional organization. Among other things, the IOTF began to invite speakers from needy archives in other countries to try to build a consciousness among the membership of a larger world meriting the attention of AMIA members as volunteers and supporters.

Whether as a result of the IOTF or other factors, it is my impression that AMIA now very decidedly regards itself as an international organization. It plays a significant and energetic part in the Coordinating Council of Audiovisual Archives Associations (CCAAA), and it organized the Joint Technical Symposiums in 2004 and 2007 with considerable success. The annual awarding of prizes and scholarships has begun to take on a more international flavor. AMIA is putting its toe in the water in Europe by conducting occasional brief events such as half-day seminars. But this must only be seen as a beginning, and we are confronted by many challenges.

One of those challenges lies just south of the U.S.–Mexican border. We have yet to achieve significant conference and committee participation from Latin America, with its numerous audiovisual archives and its diverse archival community. This surely is a matter of real concern that speaks to AMIA's relevance to the non-English-speaking world. We do, after all, share the motivations that inspire our Spanish- and Portuguese-speaking colleagues. How do we make *them* welcome? It is both a need and an opportunity.

More recently, AMIA's establishment of an Advocacy Task Force—now Advocacy Committee—was something of a first among the CCAAA associations. The committee is working on a mechanism to enable AMIA to raise public awareness and express a point of view on matters of professional principle and issues affecting moving image archiving. Having chaired this group since its inception in 2005 (and now seeking a cochair to share the load), I am beginning to see the way ahead in enabling AMIA to regularly make its voice heard on matters of interest and concern that affect the survival and accessibility of audiovisual heritage and the status of the profession.

The first outcome of the committee's work is the AMIA Code of Ethics, adopted by membership vote in late 2009. The need for a code was recognized at broad membership forums known as "AMIA at 13" and "AMIA at 14," held at conferences six and seven years ago, respectively. That leaves the second major recommendation from those forums—the adoption of some form of professional credentialing—as unfinished business, in the hands of the Education Committee. Reaching a conclusion on this matter is, in my view, an essential aspect of AMIA's coming of age as a widely recognized and influential professional association. May it be too much to hope that it might coincide with AMIA's twenty-first birthday?

So far as I can tell, there have always been a small but significant number of AMIA members in Australia. Because we denizens of Oz have always faced the tyranny of distance, we have equally felt the need to reach out and connect internationally—not through any great altruistic virtue but because as a small country (at least in population terms), we have no choice. By the same token, as moving image archivists, we are a relatively small community in global terms—and we neglect an international vision, and international networking, at our peril. My hope is that AMIA will go on to fulfill its potential as a global force of individual professionals who can change the way the world regards its audiovisual heritage.

How the AMIA Scholarships and Fellowships Program Helped Pave the Way for a New Generation of Moving Image Archivists

ROBERT DIRIG

The Association of Moving Image Archivists (AMIA) has always supported and fostered education. The organization brings together professionals who are involved with, in one way or another, the management of moving image materials. This network of archivists shares knowledge and experience through conferences, workshops, symposiums, committee work, and Listservs. Sometime during AMIA's first decade, an increasing number of graduate students became involved and were interested in becoming moving image archivists. AMIA soon started an impressive scholarship program that has grown to currently offer four scholarships, two fellowships, and an internship, funded by major film studios, laboratories, foundations, and other film-related institutions. By 2010, seventy-six students and archivists had benefited from the program and had been chosen as recipients. Former AMIA president Sam Kula summed it up well by stating, "One of AMIA's goals is to foster the education and training of young moving image professionals and the AMIA Scholarship Program is a key component to carrying out that goal."[1]

The first scholarship that AMIA offered was the Mary Pickford Scholarship in 1997. This offering was historic because it not only triggered the commencement of the AMIA Scholarship Program but was also the first scholarship ever granted specifically to students studying moving image archiving. Keith Lawrence, Mary Pickford Foundation president and CEO, approached AMIA for ideas on how his organization could help support the field. Through a conversation with then board member William O'Farrell at a conference in the mid-1990s, the idea of a scholarship for students emerged. This proposal was welcomed by AMIA and its then president Eddie Richmond. According to

Richmond, there was already a desire within the community to enhance the professionalism of people working in the field, and one way to do that would be to support education for students.[2] Richmond worked with Lawrence and the Mary Pickford Foundation in 1996 to establish and set up the guidelines for the scholarship.

The scholarship awarded three thousand dollars to the recipient, paid directly to the academic institution to be used for tuition and fees. The eligibility requirements were that the student had to be enrolled in a graduate-level program in a related field and have a grade point average of at least 3.0. Applicants had to submit an application form consisting of basic résumé-type information, an official transcript, letters of recommendation, and an essay of one thousand words or fewer describing career goals, relevant experience, and interest in moving image archives. The AMIA office gathered all of the applications, and an Education Committee Scholarship Subcommittee reviewed and selected Ann Wilkens, a student at University of Wisconsin, as the inaugural recipient. Subsequent recipients have included Rita Belda, Julie Lofthouse, Diana King, Heather Sabin, Claudy Op den Kamp, Doron Galili, Caitlin Devereaux Lewis, Thelma Ross, Sarah Resnick, Stephanie Sapienza, Heather Heckman, Walter Forsberg, and Nino Dzandzava.

Eddie Richmond would go on to play an integral role on the Education Committee beginning in 1997, helping establish two other scholarships: the Sony Pictures Scholarship in 1998 and the Consolidated Film Industries (CFI) Sid Solow Scholarship in 1999. These scholarships also awarded three thousand dollars for tuition and fees, were administered by AMIA, and had the same eligibility requirements as the Mary Pickford Scholarship. Grover Crisp, vice president of Asset Management and Film Restoration for Sony Pictures Entertainment, worked with AMIA on behalf of Sony to create a scholarship that would be endowed on a permanent basis. This not only ensured the future of the award but also symbolically demonstrated Sony's belief that educating future moving image archivists was crucial. The first recipient, in 1998, was Ann Butler, a student from Rutgers University. Subsequent recipients have included Sarah Ziebell Mann, Katie

Trainor, Laura Bradshaw, Susan Busam, Violet Matangira, Lindsay Harris, Guy Edmonds, Ishumael Zinyengere, James Gamble, Tracy Popp, Michael Araizaga, and Caitlin Hammer.

The CFI Sid Solow Scholarship was announced at the 1998 AMIA annual conference by Paul Stambaugh, vice president of CFI and named in honor of CFI's founder, Sid Solow. This was the first AMIA scholarship funded by a commercial laboratory.[3] C. Allen Giles, a student at the University of California, Berkeley, was named the first recipient. Subsequent recipients have included Heather Olson, Julio Vera, Diana Little, Emily Staresina, Julie Kessler, Tina Bastajian, Yvonne Ng, Dino Everett, Stacey Menear, and Amy Jo Damitz. It was announced in the *AMIA Newsletter* (Winter 2004) that to meet the costs of education, the three scholarships would increase their award from three thousand to four thousand dollars, thus showing the continued interest of the three sponsors in supporting graduate-level education.

The idea of enhancing professionalism through academic programs in the moving image archival field is an issue that has been discussed and debated for many years. In the landmark 1994 report *Redefining Film Preservation: A National Plan* from the Library of Congress, which involved many professionals in the field as well as the National Film Preservation Board, there is a section titled "Educating Film Preservationists." The report recommended the establishment of a graduate-level degree program in film preservation in the United States, related hands-on internships, and professional development.[4] Although not specifically calling for scholarships, AMIA felt that offering them was one way to support education and the establishment of graduate-level programs. Eddie Richmond said that because the Library of Congress report made specific mention of graduate-level education, it was helpful to the Education Committee in creating new scholarships and supporting the program.[5]

With three scholarships offered by 1999 and increased student membership in AMIA, one may wonder where all these students were studying. It had been several years since the Library of Congress's call for a master's degree program in film preservation, and there were only a couple programs in the 1990s, namely, the University of East Anglia Film Studies with

Archiving degree program and the certificate program at L. Jeffrey Selznick School of Film Preservation at George Eastman House. Many of the other students were enrolled in programs in related fields, such as library and information science, which often offered course work in archives. It is not surprising that some scholarship recipients came from such programs and still continue to do so today. Although unique in each of the following functions, the management of moving image materials, like all archival materials, involves appraisal, description and cataloging, reference and access, preservation, and collection management. Moreover, many archives have moving image materials in their collections. In fact, with the proliferation of moving image content created today, it would be difficult to find institutions (across a spectrum of fields) that do not have moving images in their archives. However, for years, moving image archives were not part of the curriculum in library and information studies and lacked course work involving the theoretical literature that was the foundation for modern archival studies. Considered so specialized and technical, students had to seek methods for educating themselves on these matters such as through internships and individual-study electives.

A paradigm shift in how moving image archivists are trained was emerging, transitioning training in the field from an apprenticeship model to an academic one. Writing about moving image archival education and the profession in 2000, Gregory Lukow stated that "the development of new generations of archivists has always relied upon unsystematic and often long-term apprenticeships that tend to focus on a limited range of specialized skills. Such narrowly defined models of archival training have generally excluded the complex social, philosophical and cultural contexts in which modern, professional archival practice is grounded."[6] Lukow echoed the Library of Congress's call for advanced programs and referred to education as "the missing link." Overall, there was support for this shift in the AMIA community. One year after the Scholarship Program began, the Education Committee, led by cochair Janice Simpson, conducted a survey asking AMIA members about the educational needs of members in the profession. The results of the survey showed that the AMIA Scholarship Program and the creation of a graduate degree program had support from a majority of the members, although there were some reservations and varying ideas as to how the programs should be designed and implemented.[7] There was enough momentum, however, to continue along the path, and the survey helped pave the way to create additional scholarships.

The Spring 2002 *AMIA Newsletter* featured a cover story article and announcement of a new scholarship sponsored by the Rick Chace Foundation. Putting this story on the front page signified the importance AMIA continued to place on the Scholarship Program. According to Rick Chace Foundation president Robert Heiber, the idea for the scholarship emerged because "Rick Chace was an excellent teacher of the practices of sound preservation and restoration. By awarding a scholarship this seemed an excellent way to recognize Rick's contribution to our field, and to continue to keep his memory a viable part of our archive community."[8] The first recipient, a student in the first class of the University of California, Los Angeles (UCLA), Moving Image Archive Studies Program, was David Gibson. Subsequent recipients have included Irene Taylor, Stephanie Stewart, Benjamin Harry, Regina Longo, Oki Miyano, Kimberly Tarr, Jennifer Blaylock, and Sean Kilcoyne.

One year later, at the 2003 AMIA annual conference, it was announced that Universal Studios would form a scholarship with AMIA, making them the second film studio to offer a scholarship in the program. Both the Universal Studios and the Rick Chace Foundation scholarships would have the same application form and eligibility requirements as the established scholarships and would also award the recipients four thousand dollars for tuition and fees. The first recipient of the Universal Studios Scholarship was Paula Felix-Didier, a student in New York University's (NYU's) Moving Image Archiving and Preservation Program. Subsequent recipients have included Jimi Jones, Baukje Stamm, Janet Ceja, Andy Uhrich, Marwa El Sahn, and Michela Russo.

With the advent of these two new scholarships, a number of graduate-level degree and certificate programs emerged between 2002 and 2005, including the UCLA Moving Image Archive Studies degree program, the NYU Moving Image Archiving and Preservation degree program, the University of Amsterdam Preservation and Presentation of the Moving Image degree program, the Charles Sturt University Audiovisual Archiving graduate certificate program, and the University of Rochester–George Eastman House degree program. Clearly the Library of Congress's call for graduate-level education was answered, and the potential pool of scholarship applicants increased.

In addition to the scholarships, AMIA currently offers three programs that answer the Library of Congress report's recommendation for integrating hands-on internships with academic programs and for offering continuing education. The three programs include the Kodak Fellowship in Film Preservation, the Image Permanence Institute Internship in Preservation Research, and the AMIA–Rockefeller Archive Center Visiting Archivist Fellowship. Even though these programs all offer students and archivists advanced training and real-world opportunities, they are unique and specialized in their own way.

At the 1999 AMIA annual conference in Montreal, Rick Utley, vice president of preservation services at the Eastman Kodak Company, announced that Kodak and AMIA would be soon announcing a new fellowship program to "foster the education and training of the next generation of moving image archivists and underline Kodak's continued commitment to the preservation of our moving image heritage."[9] Utley was challenged by Kodak to create a program that encompassed not only a scholarship but also an internship that would give students real-world experience. Utley crafted the fellowship with Eddie Richmond and then Education Committee chair Janice Simpson. One applicant would be selected and would receive a four thousand dollar scholarship, complimentary registration at the AMIA conference, and a six-week paid internship at PRO-TEK Media Preservation Services, Cinesite, and CFI. The internship was designed to give the students a glimpse into various aspects of the film preservation and restoration industry in Los Angeles, including experience at both photochemical and digital laboratories.

Whereas one application is used for the

various scholarships, a separate application was created and required for the Kodak Fellowship. Applicants need to be enrolled in a graduate-level program in a related field, have a GPA of at least 3.0, be at least twenty-one years of age, and demonstrate a strong commitment to pursuing a career in moving image archiving. Along with the application form, letters of recommendation, an official transcript, and an essay of one thousand words or fewer describing career goals, relevant experience, interest in moving image archives, and internship expectations are also required. The subcommittee awarding the scholarship also takes into consideration the applicant's academic program as it applies to moving image archive studies. Similar to the scholarships, the Education Committee subcommittee reviews the applications and makes the selections.[10] In 2000, as an MLIS student at UCLA, I was chosen as the first recipient. Subsequent recipients have included Kelly Chisholm, Elena Rossi-Snook, Patricia Rhodes, Audrey Amidon, Christopher Lane, Carla Reiter, Eva Heischler, Sandra Gibson, Jessica Storm, and Marissa Haddock.

Over the past ten years, the internship sites have changed to include Chace Audio, Laser Pacific, Technicolor, and Fotokem, always with the idea to incorporate experience in both the analogue and digital domains. These internship sites designate a mentor to work with the interns to provide individualized training. Of the various internship sites that have participated in the Kodak Fellowship program, PRO-TEK, a Kodak Company managed by Utley, has remained steadfast. The PRO-TEK facility features sophisticated temperature- and humidity-controlled vaults as well as services in inspection, restoration management, and consulting. Utley spends time with interns talking about the history of film preservation, film technologies, laboratory practices, and the business side of the field. Interns also gain experience inspecting films, looking for physical and chemical deterioration, and learning how metadata is applied as part of their inventory catalog. Students ideally take from the entire internship a better understanding of film preservation, the operation of different types of labs and facilities, and where they envision their careers.

In 2005, the Image Permanence Institute (IPI) announced a paid internship program in preservation research. Founded in 1985, IPI is a leader in the field of preservation research. Jean-Louis Bigourdan, research scientist at IPI, first conceived of the internship while attending an AMIA conference. He thought it would be beneficial for students to have the opportunity to participate in an internship focused on preservation research and that one lasting three months would best immerse the student in the field. He proposed the idea to then AMIA board member Dan Streible, then AMIA president Janice Simpson, and the Education Committee, who were all enthusiastic about the idea. The three-month program would offer a five thousand dollar stipend to cover living expenses and also cover travel costs. It would be administered by AMIA and, like the Kodak Fellowship, be awarded to one applicant and have its own application reviewed by the Education Committee Scholarships and Fellowships Subcommittee. The applicants are required to submit an application, letters of recommendation, an official transcript, and an essay of one thousand words or fewer explaining their interest in moving image archiving and career goals. Applicants also need to be enrolled or accepted in a moving image preservation or archival education program and have completed half of the program's course work before the commencement of the internship. In 2006, Justin Bonfiglio was named the first recipient. Subsequent recipients have included Timothy Wilson, James Layton, Sean Kelly, and Tessa Zdlewine.

The research projects undertaken at IPI are vast, encompassing both still and moving images. Interns have an opportunity to learn about the different research projects and also focus on one of them. One intern took part in a project testing acetate film and storage environments. Another recent intern, using special software and microscopy imaging techniques, contributed to IPI's "Knowing and Protecting Motion Picture Film Poster," which shows an overview of various film materials used over time. This educational poster "features a timeline of motion-picture technology, a wide variety of motion picture film processes, tips for material identification, and basic knowledge on film formats and soundtracks. Also included is practical advice for film examination, a glossary of technical terms, and critical information needed for long-term preservation."[11]

In 2006, the Rockefeller Visiting Archivist Fellowship was announced. This fellowship was unique to AMIA's scholarship and fellowship lineup in that it was designed for continuing education. Before joining with AMIA, the Rockefeller Archive Center already offered a similar program to archivists in developing countries that gave them archival experience at the center's archives departments as well as neighboring institutions. According to Carol Radovich, assistant director and head of archival services, the center's board was fully in support of the idea from the beginning. In 2005, Radovich began talking with Janice Simpson and Ray Edmondson on ways to collaborate with AMIA. In addition to experience at the center, they thought it would be valuable to the visiting archivist to be able to attend the annual AMIA conference to be introduced to the community, meet other professionals, and network with organizations.

Similar to the other awards, AMIA administers the program, with one Rockefeller staff member taking part in the application review. The recipient is required to be an archivist or in a related field from a developing country and needs to show in an essay how the internship will improve her continuing education and benefit her institution. Applicants also need to have a BA or equivalent, professional archival training, and two to five years of archival experience and must be able to speak and read English. The recipient receives up to thirty-five hundred dollars in travel reimbursement, complimentary registration to the AMIA conference, and a two thousand dollar stipend to cover local housing, food, and transportation costs while he is at the Rockefeller Archive Center and the AMIA conference. Ishumael Zinyengere from the National Archives of Zimbabwe was named as the first recipient in 2006. Subsequent recipients have included Peter Ugar Ogar, Ndahambelela-Hertha Lukleni, Luke Kiwanuka, Naomi Karimu, and Remi Ndour.

While at the Rockefeller Archive Center for one week, recipients have the opportunity to learn about different aspects of archives, depending on their needs and interests. Initially given an overview of the departments at the center, the visiting archivists might choose to learn more about areas such as video, film, and digital technologies; databases; environmental control; access; and administrative issues. Depending on their interests, they might take tours of nearby institutions such as the George Eastman House, MoMA, Cineric, and NYU's Moving Image Archiving and Preservation Program. During their time at the center, they will gather valuable lists of Web sites, books, and other resources that will be useful to them when they return to their home institutions. Though the visiting archivists learn a great deal during their one-week stay at the center and from the conference, the idea is that they leave with ideas that they can implement at their institutions, with contacts in the field, and with a greater sense of the professional archival community.

As with most of AMIA's committee and leadership work, volunteers are essential. The Scholarships and Fellowships Program could not have happened and continued to be so successful without the volunteerism of Education Committee chairs Eddie Richmond, Mary Ide, Janice Simpson, James Turner, Karen Lund, Karen Gracy, Frances Poole, and Lance Watsky; Scholarships and Fellowships Subcommittee chairs Eddie Richmond, Oksana Dykyj, Karen Lund, Francis Poole, Julie Lofthouse, and Snowden Becker; and all the subcommittee volunteers who were part of the review and selection process. In addition, the program owes much of its success to all the volunteer internship coordinators and mentors, who graciously provide their time and expertise.

AMIA has been fortunate to gain support from leaders in the industry to create successful scholarship and fellowship opportunities. These leaders know the importance of educating new archivists to manage and preserve moving images. Even with few educational opportunities offered in the late 1990s, everyone involved in the first several years of the program knew it would be a worthwhile endeavor. It certainly worked, with an increasing number of applicants each year originating from numerous graduate-level programs. It is not surprising to see so many students interested in studying moving image archives. Moving images

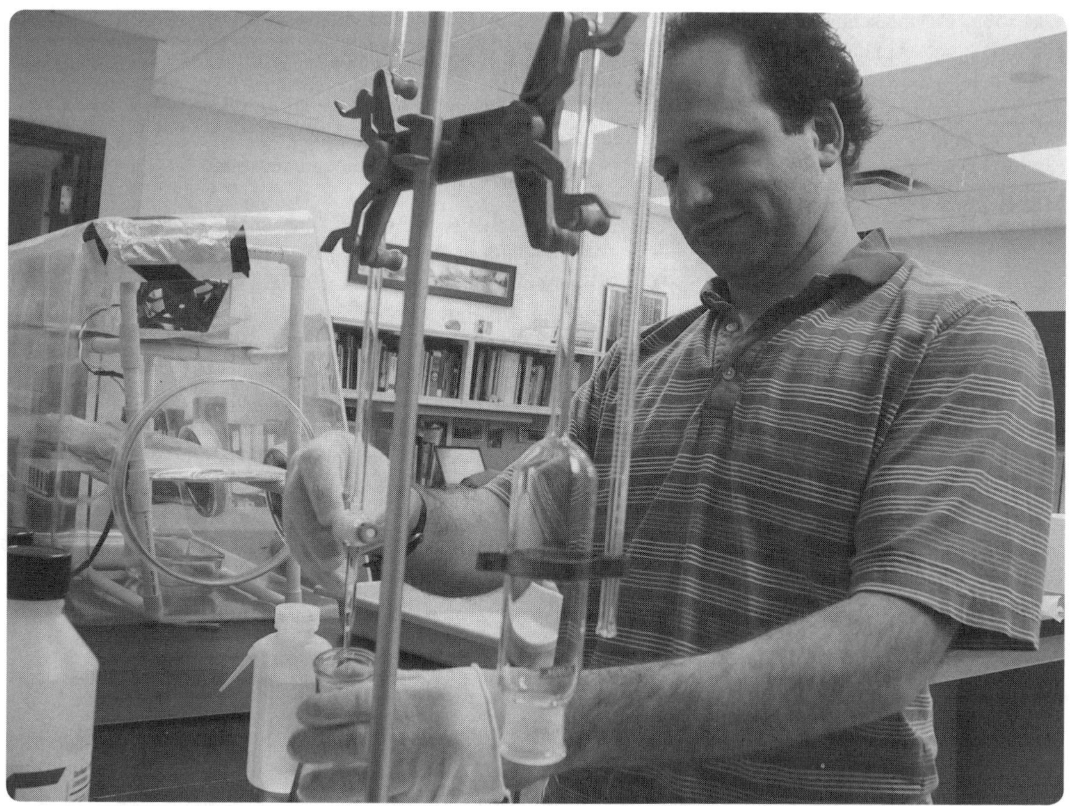

Image of the first recipient of the Image Permanence Institute internship, Justin Bonfiglio (2006 recipient), at work, 2007.

are everywhere. No longer considered a niche field in the world of archives, archivists from all types of institutions work with such materials. Many past recipients of AMIA scholarships and fellowships currently work with moving image materials. From a recent AMIA survey on scholarship recipients, over half of respondents designated that they work in an audiovisual archive (or one with audiovisual materials).[12] On the academic front, student research will likely become more collaborative, involving various other types of archives and information technology, especially with issues surrounding digital records. In addition, new scholarship and theory is being written, covering all aspects of the field. The AMIA Scholarships and Fellowships Program has played, and is continuing to play, an important part in helping to educate new moving image archivists and legitimize the academic role of moving image archival studies.

NOTES

My sincere thanks to the following people for talking and corresponding with me and for providing context and historical detail to the essay: Snowden Becker, Jean-Louis Bigourdan, Beverly Graham, Bob Heiber, Jan-Christopher Horak, Francis Poole, Carol Radovich, Eddie Richmond, Laura Rooney, Janice Simpson, and Rick Utley.

1. Sam Kula, "The Rick Chace Foundation Funds Annual AMIA Scholarship Program," *AMIA Newsletter,* no. 56 (Spring 2002): 10.
2. Eddie Richmond, telephone conversation with the author, April 6, 2010.

3. In 2000, CFI was acquired by Technicolor, adding restoration to their services. They continued to fund the scholarship.

4. Library of Congress, *Redefining Film Preservation: A National Plan* (Washington, DC: Library of Congress, 1994).

5. Richmond, telephone conversation, April 6, 2010.

6. Gregory Lukow, "Education, Training, and Careers in Moving Image Preservation," http://www.amianet.org/resources/education/ed_training_careers.pdf. Originally published in *Film History* 12, no. 2 (2000).

7. "AMIA Education Survey—Summary Results and Recommendations, 1999," http://www.amianet.org/resources/education/edu_survey.pdf. In addition to scholarships and degree programs, the survey covered workshops, distance education, dissemination of information, internships, and mentoring.

8. Robert Heiber, e-mail correspondence with the author, April 4, 2010.

9. "Kodak Sponsors Moving Image Fellowship Program," *AMIA Newsletter,* no. 47 (Winter 2000): 17.

10. For a brief period, a Fellowship Subcommittee (separate from the Scholarship Subcommittee), led by Eddie Richmond, administered the program.

11. Image Permanence Institute, "Knowing and Protecting Motion Picture Film," http://www.imagepermanenceinstitute.org/shtml_sub/filmposter_enlarge.asp.

12. "AMIA Scholarship Recipient Survey, 2009," unpublished data. Though the majority of respondents designated that they work in an audiovisual archive, other respondents (fairly evenly) marked that are working in a film lab; working with audiovisual materials (but not at an archive); teaching audiovisual archiving or a related field; working as filmmakers; or working in a different field.

AMIA's Local Television Project

KAREN CARIANI

This article describes the Association of Moving Image Archivists's (AMIA's) local television project—how it was formulated, its goals, and lessons learned from it. It was one of the first projects AMIA members undertook with outside funding to address issues of concern to the moving image community.

Much of our nation's cultural heritage has been captured by local television. From local news coverage to children's programming to arts and entertainment, local television provides a glimpse of our country's communities. As Librarian of Congress James Billington opined in 1997,

> television affects our lives from birth to death. Most Americans inform and entertain themselves through it. . . . Sadly, we have not yet sought to preserve this powerful medium in anything like a serious or systematic manner. At present, chance determines what television programs survive. Future scholars will have to rely on incomplete evidence when they assess the achievements and failures of our culture.[1]

During the 1980s and 1990s, a number of public archives and a few television stations began saving collections of local television recordings, films, and videotapes, which were deteriorating and being discarded at an alarming rate. The volume of materials created and therefore in existence from daily TV shows— particularly local news—was overwhelming to stations. From the stations' point of view, tossing it was often easier than saving it. However, much of twentieth-century culture has been documented on TV. As archivists, witnessing the destruction of these recordings of our history felt very wrong.

Professionals within AMIA discussed local television archive challenges that needed to be addressed to stem the losses, to preserve what remained, and to protect newly created material. Several conferences, studies, and meetings, such as one in Madison, Wisconsin, in 1987, outlined the problems and called for action. In 1997, the Library of Congress (LOC) issued a report titled *A Study of the Current State of American Television and Video Preservation*. AMIA members Karan Sheldon (Northeast Historic Film) and Eddie Richmond (University of California, Los Angeles [UCLA]) were cochairs of an AMIA Committee on the U.S. National Moving Image Preservation Plans, which was formed in response to the LOC report. AMIA wanted to implement projects to address issues mentioned in the report.

Karan Sheldon turned to members of AMIA's News and Documentary Interest Group to develop a project to solve specific problems related to local TV. With approval of the AMIA board, an ad hoc task force called the Local Television Case Studies/Symposium Planning Group was formed to map a strategy to address the problems of preserving local television. A small core group of committed project participants formed, including Bonnie Wilson and me as cochairs, Ruta Abolins, Steve Davidson, Lynn Farnell, Richard Fauss, Linda Giannecchini (also representing the National Academy of Television Arts and Sciences [NATAS]), Greg Lukow, Sara Meyerson, Karan Sheldon, Linda Tadic, David Weiss, and Helene Whitson. After a year of meeting at conferences and brainstorming ideas, the team formulated a project with three phases.

FORMULATING THE PROJECT

The task force's main challenge was to develop a way to raise awareness nationally about the importance of preserving these valuable materials and to stop the destruction of local television collections. Although the task force had been meeting at AMIA conferences and electronically since 1997, project planning began in earnest with a trip to Athens, Georgia, in April 1999, to the house of Linda Tadic, then director of the Peabody Collection at the University of Georgia. After working for two days and hashing out ideas of how to attack the problem at hand, a project was designed to solve the challenges.

The group felt that it was important to bring archivists and local television-producing entities together to discuss issues that affect the preservation of local television in the United States. There was a strong feeling that the content creators—the television stations (particularly the local ones)—needed to understand why it was important preserve this material and how best to do so. Without that support and understanding, the project would fall short of its goal. The task force worked on the structure, work plan, timeline, and budget for mounting a project that would inform the television community of these pressing needs.

Before determining how to stop the destruction of local TV historical materials and begin the process of preserving them, the first step was to learn what condition the collections were in and what genres were included (local news, children's programming, advertisements, local arts performances, etc.). Second was to raise awareness among the TV community about the importance of taking care of and preserving materials because of their potential historical and cultural importance. And finally, we needed to develop a guide book for stations, in non-archives speak, that would help them care for their collections and provide case studies of successful local TV archives.

Having a partner with deep ties to the TV community that could help communicate the project goals was also critical. The most productive avenue for mounting a successful project was to work in partnership with NATAS, the organization that awards the regional Emmys to TV stations and has offices across the country. NATAS is structured at the national and local levels and has mechanisms in place (regional chapters, newsletters, Web sites) that allowed the organization to reach its members to encourage them to participate in the project. In general, AMIA concentrated on reaching archivists; NATAS concentrated on reaching producers and local stations.

The project also needed separable parts that could be assigned to different task force members. This allowed everyone to participate, with no one person taking on the whole project burden. The project had three components: (1) creation of a database describing the local television holdings of public archives and stations, (2) creation and dissemination of case studies that illustrated issues of concern in forming relationships between public archives

and stations, and (3) a two-day symposium focused on the case studies, concluding with recommendations to the field. The case studies were organized around the following issues known to be important to stations and archives: (1) rights, (2) intellectual control, (3) asset protection, (4) revenue, and (5) selection. Each topic would have one or more case studies to illustrate how different archives and stations had approached, resolved, or were actively developing solutions to these issues.

Bonnie Wilson, formerly of the Minnesota Historical Society, and I, of WGBH (Boston), were asked to cochair the three-phased project. Once the shape of the project was developed, the next step was to look for potential funders and write a proposal. AMIA generously provided money to hire Greg Lukow, then at UCLA, to write a funding proposal. The National Historical Publications and Records Commission was the ideal funding source. The proposal stated,

> The long-term goal of this project is to implement a new strategy for preserving and providing access to the American local television heritage. This heritage includes a diverse range of locally originated programming, including news, entertainment, documentary, public affairs, children's, and community-based television.
>
> To help achieve this long-term goal, the Association of Moving Image Archivists (AMIA), in association with The National Academy of Television Arts and Sciences (NATAS), and on behalf of a broad range of local television archives throughout the United States, requests funding support for a project entitled "Preserving Local Television—Case Studies and Symposium." This initiative is designed to bring together archivists, broadcasters and local television producers to discuss issues of common concern, make recommendations, and collaborate on a new agenda to save America's "national collection" of locally originated television and video.

By 2001, a two-year project titled "Local Television Case Studies and Symposium" was funded and under way. In summer 2001, we hired

Sharon Blair, formerly of Connecticut Public Television, as our project manager. This was one of the first projects that AMIA administered with outside funds.

THE DATABASE

The project members believed that a survey was an essential task, to discover where local TV collections existed, how they were being kept, and the kinds of materials in the collections. The contact database started with the AMIA membership directory. The biggest hurdle was getting local TV station staff around the country to contribute information. Most had never heard of AMIA, much less thought about preservation issues. The task force designed a simple survey to gather additional information about the collections from busy station owners and staff. The survey was available online. The goal was to make sharing information about the collections as easy as possible.

Over the course of about a year, through on-site face-to-face inquiries, e-mail, phone calls, meetings, and conferences, the survey was distributed as widely as possible. A great number of saved local television collections could be found at local public television stations, and most were local news collections. The public mission–oriented stations seemed to be more likely to find a way to keep materials thought to be potentially important beyond the daily needs of the station. Direct contact with people, e-mails, or phone calls resulted in better participation.

However, it still seemed as though it was most often archivists talking to archivists and not cracking through the wall to TV stations. After two years of diligent calling, the database contained 371 records of local television collections at stations and public archives. The data was not standardized with controlled vocabularies and thus it was difficult to normalize the data with statistics about the various collections. Nevertheless, this was the first known attempt to survey local television stations across the country about their historical materials.

The database was meant to help augment the case studies, inform summit attendees, and become a resource for locating local TV collections across the country. Many of the entries in the database were used by the National Television and Video Preservation Foundation (NTVPF) to target the announcement of the first granting program. As a result, the NTVPF had over forty applicants in its first grant cycle.

THE CASE STUDIES

The case studies of existing local television archives were designed to focus on particular issues of interest to archivists and television professionals alike such as rights, intellectual control, preservation, selection, and revenue. These topics were identified by the task force survey to be the key stumbling blocks for television stations that had not yet begun an archiving program. Rights and intellectual property had to do with whether they had the rights to all the material in their collection to make it accessible, reuse it, or donate it to another institution. Preservation and selection, basic archiving activities, were jobs that currently did not exist at a station and would take additional labor. Maintaining an archive could be costly. Revenue was considered to be both money coming in to the station for sale or licensing of the collection or money spent to keep it or support it if it were to be donated to an archival repository.

As a consequence, the topics would also serve as the central concepts of the proposed two-day symposium of television industry leaders and archivists. Initially, a working group of volunteers was assigned to each of the five issues. However, it proved cumbersome to coordinate information from working groups, through the task force, and on to the project manager, so the structure of the project's input was streamlined. The eight-member task force became an overarching working group and task force all in one.

The working group endeavored to make the case studies appealing to television industry leaders by ensuring that each station could "see itself" in at least one of the studies and could use at least one of the case studies as a model for building a relationship with a public archive or starting its own collection.

At the Portland AMIA conference in November 2001, task force members started to identify potential case study subjects. Identifying examples of public archives working with one or more television stations was the ideal scenario. This gave television stations an example of how to save their materials, without necessarily having to preserve them themselves. Task force members and the project manager then spent three months conducting research and preparing written reports on potential case study subjects. The reports were reviewed by all task force members and discussed in detail in conference calls.

In early 2002, the list had been narrowed down to approximately twelve potential subjects. Simultaneously, a decision was made to hold a three-day "case study school" and meeting during the National Association of Broadcasters (NAB) conference. It was during the same time frame that the project manager was building a relationship with the NAB as a potential partner for the symposium.

During the case study school, presentations were made by task force experts in the areas of rights, intellectual control, revenue, selection, and preservation. Special advisors Dayna Deutsch, of commercial station KSTP in Minneapolis, and Brian Lockman, of the Pennsylvania Cable Network, were in attendance and made strong contributions as they reflected on the realities of stations' concerns on the issues. Those realities were the lack of time and resources local stations have to invest in archiving. For a station to divert staff and money toward the keeping of their older materials, there had to be a very compelling reason to do so. The message to the stations had to be one of potential revenue, potential savings, or great value to their audiences.

The presentations by task force members were videotaped by the project manager and are kept in the AMIA archives. Also at this gathering, the task force further narrowed the case study field to eight stations and archives. Videotaped interviews were made at most of these sites.

The local television task force meeting at the Boston AMIA conference in November 2002 was devoted to work related to the symposium and discussion and review of the case study drafts. The case studies became part of the guidebook that took shape during the project extension periods.

THE SYMPOSIUM

The challenge of attracting television industry leaders to a two- to three-day symposium on the subject of local television archiving was daunting. What follows is an outline of the project's attempts to convene such a symposium and the resulting compromise. Advisers Lockman and Deutsch, along with television professionals Giannecchini and Blair, stressed that industry leaders have several priorities that rank above saving historical material such as getting daily programs on the air. So how could we get them to attend a multiday symposium?

Originally conceived as a two-hundred-person symposium, the task force downsized the symposium to fifty to seventy-five attendees, made up of television industry leaders, archivists, and policy makers and funding agencies with interests in archives and history. The symposium became a "summit," primarily to sound less like a scholarly meeting and more like a meeting of action and substance to the television industry leaders the project hoped to attract. The consensus was that a targeted, more personal meeting might have more impact.

The project manager attempted to solidify a relationship with the NAB and its Educational Foundation (NABEF). She proposed to the NABEF that its June 2003 Service to America Symposium and Awards event in Washington, D.C., focus on the subject of local television and that awards be given to television stations exhibiting proficiency in archiving. This could be a way to promote the goal of archiving to the television community. Perhaps a core group of industry leaders, already attending the Service to America event, might remain in the Washington, D.C., area and attend a summit on subsequent days.

An attempt was also made to hold the summit in association with the Library of American Broadcasting at the University of Maryland. Although primarily a repository of documents relating to early public television, the library has a history with the NAB, holding archival materials originally held by the NAB.

At AMIA's Boston conference in November 2003, a representative of the Library of American Broadcasting, Suzanne Adamko, addressed the task force. She presented the facilities and other support the library could provide for the summit. Over the next two months, progress in solidifying the summits with either NAB or the library was at a standstill.

Without giving up on the possibility of NABEF support for a June summit, the project manager proposed that up to four mini-summits be held, all in conjunction with other television industry meetings already scheduled and attracting participants from all over the country. With task force approval, the project manager began investigating summits with four organizations in four locations: the Public Broadcasting Service (PBS) in Miami, Florida; NATAS trustees in Washington, D.C.; the NABEF in Washington, D.C.; and the National Cable Television Association (NCTA) in Chicago, Illinois.

It was late April before it became clear that neither the PBS nor NCTA meetings were viable events to which we could attach our summits, although staff organizers of both meetings were supportive of our efforts and attempted to accommodate the project. However, inquiries to cable industry leaders were falling on deaf ears, except for task force member Susan Madison (who was also leaving her position with the Cable Center in Denver) and advisor Brian Lockman of the Pennsylvania Cable Network.

Once again, there were positive responses from public television station managers about the importance of station archives and participation in a summit. However, the schedule and attendance for the PBS meeting were still in such flux that there was great difficulty in scheduling a multihour mini-summit on June 6 during a meeting at which public television funding crises would dominate the proceedings.

By early May, the symposium–summit activity was reduced to two summits, one in conjunction with NATAS on June 8 and one adjacent to the NABEF's Service to America awards and symposium on June 9, both in Washington, D.C. The yearlong effort to engage the NAB administration was dashed when internal liaison Howard Marcantel left for the Discovery Channel. The historically powerful NAB was also being challenged by the industry over the NAB's position on Federal Communications Commission changes to group ownership rules. In other words, supporting the creation of local station archives was the last thing on the mind of NAB officers.

On Sunday, June 8, 2003, the summit was held with NATAS administration and national trustees, who are charged with developing and maintaining policy regarding NATAS national awards, educational projects, and the activities of the eighteen local NATAS chapters around the country. The goals for this summit were to convince the trustees and national staff of the importance of creating local television archives and to make the promotion of archiving an ongoing activity of both the national organization and its local chapters.

The group of television leaders—many of them pioneers in the industry—and the task force were able to hear war stories about lost material. According to task force member and NATAS national officer Linda Giannecchini, several of the NATAS trustees waxed enthusiastic as they described the summit to their colleagues who were unable to attend. This meeting was invaluable and helped solidify the relationship with NATAS and its chapters across the country and raised awareness within the group of the need to preserve this material.

On Monday, June 9, the project summit was with the station industry leaders who had traveled to Washington, D.C., as recipients of Service to America awards, to be granted that evening. The two exceptions were the acting general manager of Howard University's television station and the general manager of the University of North Carolina Television Center. It was a gathering at which the station managers expressed interest in creating archives; bemoaned the lack of time and money with which to do the work; and asked for short case studies, simple tool kits, and ideas about funding possibilities.

Although some were disappointed with the shift from the original idea of a two- to three-day summit–symposium of archivists and TV professionals to a two-day summit, in the end, we got what we needed from the meetings. After a year of struggling to get the attention of TV professionals and the NAB, the focus was shifted from a large three-day symposium that would likely have been underattended to smaller, more intimate group meetings. The larger summit would have taken place after September 11, 2001, when the resulting slide in the economy meant that most local TV stations would be struggling to keep jobs rather than preserve materials.

COMPLETING THE PROJECT

During the two years of summits and discussions with the industry, requests for models, simple tool kits, and funding sources were made loud and clear. The task force responded by expanding the project. With approximately thirty thousand dollars still left in the budget, a six-month extension was requested to develop a guidebook of simple tools that expanded the case studies to help local stations figure out how best to keep and preserve their materials.

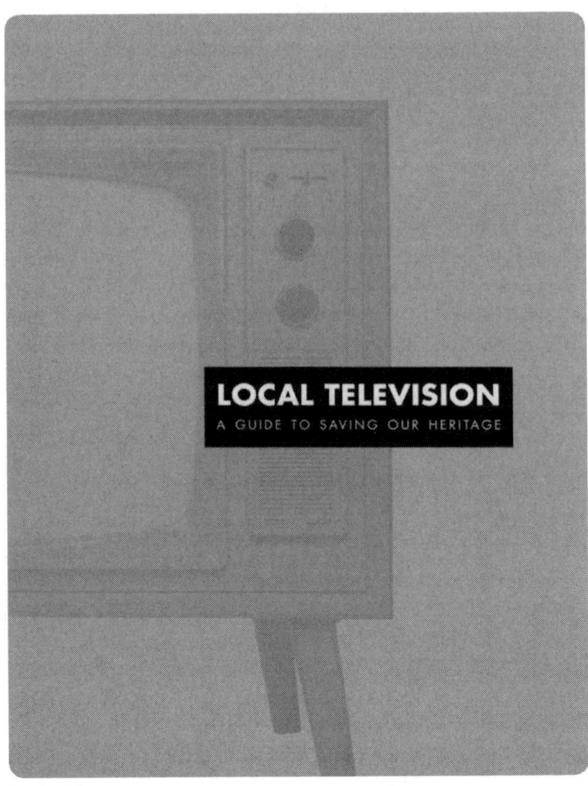

The cover of *Local Television: A Guide to Saving Our Heritage,* put out by AMIA members in 2004.

In September 2003, the project codirectors attended a meeting with the NATAS presidents and administrators to find out specifically what tools these professionals would find useful and how to expand communications with the NATAS community. NATAS's foremost concern was preserving the Emmy winners, the best of the best in their field. They also wanted a map of archival contacts whom they could call for advice and help on preserving their materials.

An opportunity to bring NATAS members to the AMIA conference to interact with AMIA members and to learn more about AMIA's efforts and basic archiving issues proved to be especially important in planning for the guide. The NATAS representatives could also work closely with the task force to shape the guide. A NATAS chapter president from Denver was sponsored to attend the AMIA conference in Vancouver. NATAS administrators and chapter presidents and other people affiliated with NATAS heard about the project and asked about becoming involved.

The meetings and discussions made it clear that stations needed very simple directions regarding what to do with their materials. The directions needed to be easy to read and nontechnical. The target audience for the tools were television professionals who knew nothing about archiving but who wanted to follow the correct path to preserving their materials, even with modest resources.

The resulting tools—including the five case studies and a practical step-by-step guide with a list of archiving resources—were published in 2004 as *Local Television: A Guide to Saving Our Heritage.* This guide was distributed by mail to over six hundred people: everyone in the database whom the task force had contacted, case study participants, NATAS representatives, and state broadcast associations. NATAS requested several boxes of the guide to distribute among its members. All four hundred remaining copies have been distributed, and the guide is now available on the AMIA Web site.[2]

After the publication of the guide, the project concluded in spring 2004, at which point the task force was dissolved. However, it quickly morphed into the Television, News, and Documentary Committee of AMIA, which, it is hoped, will carry on the project goals.

CONCLUSIONS

The primary challenge the project faced was getting the attention of television industry leaders on a subject that does not contribute significantly to a station's bottom line. Every industry leader expressed wishful interest in the subject of preserving local television. Once engaged, many of them asked for guidance and practical tools with which to preserve local television as money and time allowed.

The value of any project lies in what was accomplished and learned. This project succeeded in raising awareness of the urgency to preserve local television among industry leaders via the NATAS. It attempted to get the attention of the NAB as well. However, task force members learned that some industry leaders must be persuaded one by one. Therefore the most successful communications occurred under a dynamic and committed leader like Peter Price of NATAS and through personal contact with individuals like Liz Cheng of WCVB, Boston, and Alison White of the Corporation for Public Broadcasting. We learned that people involved in the producing and broadcasting of television are interested in archival knowledge and expertise but need quick answers to immediate problems. Therefore it was a challenge to make an impact on the industry but helpful to single out individuals who would listen to the project hopes and goals as well as help spread the word in the future.

Over the past several years, there has been a growing awareness of the importance of local materials that coincides nicely with the fifty-year anniversary of many TV stations. A number of articles have been written about this rich history and the importance of keeping it. Just this past year, an initiative has been launched out of the Corporation for Public Broadcasting to develop an American Archive of materials created for and by public television and radio stations. The goal is to begin preserving these great collections of materials across the country at local public stations that document our rich national history. Perhaps this project helped contribute to this awakened consciousness. Perhaps the project just happened at the right time. Success cannot be adequately measured so soon; it will be a long-term endeavor to pursue the ideas set out and assess what has been achieved by our efforts to preserve local television.

2004 AMIA Local Television Project Task Force:
Karen Cariani (WGBH, Boston) and Bonnie Wilson (Minnesota Historical Society), co-chairs
Lisa Carter, University of Kentucky
Paul Eisloeffel, Nebraska State Historical Society
Lynn Farnell, Moving Images
Richard Fauss, West Virginia State Archives
Linda Giannecchini, National Academy of Television Arts and Sciences
Additional task force members:
Greg Lukow, Library of Congress
Mark Ritchie, Kitchener, Ontario

NOTES
1. Library of Congress, with a preface by James H. Billington, *Television and Video Preservation 1997: A Study of the Current State of American Television and Video Preservation,* vol. 1 (Washington, DC: Library of Congress, 1997).
2. See http://www.amianet.org/resources/reportsnologin.php?accesscheck=%2Fresources%2Freports.php.

A View from the Booth
Archival Screening Night

KATIE TRAINOR

Archival Screening Night (ASN) takes place on the Friday night of the annual Association of Moving Image Archivists (AMIA) conference. In the months approaching the conference, AMIA members are invited to submit a treasure from their collections to be included in the program lineup. Submissions might include news clips, home movies, travelogues, commercials, restored classics, and experimental films. A wide array of archival gems are then put together into a program that warms the room with shared laughter, delight, and sometimes somber reality. It is almost impossible to encapsulate ASN without bringing my personal insight into this amazing gathering of archivists, scholars, students, and technicians. I look forward to the AMIA conference every year, and I specifically recall the moment I knew I wanted to be involved in what many refer to as a highlight of their conference experience.

Los Angeles, November 2000: I was a student in the L. Jeffrey Selznick school of Film Preservation at the George Eastman House and attending my first AMIA conference. Many of us recall the grandeur of the Samuel Goldwyn Theater on Wilshire Boulevard, where the ASN was held that year: the more-than-life-sized Oscars bookending the red-curtained stage and the excitement of what would enfold before our eyes. I had been to many film festival screenings before, but there was something different about the energy of the room. Of course, I was a starry-eyed student of film preservation and had never been to the Academy before. It was during the intermission, when I was standing in line for refreshments, that I recognized the evening's organizer, Ruta Abolins, who had at that point been commandeering the screening night for many conferences past. In my young, naive way, I immediately introduced myself and offered my services for screening nights to follow. I explained to her my love for and involvement in film projection and that I had worked at a few film festivals as both projectionist and programmer. I could "help tighten the show" perhaps. I even had "a few ideas that would smooth presentation." Oh, how bold and inexperienced I was! Ruta listened patiently and then calmly said, "Here's the baton. It's yours." What did I just do? Could I follow in such esteemed footsteps? Lo and behold, the next year, AMIA was in Portland, Oregon, and I took that baton. Ten years later, I am still organizing and now co-organizing what will remain a very special evening of our annual conference.

ASN evolved from a previous incarnation. Before AMIA was AMIA, it was the Film and Television Archives Advisory Committees. They, too, held screenings. Current AMIA president Wendy Shay (Archives Center, National Museum of American History) recalls an early gathering from 1985 in Wisconsin at which attendees viewed video footage from the Austrian Film Archives, during which they took nitrate out and started burning it, an undoubtedly legendary screening in the event's history. Those who started this organization, then, screened films at their annual gatherings from the very beginning. What was initially an informal screening of ten to fourteen films and videos became a more formalized annual screening event based on submissions of recent archival acquisitions, discoveries, and restorations. By 2000, the event was officially titled "Archival Screening Night." As the membership grew, the need for bigger venues increased as well. Needless to say, the amount of material that members wanted to show and see similarly escalated.

Thankfully what is most remembered about ASN are the films that were screened and not the very few technical mistakes (and resulting delays) that *may* have occurred! We have seen clips of old news programs, restored classics, home movies, experimental and avant-garde treasures, travelogues, poignant interviews, industrial and educational classics, superb trailers, and musical wonders. Some memorable moments include the 2002 Boston conference, for which Margie Compton (archivist at the University of Georgia Media Archives) dressed in a green go-go outfit to go along with a clip from *Now Explosion* (1970), a popular TV show in Atlanta that featured music of the time. At that same conference, Francis Poole (University of Delaware Library) presented

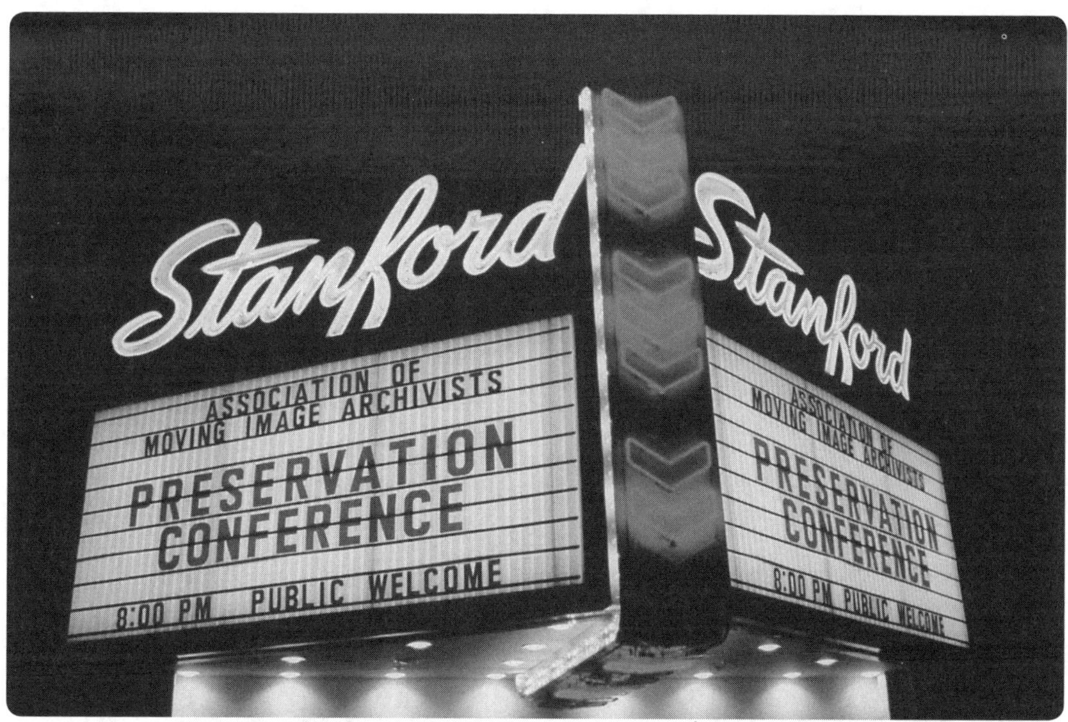

The annual evening of archival screenings was held at the second annual AMIA conference on December 11, 1992, at David W. Packard's Stanford Theatre in Palo Alto, California, where the theater marquee announced the event. Photo courtesy Gregory Lukow.

a clip from *Bodies* (early 1970s), an educational film that showed Teaneck, New Jersey, kids in the nude. This was immediately followed by the wonderful Barry Allen (Paramount), who did not realize why everyone was (still) laughing when he started his introduction to the preservation of *Trigger, Jr.* (1950).

We have been fortunate to have the late archivist, mentor, and friend Bill O'Farrell present, on several occasions, the rare 9.5mm format (9.5mm was introduced by Pathé Freres in 1922, mainly for home use) blown up to 35mm. Jeff Joseph (SabuCat Production Archives) presented a program of "3-D rarities from the 1930s" in Vancouver (glasses included!). At the 2008 Savannah conference, Marc Toscano of the Academy Film Archive (AFA) presented the psychedelic journey of socks and other Sears apparel, *Sears' Sox* (1968). This commercial, commissioned by Sears, was made by experimental filmmakers Chick Strand, Pat O'Neill, and Neon Park and was restored by the AFA. For the TV lovers out there, AMIA audiences were privy to the oldest surviving color videotape of the *Tonight Show,* starring Johnny Carson in 1968. In Austin, Texas, current AMIA board treasurer Alan Stark dressed up in amazing Asian attire for his introduction to *The Mask of Fu Manchu* (1932). We caught a rare glimpse of African American baseball player Satchel Paige's pitching, courtesy of Lynne Kirste at the AFA, as well as many Technicolor clips and screen tests provided by the George Eastman House over the years. In 2010, AMIA board member Dennis Doros steered the project of gathering the past AMIA screening night brochures and scanning them, so those who were not able to attend certain conferences

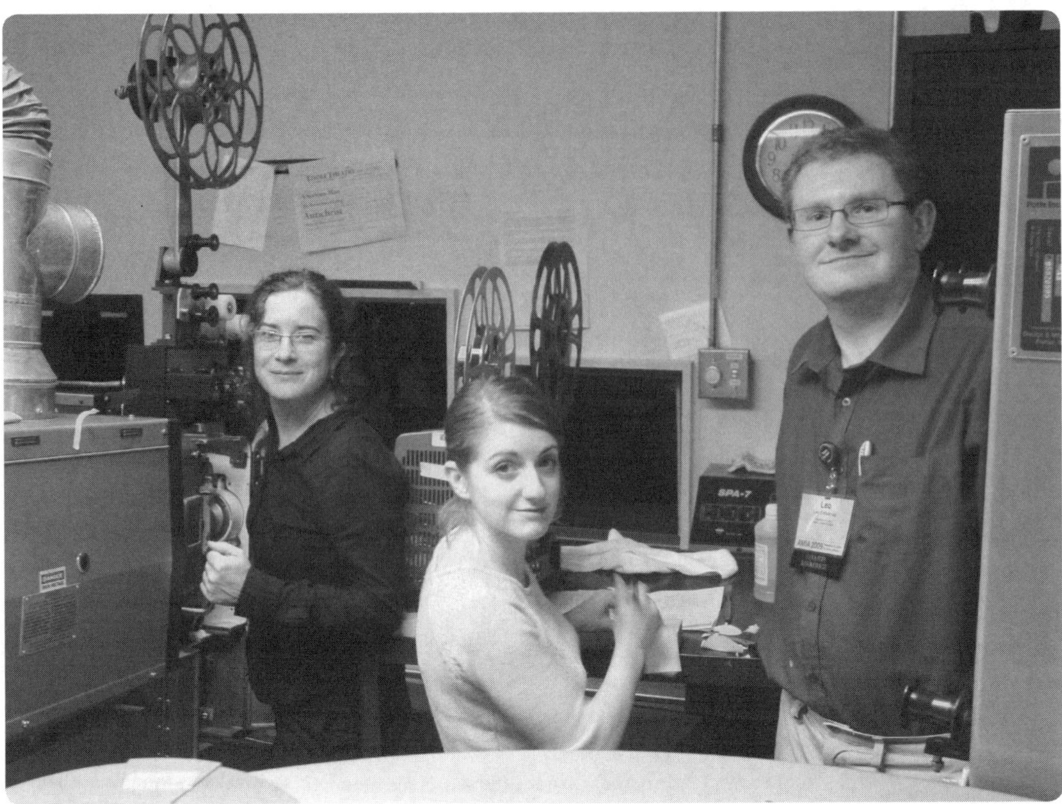

or who just want to remember what played each year can access the program brochures for all conferences going back to 1990.[2] Most of the films listed include title, year, format, institution, and a brief description—information that each year's ASN organizers compile and distribute in program form to the audience at the event.

Despite this impressive record of the ASN, what I cannot recall, sadly, is the content of many of the titles that have been screened over the years. I have certainly been able, from time to time, to peek my head out and enjoy the images on-screen or hear audience laughter bubbling up to the booth, but from my position, what I have mainly been concerned with is how the audience has seen the images. Is the masking correct? Do we have the proper lenses and aperture plates? Is it sound or silent? Did we cue the tapes correctly? There is plenty of lively booth dialogue (as some attendees may have heard from thin porthole glass in the back of the auditorium): "Make sure they don't see any blue screen!" "Is the projector running at the right speed?" "Shhh! They can hear us out there."

An ASN comes together through a feat of collegial collaboration that begins a couple months before the November meeting. As of 2010, the ASN group consists of Antonella Bonfanti (George Eastman House), Paul Rayton (American Cinematheque), Leo Enticknap (University of Leeds), and me. There is an open call, and any member is allowed to submit, granted they adhere to ASN criteria. Submissions must either be new preservation work, footage from a recent discovery, or an acquisition of historical interest. We accept 35mm, 16mm, and a variety of video formats. We are not capable of watching content ahead of time because of time,

What the audience never gets to see during AMIA Archival Screening Night: the projectionists working behind the scenes. From left to right: Katie Trainor (MoMA), Antonella Bonfanti (George Eastman House), and Leo Enticknap (University of Leeds) in the booth of the Tivoli Theater at the 2009 Archival Screening Night in St. Louis, Missouri. Photograph courtesy Paul Rayton.

money, and location constraints; therefore we put together a program that involves curating many different formats that we "view" only on paper. To include as many submissions as possible, we limit submissions to six minutes in length so that the audience's attention is grabbed within a reasonable time frame. This has been a difficult decision to which to adhere because we often wish we could screen submissions in their entirety. But to highlight work from as many institutions as possible, we have to have a strict time limit. We try to put a varied program together, switching between film and video, sound and silent, and various levels of emotional content. We cut off the screening total at around twenty-five submissions to keep the program length reasonable.

Because AMIA does not meet in the same city in consecutive years, venues are always part of what makes putting on this show a challenge. We are often met by limitations in terms of a given theater's technical requirements. The ASN group, along with the conference organizers, make informed decisions on what theaters to choose and why. This is getting increasingly tougher as many of the theaters we once loved have met their demise. We have been challenged by new technology as we enter into a different phase of presentation with the advent of digital cinema, which is entering the exhibition arena at an alarming pace and pushing aside mechanical film projectors, which gather dust in the corners. But as we all have

heard many times before, "the show must go on," and those of us who remain dedicated to screening our archival gems must continue to figure out how best to share these materials with AMIA conference attendees every year.

As I write this now and have even more film festivals under my belt, I can honestly say that this night at AMIA is, and will remain, the hardest show to pull off. We organizers have the toughest audience in the world sitting in a darkened theater. We want to please everyone and make this evening special. We all settle in for two and a half hours to enjoy rarities from our archives. The pressure to put on a good show is immense: this audience, perhaps more than any other, deserves the best presentation we are capable of executing. What is wonderful about our field is that we will never run out of things to show.

NOTES

In researching the history of this annual event, I polled many longtime members for their recollections. I want to thank Margie Compton, Wendy Shay, Dennis Doros, Laura Rooney, Leo Enticknap, and Paul Rayton.

1. See http://www.amianet.org/events/past-conference.php.

I Am an Amateur Moving Image Archivist

ROBBINS BARSTOW

I am a ninety-year-old amateur moving image archivist. All my life, I have had two irresistible impulses—to record and to preserve moving images of life around me—not for money, just for fun. I am a relatively new member of the Association of Moving Image Archivists (AMIA), but it has opened up to me a whole new world of fellowship with professional film preservationists from all over the country and, indeed, the world.

I have always been a movie buff. My earliest film hero was the swashbuckling adventurer Douglas Fairbanks Sr., with his 1920s silent versions of epic stories like *The Three Musketeers* (1921), *Robin Hood* (1922), *The Thief of Bagdad* (1924), and *The Black Pirate* (1926). In the 1930s, at the start of my teen years, Tarzan took over as my favorite movie hero, as embodied by Johnny Weissmuller in the series of feature films produced by Metro-Goldwyn-Mayer, including *Tarzan the Apeman* (1932), *Tarzan and His Mate* (1934), and *Tarzan Escapes* (1936). My two younger brothers and I would play Tarzan games in the park across the street from our Hartford, Connecticut, home.

At about this same time, I developed a great interest in home movies. My parents got me a small, hand-cranked 16mm Kodascope film projector, and I would buy short reels of cartoons and silent comedies and charge neighborhood kids five cents to come and watch them projected on a sheet hung on our basement wall. Then I acquired an early Eastman 16mm boxed movie camera and started taking family movies on my own. I always tried to make them interesting, with little stories or incidents and humorous tricks involving the whole family. And I didn't want simply to expose the film, look at it a couple times, and then throw it out; I wanted to preserve these visual, moving records of little pieces of our lives so that they could be recalled and reenjoyed in future years. I got a small editing machine or splicing block, with brush-applied film cement, which I used to sort out the various film scenes and piece them together in suitable sequences, generally with very little leftover film to be thrown away.

This all came together in 1936, when I produced my first, major, home-made movie epic, *Tarzan and the Rocky Gorge*.[1] While visiting some family friends who had a cottage in the woods in the small, rural town of Granby, Connecticut, northwest of Hartford, we came across a tall natural gorge, with rocky sides at least fifty feet high and a small stream running along the bottom with several deep pools. "What a great setting for a Tarzan movie!" we all exclaimed.

So we three brothers got together to dream up an original story. At the age of sixteen, I was the oldest and tallest, so naturally, I would be Tarzan. We decided on the simple plot framework of having a young adventurer go to Africa to see Tarzan in person. We named this eminent African explorer Paulus Rufus Barstinio, a variation of Paul Rogers Barstow, age ten, the youngest of us three brothers. Of course, we needed some kind of a villain, to provide suspense and excitement. Our middle brother, John, age fourteen, took quite seriously the fun challenge of playing the treacherous Mahahatmi Slinkaround, who would try to thwart Paulus's jungle quest. To balance us three male characters, we persuaded three neighborhood girls to go with us on our filmmaking excursion as members of Paulus's safari. I bought several hundred-foot reels of 16mm black-and-white film and loaded the camera, and we all set out to spend an entire day of creative filmmaking at the rocky gorge location.

We had plotted out ahead of time the general story line, but we had no script. We made things up as we went along, depending on the varied opportunities the natural setting provided. I had to get one of the other participants to take the scenes in which I appeared as Tarzan. But everybody was highly cooperative, and it was a very fun experience for all.

When the films were developed, I had the further fun of editing them into finalized form. I worked out a standard narration, which I recited live every time we showed the film. The resulting twelve-minute, black-and-white, fictional home movie became a family classic, bonding us brothers literally for the rest of our

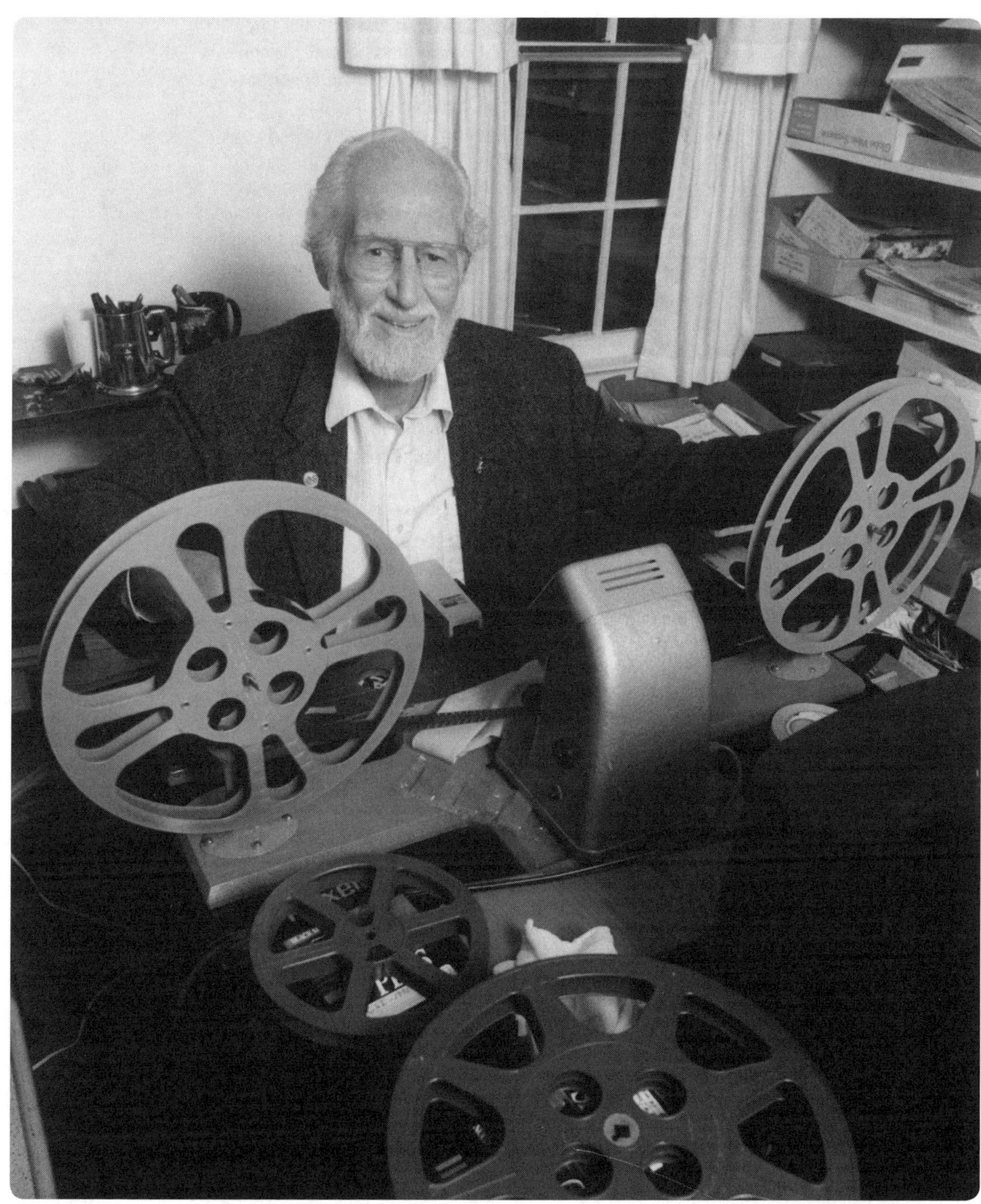

Amateur moving image archivist Robbins Barstow editing 16mm film at his Wethersfield, Connecticut, home (circa 1990). Photo courtesy Robbins Barstow.

lives. It was shown and reshown time and time again, with live narration and great laughter and cheers, at family gatherings and even at outside performances for friends, relatives, and community groups. It became an integral part of all our lives.

But we never dreamed it would go global.

THE IMPACT OF AMIA

After graduating from Dartmouth College in 1941, I married Margaret Vanderbeek. We had three children, and in 1951, we moved into a new home we had had built in Wethersfield, Connecticut, a suburb of Hartford. For thirty-four years, I served on the staff of the Connecticut Education Association, until my retirement in 1984.

During all these years, I was fortunate enough to be able to "follow my bliss" as an avocational home movie maker. Over the years, I produced dozens of family chronicles, travel adventure films, whale and dolphin documentaries, and other moving image records. I carefully preserved all these works and considered them to be a legacy. I was a nonprofessional archivist.

Now, what about the impact of AMIA? As a boy making the Tarzan movie, I became a youthful member of what was called the Amateur Cinema League and received their publications with helpful information about making effective films. But after my teen years, I lost contact with outside film groups and did my continuing periodic family filmmaking quite independently.

In 1989, after nearly sixty years of using 16mm film, I finally switched over to videomaking. With this technological advance, I was able to have my films, including the original Tarzan, transferred to VHS video, on which I could record my traditional narrations. This made them available for showing anyplace, and a number of them were broadcast over our local Wethersfield public access television channel.

My relationship to AMIA began in 2001, when my wife and I attended a showing in New London, Connecticut, of the classic film *A Touch of Evil* (Orson Welles, 1958), sponsored by the National Film Preservation Board of the Library of Congress (LOC). I found out about the LOC's moving image archival work and learned that

they were concerned not just with the fate of past Hollywood feature films but with the entire spectrum of the American movie experience, including home movies.

I subsequently wrote directly to Dr. James H. Billington, the distinguished Librarian of Congress, telling him about my extensive collection of family home movies chronicling our middle-class suburban family's lives, travels, and experiences during the 1940s, 1950s, and 1960s. Dr. Billington referred me to Dr. Mike Mashon in the library's Motion Picture, Broadcasting, and Recorded Sound Division. After a number of follow-up contacts, I eventually took down to Mike's office in Washington, D.C., copies of a few of my productions in VHS and DVD format. On learning that I had carefully preserved all the original 16mm film footage, he expressed great interest in acquiring these for the library's archives.

Actually, it took me several years finally to put together in properly edited form all the approximately nine thousand feet of film, with complete transcribed narrations, that appeared to be suitable for this purpose. In April 2007, I formally donated to the LOC a total of twelve moving image programs constituting "The Robbins Barstow Collection of 20th Century Family Home Movies." These are now stored at the LOC's new National Audio-Visual Conservation Center in Culpeper, Virginia.

Meanwhile, Mike Mashon had put me in touch with Dwight Swanson and the newly organized Center for Home Movies (CHM), which was undertaking to sponsor an annual Home Movie Day in multiple locations around the country. I took my Tarzan film to a Home Movie Day in Boston, Massachusetts, on August 16, 2003, and was subsequently invited to present it at a Northeast Historic Film Summer Symposium in Bucksport, Maine, in July 2005. It was there that I first became aware of the existence of AMIA, through such new CHM friends as Liz Coffey, Snowden Becker, and Katie Trainor. On becoming a member of AMIA, I was immediately impressed with the quality and quantity of the association's programs, projects, and publications.

Attending the AMIA annual conference in Rochester, New York, in September 2007 was one of the high points of my entire filmmaking life. The organization gave validation for all

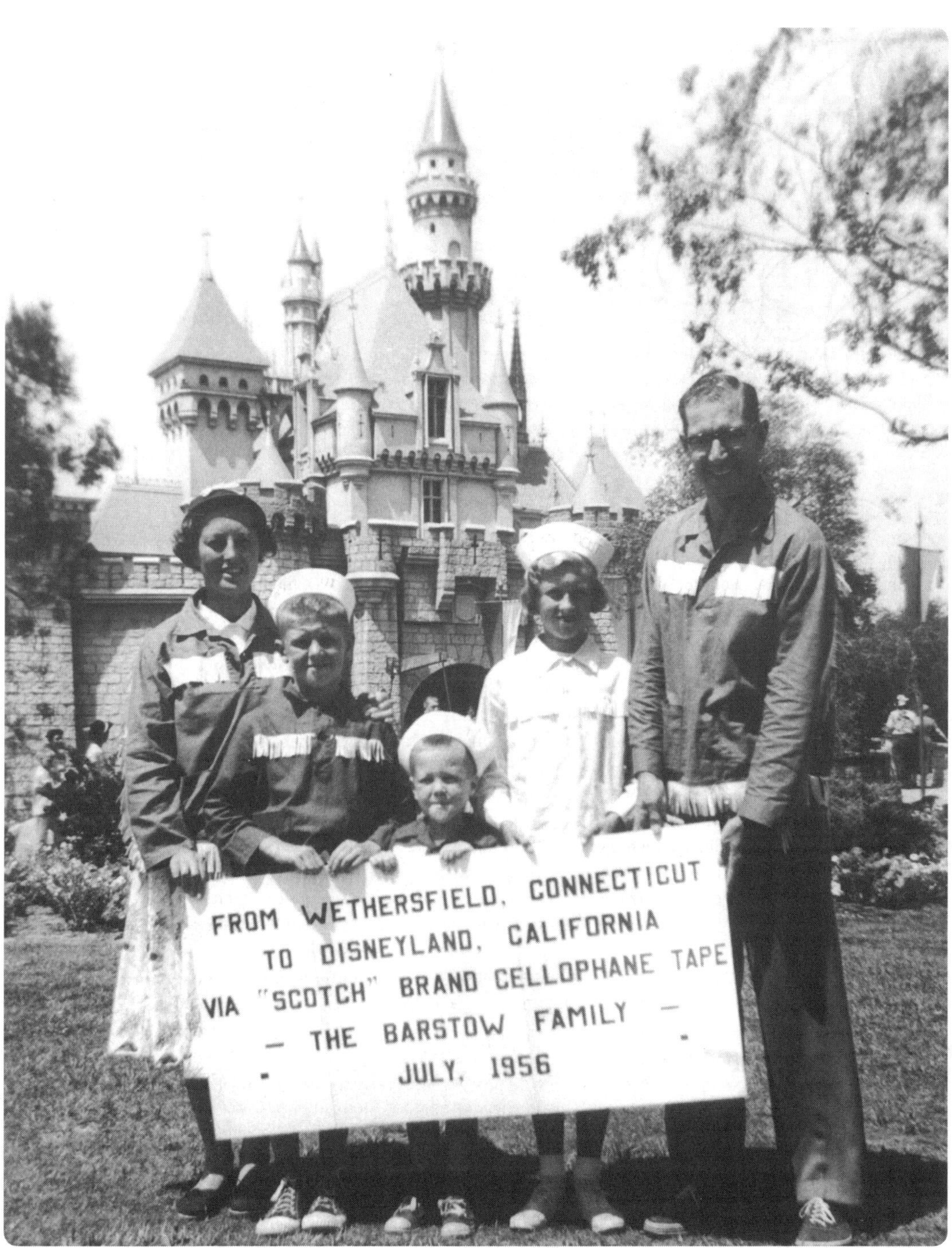

Barstow family at Disneyland (1956). Photo courtesy Robbins Barstow.

my lifelong film saving, and I reveled in the company of so many joyous, kindred spirits who were in the business of what for me had been an avocational pursuit. I benefited greatly from all the presentations, discussions, and other activities during the well-planned week.

I came to realize that there is more to film archiving than simply keeping carefully assembled reels of original film footage in large cans stored on a closet shelf. I was made conscious that 16mm film inevitably deteriorates over many years and that special technologies are constantly being developed by professional archivists, such as those in AMIA, to protect and prolong the life of these treasured moving images. I learned, after a lifetime, that it was not enough to be an amateur film archivist if I really wanted my collections of family home movies to constitute a living legacy. This is what led me to seek out the LOC as a recipient of what I wanted to be truly preserved and maintained in some lasting form for future generations, and it has led me to donate to the CHM a large number of additional Barstow film production reels.

I must say, however, that the most exciting breakthrough for me personally at the 2007 AMIA annual conference in Rochester came from my meeting Skip Elsheimer, a self-styled audiovisual geek who does digitizing work for the massive Internet Archive. He had been working with Dwight Swanson and the CHM to get uploaded on that site a DVD of films selected from various Home Movie Days that they called *Livingroom Cinema* and that included my Tarzan film. It was absolutely mind-blowing to me to learn that he could upload to Archive.org any of my home movie films and that they then could be viewed and downloaded free by any person any place in the world who had access to the Internet. Skip offered to convert and upload any of my films that I had on DVD. Eventually, we ended up with a total of sixteen of my "Barstow Travel Adventure" film and video productions being posted on Archive.org. *Tarzan and the Rocky Gorge* has proven to be the most popular of these, with 148,625 viewings recorded by April 2010.

The ultimate attainment of archival glory occurred for our family on December 30, 2008. The most outstanding production in my LOC home movie collection and among the Internet offerings is a film we made in 1956, telling the story of a fabulous, real-life, weeklong trip my wife and I and our three young children made to Walt Disney's newly opened Disneyland in Anaheim, California.

We had all submitted entries in a nationwide contest sponsored by Scotch Brand cellophane tape. The reason given for liking Scotch tape by then four-year-old Daniel Barstow—"because when some things tear I can just use it"—had been selected as one of twenty-five winners of a free family trip to Disneyland. We called the filmed record we made of this trip *Disneyland Dream.*[2] Since its posting on Archive.org, it has been downloaded more than seventy thousand times. Each year since 1988, the LOC has been required by law to name to the National Film Registry twenty-five American films that are "culturally, historically or aesthetically" significant, to be "preserved for all time." In December 2008, Dr. James H. Billington named *Disneyland Dream* as one of his annual selections to this most prestigious archive.

The purpose of archiving may be said to be to give a degree of immortality to certain persons, places, and events. It is to maintain the memory of them and to make them recoverable by future generations. Perhaps the most meaningful and true-to-life form of archiving is moving image archiving. This has been technologically possible only for a little more than the last century of human history. Long live moving image archiving and the association that promotes and perfects it!

NOTES

1. *Tarzan and the Rocky Gorge* (1936) is available for viewing and download at http://www.archive.org/details/homemovie_tarzan_and_rocky_gorge.

2. *Disneyland Dream* (1956) is available at http://www.archive.org/details/barstow_disneyland_dream_1956.

On the Role of AMIA in Reshaping the Field of the Moving Image

GIOVANNA FOSSATI

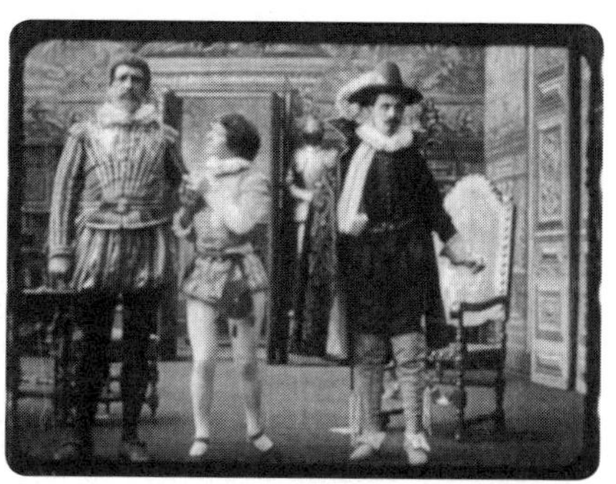

Film frame from *La Dette* (Pathé, France, 1910; stencil color). The film was digitally restored by EYE Film Institute Netherlands at Haghefilm Conservation in Amsterdam. The restoration was presented at the Film Biennale 2010 in Amsterdam during The Reel Thing, held in conjunction with the AMIA seminar. Courtesy EYE Film Institute Netherlands.

In these pages, I would like to address the unique role of the Association of Moving Image Archivists (AMIA) within the field of moving image archives in relation to the ongoing transition from analogue to digital. In recent years, I have investigated the interplay between film and media theory and film archival practice in this time of transition. I have come to believe that film and moving image media in general are transitional in nature.[1] The current transition is characterized by a high degree of hybridization between analogue and digital technology. The transitional nature of film is deeply related to the notion of film as the site of interpretive contestation. From this perspective, film is not only transitional as it changes over time but is also subject to various interpretations at the same time.

This has been the case in various instances in film history. In the case of color in silent cinema, for example, once black-and-white film became dominant in the 1930s, coloring techniques such as tinting, toning, and stenciling were abandoned by mainstream film production. Early colored films even risked disappearing retrospectively because they were often duplicated onto black-and-white film. In the 1980s, however, archives and film scholars rediscovered color in silent cinema; the practice of duplicating colored films to black-and-white film stock was challenged, and new techniques for restoring the original colors were developed.[2]

Something similar is likely to occur in the transition from analogue to digital. Once digital film becomes dominant and replaces photochemical film, reducing it to a niche technology, new criteria will emerge that will retrospectively redefine the role of photochemical film and reinterpret some of its technological and aesthetical characteristics. The characteristics of film, as we had known them before the digital came about, may even be temporarily neglected, as has been the case before,

for instance, with early coloring techniques. As the transition from analogue to digital is ongoing, film has become a hybrid medium between analogue and digital. But transition has always been a characteristic of film, and if we look back, we realize that analogue was never a well-defined concept to begin with. It is hoped that the full replacement of photochemical film by digital film will happen after proper solutions are developed to tackle the technical problems related to digital film (e.g., long-term preservation issues, obsolescence of hardware and software, instability of standards), and AMIA will be at the forefront of helping to facilitate these solutions.

As film changes, so do the people working with and reflecting on it, as they are part of the same transition. Technological transitions cannot be analyzed outside their social framing. Social groups and players influence and are part of these transitions, and AMIA is one of the major players of the transition to digital within the film archival field. On the occasion of AMIA's twentieth anniversary, I would like to offer food for thought on AMIA's role as a very special player in the moving image field. The field of moving image archives comprises a wide spectrum of relevant social groups. It includes film archives, the commercial film industry, film and media scholars, and policy makers in the cultural sector. There are also the hardware and software manufacturers; film laboratories, some of which are specialized in film restoration; and other special interest groups supporting digital initiatives, together with a broader array of cultural institutions. Certainly no less important are the film audiences and the media users, who range from filmmakers and media artists using archival footage to the film archivists, scholars, and students accessing archives for research purposes to film enthusiasts and online users in general.

These social groups, so different in their nature and objectives, are influenced by the current transition from analogue to digital, and in turn, they all contribute to it. Some are closer than others to the moving image artifacts and therefore have a more direct influence on the artifacts' lives. The social groups that have a direct and material influence on "the archival life of film"—by which I mean the life of film and of moving image artifacts in broader terms, once they have entered the archive and undergone the processes of selection, preservation, restoration, and exhibition—are mainly archivists, laboratory technicians, and scholars, at least those devoted to researching and teaching the archival dimension of the medium, all of whom are very well represented within AMIA.[3] These individuals have an obligation to address issues concerning preservation, restoration, and access to film heritage.

Jay David Bolter and Richard Grusin have pointed out that new media "emerge from within cultural contexts, and they refashion other media, which are embedded in the same or similar contexts."[4] Technological transformations as well as economic and cultural shifts do not happen in a vacuum; rather they originate and are further reshaped within a social framing. In this respect, the role of AMIA as a social group during the transition from analogue to digital is important and quite unique. In the first place, AMIA, twenty years young, is about as old as the discourse regarding the transition to digital. This gives AMIA and its community an extraordinary point of view on the transition, as the changes in archival practice and the debate around it have started and grown to-

gether with the association. AMIA's first twenty years—documented in its e-mail discussion list, the newsletter, and *The Moving Image* journal—are an ideal source for researching the transformation within the archival field during this transition.

In addition, AMIA's membership is based on individuals, whereas most other international organizations in the field, such as the International Federation of Film Archives (FIAF) and the International Federation of Television Archives (FIAT), are based on institutional members. As a consequence, AMIA, as an organization, covers a much larger scope of the field, both in terms of specializations within the same institution (the archivist, the projectionist, the restorer, the archives director) and of different areas within the field (the collector, the scholar, the distributor, the exhibitor). In this way, AMIA represents an exemplary cross section of the field for analyzing the interplay between the practice and the theoretical discourse in the transition to digital. However, there is still one geocultural limitation of the organization, as the majority of AMIA's members are based in North America. Although this has been changing in recent years, with more members joining AMIA from outside the United States and Canada, it is still an aspect to be worked on to fulfill the international ambition of the organization and make it fully representative of the field.

Social groups also contribute to and shape the field at large via interaction. The places where they interact are manifold and different in character and mission, from professional organizations to archival film festivals, from academic programs to international conferences and symposia. AMIA is only one such place, but it also covers a uniquely broad spectrum of the field, gathering film archivists, scholars, and professionals and crosscutting the whole moving image media landscape. In this way, AMIA bridges the traditional gap, still clearly present in other professional organizations, between different moving image media, from film to television, from video to new digital media.

The dialogue between different fields is of great importance as it helps the field raise questions, recognize common problems, and work together to find new ways for preserving and promoting moving image heritage. This is especially true in this time of technological transition, when archival practice is changing together with its own objects, the audiovisual artifacts themselves. Furthermore, the very role of the moving image archivist is changing, and as I have indicated, AMIA offers an extraordinary forum to reflect on and shape such change. Another unique aspect of AMIA's membership is that it brings together nonprofit (archival and academic) and commercial bodies, alongside vendors providing services to the whole field. This differs remarkably from, for instance, FIAF, which is based on institutional membership and allows full membership only of nonprofit film archives and partial membership (i.e., "associate") of nonprofit organizations devoted to the preservation of audiovisual collections in a broader use of the term. Commercial film and audiovisual collections or service providers in the field can only become FIAF "donors."[5]

AMIA has been addressing the changes and issues brought about by this transition to digital and its resulting hybridization in many different ways in conferences, workshops, symposia, and online forums via task forces and committees. These initiatives show how the transition is influencing AMIA and, in turn, how AMIA is affecting (and at times even stewarding) the transition. The Digital Initiatives Committee, for instance, works toward the identification of relevant issues in relation to the digital turn within the moving image and audio fields. The committee, created in 2003 as a result of the preliminary work carried out by the Digital Issues Task Force, in operation since the early 2000s, promotes the study and formulation of recommended practices and acts in close collaboration with other groups within AMIA such as the Preservation and Access committees.[6] The coexistence of and collaboration between different committees is one of the most effective instruments of AMIA. A clear example of this is the coexistence of a committee devoted to nitrate film, a format that has been obsolete for half a century, and of the Digital Initiatives Committee, dealing with new formats that in many cases are just a few months old (and too often become obsolete in a matter of years). Typical of AMIA, some of the members of the one committee collaborate closely with members of the other.

The workshops that have been offered in the past decade at the annual conferences provide examples of the work being done by AMIA committees in the area of digital technology. At times, a workshop on film preservation is followed by another on emerging digital formats, as was the case at the 2005 conference held in Austin, Texas, with the Film Collection Management Workshop, provided by the Image Permanence Institute, and the Digital Basics Workshop, held by the Digital Initiatives Committee. Another example, this time of the transitional spirit of AMIA's initiatives, are the two editions of the Joint Technical Symposium organized in Toronto on behalf of the Coordinating Council of Audiovisual Archive Associations in 2004 and 2007, with the titles of the two symposia being "Preserving the Audio Visual Heritage—Transition and Access" (2004) and "Audio Visual Heritage and the Digital Universe" (2007). In 2004, different presentations involved projects focusing on the hybrid use of the best tools available at the time from both analogue and digital technologies, as in the case of the Cinemascope 55 restoration of *The King and I* (1955) by Twentieth Century Fox, carried out at Cineric (New York). The restoration was an exemplary case of retroengineering, as a 4K scanner was used after adapting a wet-gate system to cope with the characteristics of the obsolete widescreen format.[7]

Looking back at my personal experience with AMIA, which started in 2002, with the conference held in Boston, I can certainly say that it has broadened my perspective both as a film archivist and as a film scholar. Thanks to AMIA's conferences, I stay connected with a large and varied community, different from the very specific one I was used to, for instance, at FIAF conferences or festivals such as Le Giornate del Cinema Muto in Pordenone or Il Cinema Ritrovato in Bologna. It is also thanks to AMIA that I have been led to recognize the extraordinary importance of the social construction in the technological transformation of the film medium, in particular in the field of film archiving and in the current transition from analogue to digital. A particularly important experience with AMIA has been the seminar held in Amsterdam during the Film Biennale in 2007 and 2010, in collaboration with EYE Film Institute Netherlands (formerly known as Nederlands Filmmuseum) and with the organizers of

The Reel Thing, which brought together different key figures from the field. In both editions of the seminar, the participants shared experiences on the collaboration between film archivists, filmmakers, and scholars (in 2007), and were confronted with a number of emerging forms of online audiovisual archives (in 2010). As part of the organizing team, I noticed on both occasions how archivists, in particular, appreciated the opportunity to share personal experiences and knowledge with professionals from other fields. Both in 2007 and 2010, requests for participation in the seminar exceeded availability, and the enthusiasm lasted long after the event, leading also to new applications for AMIA membership.

I am also confident that these experiences and exposure to colleagues from such diverse backgrounds and areas of application have contributed to the professional development of my colleagues at EYE and of my students in the MA program Preservation and Presentation of the Moving Image at the University of Amsterdam. We all benefit from the exchange of knowledge and experience and the reflection on the practice of moving image archiving these interactions can provide.

Film, as an idea and as an object, has been interpreted differently throughout its history. This is again the case with the transition to digital. Film has been and certainly still is considered differently by different social groups. This is even truer of archival film. Because of this plurality of interpretations, different frameworks are applied to (archival) film, even by the same archive, and not necessarily in contradiction with each other.[8] This plurality of interpretations coexists and is manifest within AMIA, whereas other professional organizations are traditionally prone to favor one interpretation.

This brings me to what I consider to be the extraordinary perspective we have now—looking at film while it is transitioning from analogue to digital technology—and to the privileged point of view of AMIA and its members. From a curator's perspective, in particular, I appreciate AMIA as a platform to promote ideas and initiatives close to the archival field. One way of making AMIA even more representative of the whole field would be to ensure wider participation from outside North America. This would be important not only for AMIA but also for the broader field of moving image archives at large.

NOTES

1. Refer to Giovanna Fossati, *From Grain to Pixel: The Archival Life of Film in Transition* (Amsterdam: Amsterdam University Press, 2009).

2. For a discussion on color in silent films, refer to Daan Hertogs and Nico de Klerk, eds., *"Disorderly Order": Colours in Silent Film* (Amsterdam: Nederlands Filmmuseum, 1996).

3. Refer to AMIA's Web site, which reads, "AMIA's members range from those who work solely with moving images to organizations where moving images are only a small part of their collection to individuals who want to protect their personal collection—home movies or small gauge or video—to film buffs concerned with losing our visual heritage." http://www.amianet.org/.

4. Jay David Bolter and Richard Grusin, *Remediation: Understanding New Media* (Cambridge, MA: MIT Press, 1999), 19.

5. Refer also to membership information on the FIAF Web site: http://www.fiafnet.org/uk/members/cat_affilation.cfm.

6. Refer to http://www.amianet.org/groups/committees/digital/diginits.php and to http://en.wikipedia.org/wiki/Association_of_Moving_Image_Archivists.

7. For more information on this project, see the film *Restoring a CinemaScope Picture in CinemaScope 55* (2004), made by Simon Lund, which can be viewed online at the Video Aids for Film Preservation Web site: http://www.folkstreams.net/vafp/clip.php?id=42. For more information on the JTS editions of 2004 and 2007, refer to Giovanna Fossati, "Notes on JTS 2004 Preserving the AudioVisual Heritage—Transition and Access," *FIAF Journal of Preservation* 68 (2005): 25–31, and David Walsh, "Joint Technical Symposium 2007 Audio-Visual Heritage and the Digital Universe—(28–30 June, Toronto)," *FIAF Journal of Preservation* 74/75 (2007): 57–60.

8. Frameworks indicate the conceptual framings within which theories and policies are formulated and practices are carried out. In my research, I have proposed a number of such frameworks, namely, "film as art," "film as *dispositif*," "film as state of the art," and "film as original." Fossati, *From Grain to Pixel*.

REVIEWS

Books

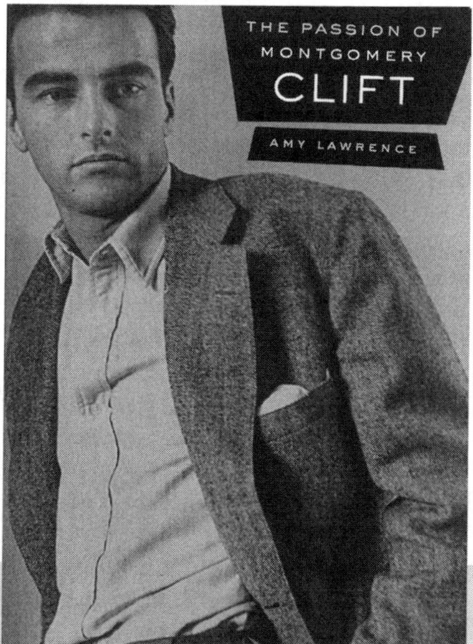

The Passion of Montgomery Clift
BY AMY LAWRENCE
UNIVERSITY OF CALIFORNIA PRESS, 2010

Kate Fortmueller

In the introduction to *Heavenly Bodies,* Richard Dyer explains that star images have histories that surpass the life span of the star and that the star text is continuously produced after the star has stopped working. With *The Passion of Montgomery Clift,* Amy Lawrence takes up a study examining the creation of Montgomery Clift both as an object of Clift's self-production and as a production of fan desire. The idea for this project stemmed from general thoughts about how fans remember films and assimilate them into their daily lives; Lawrence was drawn to Clift because of a single charged moment of performance in *I Confess* (1953). Montgomery Clift's fans function as a key point of analysis throughout the book, but the dual focus on how fans and stars produce star images resonates strongly with Dyer's point about star histories. Lawrence traces the subject and the image of Montgomery Clift both from a historically specific perspective (how Clift was perceived during his life and how Clift was working to fashion his own image and persona) and from the perspective of how these images get remade in light of new information about Clift and at different points in time with newer fans. However, this ambitious approach toward various star narratives is not the only resonance with Dyer's book. Both works evoke religious language in their titles, and though Lawrence notes the ironic tone that Dyer takes with the title *Heavenly Bodies,* she is sincerely interested in considering how fans appropriate religious language to talk about stars, something that Lawrence claims represents a "disjunction between ethereal imagery and earthly biography" (4).

Although the book proceeds chronologically and addresses the milestones in Clift's early years and Hollywood career, *The Passion of Montgomery Clift* is not merely a biography. The book draws on biographic information throughout, but Lawrence is more concerned with how fans make use of biographic material than with verifying facts of Clift's life. Lawrence carefully draws from the 1970s biographies of Clift by LaGuardia and Bosworth,[1] noting the tones of each biography, their respective sympathies (especially in relation to Clift's sexual relationships), and the noteworthy differences between the two, but she does not overemphasize extraneous information or trivia about his life. Her historical research is focused on Clift's on-set behavior, which is documented in a combination of primary archival research and secondary sources. The book is carefully researched, but the strength in her argument about the quality of Clift's acting and her statement about the perceived shifts in its quality arises from the combination of research and compelling visual and aural analysis.

The chronological structure determines that the book culminates with Montgomery Clift's critical failures, but the close film analysis that accompanies each one of Clift's films serves a recuperative function. Lawrence repeatedly warns against the fan practice of collapsing the actor into the character that he plays, concisely stating, "Biography does not trump labor" (142). She argues that the tendency of fans to see characters and films as biographical fuels the perception that Clift's acting deteriorated after his accident in 1956. To challenge this assumption, Lawrence uses comparative visual analysis to contrast Clift's performances at different points in his career (pre- and postaccident). One particularly clear example of this approach is in her comparison between the courtroom sequences of *Judgment at Nuremberg* (1961) and *A Place in the Sun* (1951) (212–17). Previous discussions of Clift's performance in *Nuremberg* have claimed that his trembling and sweating indicated that he was struggling with alcohol withdrawal. Through close analysis of each performance, Lawrence contends that Clift's specific movements and gestures in *Nuremberg* are voluntary and conscious, based on their similarity to his movements in the courtroom scene in *A Place in the Sun*. Ultimately, the warnings about collapsing biography and labor create a tension with the overarching points about how fans compose star biographies, especially in the second half of the book. By focusing on the labor of acting and the effort Clift put into his performance, Lawrence seems to be implicitly criticizing fan readings that generate narratives through gossip or biographical information.

Lawrence draws on a wide field of media that extends beyond Clift's films such as Noel Alumit's *Letters to Montgomery Clift,* Steve Erickson's *Zeroville,* REM's "Monty Got a Raw Deal," the Clash's "Right Profile," and a number of Clift's recorded radio broadcasts. Lawrence explains similarities between fan experiences of Clift's performances, but she also demonstrates the wide range of ways in which fans relate to Montgomery Clift (the REM and Clash songs contrast particularly well). The juxtaposition of these fan texts and experiences seems chaotic, but Lawrence demonstrates how this array of productions, in addition to her analysis of film and audio texts, constructs narratives about the star and his biography. The cumulative effect of these examples fills out the visual analysis and speaks to the way that star texts, histories, and legacies are produced through a variety of media forms.

Star studies have been approached from a variety of different angles: they have explored representations and the construction of stars, taken up issues of labor, and looked at the relationships between fans and stars such as Richard Dyer's discussion of gay men and Judy Garland and Jackie Stacey's study of British women and classical Hollywood stars (6). *The Passion of Montgomery Clift* approaches the subject of Clift from each of these angles at various points throughout the book, but what distinguishes Lawrence's approach to the fan–star relationship is her emphasis on casual, individual fan engagement as opposed to exceptional fan practices or select groups of fans. In her discussion of bobby-soxers, Lawrence uses her mother as an example of a Clift fan, explaining that her mother "has not seen every film Clift ever made, nor does she intend to" (55). Lawrence goes on to use this example to stress a point about how fans felt bonded to Clift, regardless of their tempered behavior and casual consumption of his films. This example stands out not only because it is the author's mother but because it seems like an anachronistic use of the word *fan*. Contemporary media scholars often pay more attention to exceptional or more active fan practices that engage with film, television, or stars by producing media or texts as responses. Typically the title of "fan" is bestowed on people who commit more fully to a text and feel that it is necessary to see every work of a given star or property. What Lawrence points to in her discussion of Clift is what might be termed a *banality of fandom*. Although Lawrence never develops a sustained theorization of these types of fan relationships, her specific examples of banal fan practices constitute a compelling object of study, not necessarily as exciting as the exceptional cases of Dyer and Stacey but disarming in their familiarity. Most people will not participate in an active fan object of analysis, as most filmgoers have experienced feelings of intimacy with a particular star (even if it is only in one or two films).

Lawrence's primary focus is on how stars are created through fan and self-production, but *The Passion of Montgomery Clift* also has several other theoretical threads, including treatments of religious language, indexicality, language of the body, and the materiality of star bodies. Each chapter addresses a larger theoretical issue, which Lawrence discusses cogently; but at times, some of these larger questions do not clearly resonate with the issue of star narrative construction that frames the book. In chapter 3, Lawrence poses a question about Clift's performance: "Are we engrossed by Clift's performance as an actor or enraptured by the face of a saint?" (86). The discussion of photography and the representation of saints that emerge from this question tend toward hagiography and never fully come back to answer her initial question. This is an interesting digression, but it needs to be more fully connected to her overarching points about Clift.

The Passion of Montgomery Clift is broadly applicable for film scholars because it addresses a wide range of questions and theoretical issues and offers a nice methodological model for how to juxtapose archival research with performance analysis. The book raises a number of questions in relation to both star studies and the perceived excesses of fan practices; however, the wide range of questions posed throughout the book occasionally comes at the expense of answers. An academic reader might want more resolution, but the central ideas about fandom and the saintliness of Montgomery Clift are ones that have much wider and nonacademic appeal. The great success of this book is in its ability to serve both an academic and a popular audience through its dual arguments; one argument is about fans and star narratives, but there is also a more basic (and controversial) argument about the trajectory of Clift's career. Lawrence's rich descriptions of Clift's performances and films keep the book

lively, and her close textual analyses make a convincing argument against the commonsense assumption that Clift's acting abilities declined after the accident.

NOTE

1. Robert LaGuardia, *Monty: A Biography of Montgomery Clift* (New York: Avon Books, 1978); Patricia Bosworth, *Montgomery Clift: A Biography* (New York: Harcourt Brace Jovanovich, 1978).

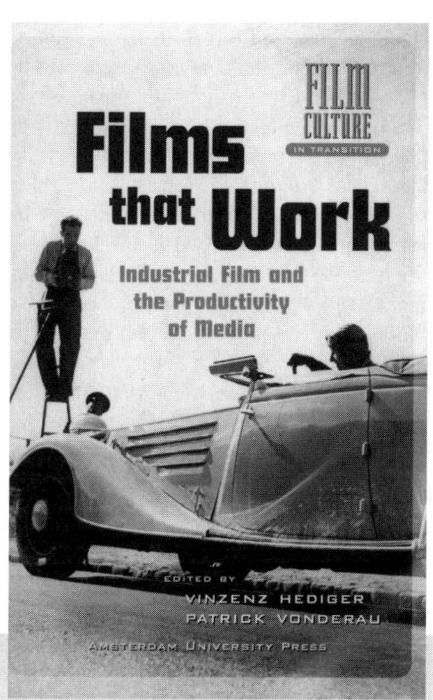

*Films That Work:
Industrial Film and the
Productivity of Media*
EDITED BY VINZENZ HEDIGER AND
PATRICK VONDERAU
AMSTERDAM UNIVERSITY PRESS, 2009

Martin L. Johnson

The industrial film is one of many so-called orphan genres, like amateur film or science film, that were largely ignored in the early decades of cinema studies. But though these companion genres are finding homes in new subfields of the discipline, the industrial film has remained relatively neglected, despite the availability of extensive archival collections holding thousands of films. *Films That Work,* edited by Vinzenz Hediger and Patrick Vonderau, attempts both to explain the absence of scholarship on the industrial film and, more important, to show the possibilities for such scholarship to challenge how scholars in cinema studies think about the role of media in social institutions and organizations.

In their introductory essay, Hediger and Vonderau claim that many industrial films lack visual interest and therefore are not suited for the aesthetic and auteurist approaches to criticism that formerly helped scholars resurrect forgotten directors and genres. Instead, the authors propose that analysis of industrial film should focus on the circumstances in which the films were produced and used. Repeating a formula first used by Thomas Elsaesser, the editors argue that films have an *Auftrag* (occasion), *Anlass* (purpose), and *Adressat* (addressee) and that the scholar's task is to locate industrial films in these three contexts. In addition, the editors argue that industrial films serve one of three purposes in industrial organizations: "*record* (institutional memory), *rhetoric* (governance) and *rationalization* (optimizing process)" (11). In more than twenty essays, covering a wide spectrum of historical periods, methodologies, and film producers, scholars from the United States and Europe use extensive archival research to write new histories of an underdescribed and undertheorized mode of production.

In the opening essays of the volume, Elsaesser, Hediger and Vonderau, and Rick Prelinger remind us just how difficult the industrial film is to define as a genre. Hediger and Vonderau argue that the industrial film is not a genre at all but a "strategically weak and parasitic form," one that can become an educational film, a documentary, or a scientific film (46). Elsaesser suggests that by considering industrial films as events rather than as texts, scholars can consider them as part of a "network" in which social and historical relationships between film-events are formed. Prelinger, in an interview conducted by Vonderau, argues that the field of industrial films is so large and diverse that it

is "almost fruitless" for a scholar to understand the work as a whole (53).

Subsequent chapters in the book are narrowly defined inquiries into various aspects of industrial film. In one clever essay, Frank Kessler and Eef Masson challenge traditional accounts of the formation of nonfiction film genres by comparing two films about cheese making: one a 1909 Pathé film set in Holland and the other a 1920 film set in Britain. Though both are process films, the Pathé film shows cheese making as a traditional practice, one bound up with Dutch identity, whereas the British film focuses on the modern manufacturing processes used in cheese production. Owing to these differences, Kessler and Masson show here that the Pathé film overlaps with the travelogue form, whereas the British film resembles instructional films used to educate employees about industrial processes. These two films were screened to general audiences as well as in educational arenas, thereby occupying different genre categories dependent on the circumstances of their exhibition. Kessler and Masson use these cheese-making films to show that the industrial film is not just film *about* industry, sponsored *by* industry, or screened *for* industrial purposes but rather a more mutable and complex category of film production and exhibition. Indeed, according to the authors, industrial films are often deliberately produced as open texts, ones that can be readily adapted for a range of exhibition sites and contexts.

This final point is emphasized in a number of studies of industrial film sponsors and producers. Yvonne Zimmermann analyzes Swiss corporate films as both the lifeblood of the country's film industry and, in many cases, as the principal way in which Swiss identity is represented inside and outside Switzerland. Other essays examine industrial films produced by Renault, Shell, and intriguingly, the Bat'a Corporation, a shoe manufacturer in Zlin, Czechoslovakia. In his essay on Bat'a, Petr Szczepanik shows how the company used industrial films as part of a multimedia strategy in the factory to increase worker productivity and boost the company's national and international image. Three industrial film producers—Jam Handy, Centron, and McGraw-Hill—are also profiled, reminding the reader that in the broad field of industrial film, specific producers specialized in certain visual and narrative techniques, such as animation in the case of McGraw-Hill's management films.

In addition to selecting wide-ranging analytic essays on industrial films in the United States and Europe, the editors include an eighty-page annotated bibliography, compiled by Vonderau and Anna Heymer, that features summaries of many dissertations and little known books on industrial film. Rather than undermining the editors' claim that the industrial film suffers from a lack of scholarly attention, the articles, magazines, dissertations, and books listed offer scholars interested in the industrial film a set of readings that fall outside the traditional provinces of cinema studies. By proposing that scholars focus on the role industrial film plays in visualizing and shaping social relations in organizations and corporations, Hediger and Vonderau set out a new agenda for inquiries into industrial film that goes beyond auteurism and genre categorization. *Films That Work* is the rare anthology that both defines a new field of study and offers numerous examples of just what that field might look like for years to come.

DVDs

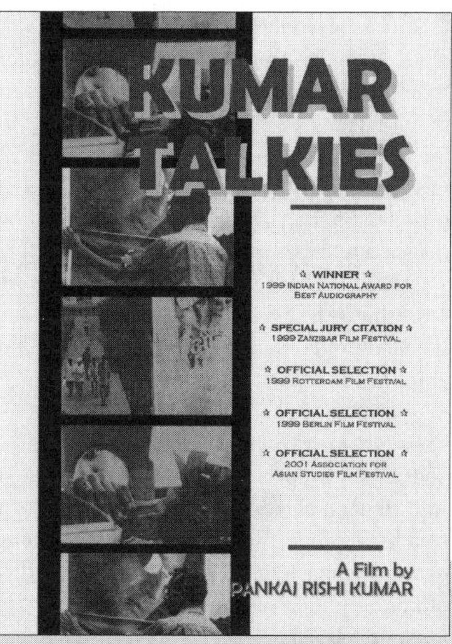

Kumar Talkies (1998)
DVD-R DISTRIBUTED BY FIRST RUN/ICARUS FILMS, 2000

Ashish Chadha

Kumar Talkies is a meandering documentary about the only cinema theater in Kalpi, a nondescript, inconsequential town in northern India. Kalpi lies at the forgotten margins of postcolonial India, away from the alluring metropolitan center of Indian cultural modernity. A medieval market town shorn of its premodern imminence and now a waylaid bazaar of local agrarian produce and minor industries, it is here that the rustic Indian masses that consume the affective sensorium of Hindi cinema toil and subsist. Kalpi's historical self-imagination is represented by this popular cinema as the battlefield where the rebellious queen of Jhansi valiantly fought the British during India's first war of independence in 1857. Immortalized in the popular Hindi film *Jhansi Ki Rani* (1952), Kalpi sits on the edge of the Chambal Valley, a site often featured in 1960s *dacoit,* or "bandit," films. Cinema in Kalpi is a part of the everyday banality of discreet pleasure and wasted desire. Cinema is indispensable for Kalpi, but it has an ambivalent relationship to its people, who watch it on cable in the privacy of their bedrooms or in the town's only theater. Kumar Talkies is their only source of public entertainment. Audiences trot to this ramshackle theater three times a day to see soft porn movies or gratuitous B-grade Bollywood masala fare. Often abruptly interrupted by power outages or missing scenes, these fragments of discontinuous cinema are conspicuously consumed by the subaltern working class of Kalpi. Projecting scratched and faded celluloid through a rickety projector with screechy sound, Kumar Talkies is a family operation catering to the unfulfilled gratification of the town's apathetic men folk.

Director Pankaj Rishi Kumar enters this social sphere of debased pleasure and inconsequential propensity to document, almost with ethnographic acuity, the place of cinema in small-town India, far away from the glamorous enthrallment of Bombay into the dusty turgidity of northern India. Trained as an editor at the Film and Television Institute of India, Kumar began his career as an assistant editor on the celebrated film *Bandit Queen* (1994). Subsequently disillusioned with the mainstream Indian film industry, he made this 16mm documentary with his own money to fathom the seductive allure of the cinematic pleasures that had ensnared him.

Kumar Talkies begins as a seemingly conventional documentary intervention to unobtrusively explore the role of cinema in a provincial, nonmetropolitan India, but slowly and unmindfully, the film descends into the domain of the personal. The decrepit, monkey-strutting, pigeon-infested theater was actually a gutted lentil mill that Kumar's father inherited and, in 1969, transformed into a talkie. Kumar uses the theater as an emotional conduit to make forays into his own family history, both to examine his quirky love of cinema inherited from his father, a retired government official, and to explore the role of cinema in Kalpi during the emerging twenty-four-seven cable television onslaught of the late 1990s. Kumar adeptly excavates the pedestrian geography of his ancestral town to make a documentary that navigates his autobiography to tell a tale about cinema. In the film, his obsession with cinema, his father's fetish with films, and Kalpi's love for cinema all collapse into a single narrative that comments on the affective role of cinema in contemporary India.

The family in *Kumar Talkies* provides the film with a personal locus around which the affective narrative of the documentary is woven. Kumar's father had recently died, and Kumar uses the documentary as a memorial to his father's fascination with cinema as well as to address his own susceptibility toward the medium. Kumar subtly ties his infective relationship to cinema as a filmmaker to the emotive bond that he shared with his father as the only one of three sons to choose cinema as a profession. The search for what cinema means to Kalpi's inhabitants becomes a metaphor for Kumar's own quest, mirrored in his delicate excavation of his deceased father's eccentric obsession. The documentary is driven by a sense of poignancy—the story of a crumbling theater in a collapsing town compounded by the absent father figure. It is in the invocation of this familial loss, as depicted by Kumar and his mother's entry into the theater courtyard, that the personal is powerfully summoned to affect the documentary. Her reminiscence of her husband's idiosyncratic decision to move away from metropolitan Delhi into the disheveled backyard of his ancestral home to start a theater supplants the sociological impetus of the documentary with an exploration of the personal.

Kumar's longing for his dead father mirrors his nostalgia for cinema, and this is astutely indexed when he invokes his father in the first frame of the film. Kumar announces the genesis of his documentary in a voice-over as one of the earliest moving images in the history of cinema, the Lumière Brothers' iconic *L'arrivée d'un train à La Ciotat* (1896), appears on-screen. This double nostalgia is later evocatively portrayed through the introduction of Super 8mm footage shot by Kumar's father, thus firmly locating the film within the domain of the personal. Faded images from home movies that Kumar's father shot in the 1960s are projected as we listen to a telephone conversation between the filmmaker and his mother talking about their discovery. It is here that Kumar effectively employs the affective valence of the personal to index nostalgia for cinema. For him, the dwindling audiences in his father's theater, together with his own disillusionment in the Bombay mainstream film industry, are mirrored in the film's nostalgic Super 8mm footage. Kumar successfully employs the self-referential indexicality of cinema by intertwining it with autobiographic self-reflexivity to discover the affective meaning of cinema. *Kumar Talkies* thus is both a pursuit of cinema's sprit in an innocuous northern Indian town and an inquiry into the meaning of cinema by the filmmaker. He evocatively maps his own personal history onto the history of cinematic modernity in postcolonial India.

Very few Indian documentary films are available in the international DVD market. This is unexpected because India has a politically active independent documentary film tradition, and since 1948, the state-funded Films Division has produced close to eight thousand films, many of which deserve to be widely seen. Therefore the DVD of *Kumar Talkies* is an important step in bringing this vibrant Indian documentary scene to the American market. Though the DVD released by Icarus Films in 2000 is not of sterling quality, its standard-definition Telecine transfer from the original 16mm is very watchable. The DVD is devoid of any extras or features, which is a disappointment. Having interviewed Kumar a number of times about this film, I think a director's commentary about its making would have greatly enriched the DVD and been very useful for those academics, archivists, and enthusiasts interested in the history of non-Western documentary production practices. *Kumar Talkies* was the first and the last 16mm film that Kumar made and also perhaps one of the last 16mm documentaries produced by a major Indian independent documentary filmmaker. Subsequently, Kumar and a number of other independent documentary filmmakers, including Anand Patwardhan, Sanjay Kak, Ranjan Palit, Vasudha Joshi, and others, have switched to digital video. Thus this DVD is an important record of a filmmaking practice that characterized poststatist independent Indian documentary since the mid-1970s, a practice that was fundamentally dependent on portable 16mm cameras.

The release of the DVD is also important because *Kumar Talkies* is one of the few documentaries of the 1990s that made a concerted effort to distance itself from the political as it unhesitatingly attempted to interrogate the social with a subtle contemplation on the family. This move away from the political is itself a political choice. *Kumar Talkies* is not a film that ostensibly tries to investigate the political in the personal or to transform the personal into the political; rather it is interested in exploring the social through the personal. By diving into his family history, Kumar makes the self-reflexive move to investigate the valence of cinema for cinema. He wants to locate the political in the familial and the autobiographic. For him, the history of cinema cannot be comprehended without exploration of that very desire that led him to become a filmmaker. Thus *Kumar Talkies* is not only an exploration of the cinematic pleasures in a town at the margins of modernity but also an attempt to comprehend the filmmaker's desire for cinema through his family history. The common love for cinema becomes the emotive kinship through which Kumar the filmmaker; his father, a deceased theater owner; and the subaltern audiences of Kalpi are inexorably tied in a subtle narrative thread. Kumar artfully mirrors the biography of a crumbling theater with his own autobiography to articulate the affect for cinema in postcolonial India at the end of twentieth century.

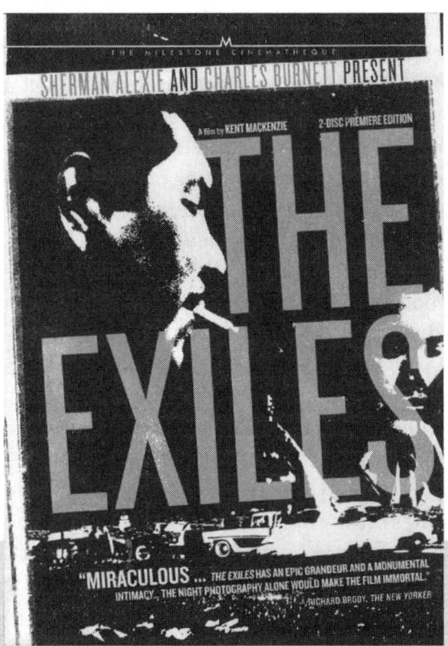

The Exiles (1961)
DVD DISTRIBUTED BY MILESTONE FILMS, 2009

Josh Glick

Shot between 1958 and 1961, just before urban renewal initiatives razed much of Los Angeles's downtown core, *The Exiles* offers stirring views of a now nonexistent Bunker Hill neighborhood and a complex portrait of a small group of Native Americans struggling to negotiate their identities within the city. Milestone Films's two-disc Premiere Edition DVD contains a meticulous restoration of director Kent Mackenzie's 1961 release and a wealth of supplementary materials that provide insight into its production and the broader historical context in which it was conceived.

After playing on the international festival circuit and then receiving limited nontheatrical distribution through Pathé Contemporary in 1964, *The Exiles* resurfaced in 2003 when Thom Andersen featured some of its scenes in his epic compilation documentary *Los Angeles Plays Itself*. The evocative sampling (included on the DVD) piqued the interests of Milestone's Cindi Rowell, who located the only existing 35mm print of *The Exiles* at the University of Southern California's (USC's) Cinema Archive.

Rowell and USC archivist Valarie Schwan took the negative to UCLA Film & Television Archive preservationist Ross Lipman, who, with the help of original crew member John Morrill and such companies as Fotokem, Audio Mechanics, and NT Audio, performed the restoration. The resulting viewing experience attests to their labor. Sharp black-and-white tonal contrasts register the graceful night photography of cinematographers Erik Daarstad, Robert Kaufman, Morrill, and Mackenzie. Voice-over monologues, intertwined with the blistering rock and roll music of the Revels, give the overall sound design an intimate and visceral quality.

Selections from the supplementary materials ground the origins of Mackenzie's filmmaking in his student years at USC. It was there that he completed *Bunker Hill–1956,* a short documentary about a community of pensioners in Los Angeles and the municipal construction plans that threatened to displace them. Additionally, the inclusion of the four drafts of the script for *Bunker Hill–1956* reveals the project's development, from the initial treatment that describes the atmosphere of the locale to the final release script that focuses on the residents expressing their commitment to the homes they have made for themselves and their anxieties over having to move.

Mackenzie began working on *The Exiles* following graduation. Among the items on the DVD that directly relate to the film is his master's thesis, submitted to USC in 1964. The document does much to elucidate the film's path to production. After reading an article in *Harper's Magazine* about the difficulties of contemporary Native Americans in the United States, Mackenzie envisioned making an educational film about the move of an Apache family from Arizona to Los Angeles through the controversial Relocation Program. The document "The Exiles Funding Proposal," also on the DVD, details Mackenzie's initial research into the venture. The practicalities of making the film, combined with his own desire to steer clear of a didactic model of documentary, led him to embark on a cinematic project that explored the nightly social activities of a group of Native Americans in and around Bunker Hill and Main Street.

The thesis also provides a better understanding of how Mackenzie and his crew, drawing from an eclectic group of directors such as Robert Flaherty, Sidney Meyers, and Vittorio De Sica, pursued an innovative mode of stylized realism. Their production method involved location shooting and the use of nonactors (who had a large amount of input into their own lines), while at the same time planning scenes and editing to ensure thematic unity for the overall film. The six drafts and the final script provide a more nuanced sense of the later stages of the film's evolution and reveal the various permutations of the title, from *The Trail of the Thunderbird* to *The Exiles*.

The multivocal audio commentaries on the DVD feature crew members such as Daarstad, filmmakers such as Charles Burnett, writer–director Sherman Alexie, and Milestone co-founder Dennis Doros. They reinforce the notion that Mackenzie was deeply invested in all aspects of production, while also emphasizing the film's highly collaborative aspects. Both the crew and the Native Americans contributed to, rather than worked under, the social and aesthetic vision of *The Exiles*. The commentators' remarks are valuable; however, they could have more rigorously situated Mackenzie in relation to the emerging international scene of alternative filmmaking, as the era saw direct cinema in the United States, Free Cinema in England, cinéma direct in Canada, and New Wave cinema and cinema verité in France.

The inclusion of three of Mackenzie's later films allows scholars and enthusiasts to trace a loose professional trajectory. *Story of a Rodeo Cowboy* (1962), made for the Hollywood documentary television producer David Wolper; *A Skill for Molina* (1964), made for the U.S. Information Agency; and *Ivan and His Father* (1970), made for Dimension Films, lack the blend of complexity and conflict that so permeated the narrative texture of *The Exiles*. However, these films do reveal Mackenzie's sustained interest in following individuals and groups at odds with the mainstream of contemporary American society. These films also speak to his responsibility to the institutions for which he worked and to the financial difficulties of pursuing independent documentaries in Los Angeles during this time period.

As Mackenzie confronted film industry pressures throughout much of his career, until his death in 1980, the booklet "The Jug Band Man," dated 1972, appears as the most curious part of the DVD. Described by Mackenzie as "A Journal of an Attempt to Capture in a Film Treatment the Actual Life and Feelings of a Wandering Youth," the 430-page document brings together photography, prose and poetry, and the transcription of conversations into a chronicle of the self reflective musings and interactions of a young man named JM living in California. The project was axed because of a stalling of creative momentum and JM himself losing interest. It nonetheless showcases Mackenzie's empathetic eye and ear for observation and would reward further examination as a work of experimental documentary media in its own right. "The Jug Band Man" makes one wonder what Mackenzie would have created had he completed the project.

Other films included in the supplementary materials broaden our understanding of the history of Bunker Hill. Greg Kimble's *Bunker Hill: A Tale of Urban Renewal* (2009) describes the area's nineteenth-century past as a home to Los Angeles's elite, the demographic shifts that took place, and the mid-twentieth-century municipal plans for redevelopment. Robert Kirste's home movie footage of the last day of operation of Bunker Hill's funicular tramway in *Last Day of Angels Flight* (2009) gives a more personal account of how one of the area's defining technoarchitectural landmarks was used by Angelinos.

Also present on the DVD is James Youngdeer's short fiction film *White Fawn's Devotion* (1910), allegedly the first Native American film ever made. The film shifts the main discursive terrain of the DVD from the representation of Los Angeles and the presence of Native Americans in the city at mid-century to questions about their representation in early mainstream film and even their presence behind the camera. The film adds another facet to the issue of native cinema that Sherman Alexie discusses on one of the audio commentaries.

Milestone's DVD provides a rich archive that will allow scholars to place Mackenzie within a chronology of documentary and realist film practice. One will definitely want to track down his 1971 film *Saturday Morning* as well his still photographic projects to gain added insight into his creative profile. A main virtue of the Milestone DVD is that it encourages interdisciplinary study. Understanding Bunker Hill, urban renewal, and the lives of Native Americans in the Relocation Program enhances and expands the power of the film, just as the film illuminates the social history of Los Angeles.

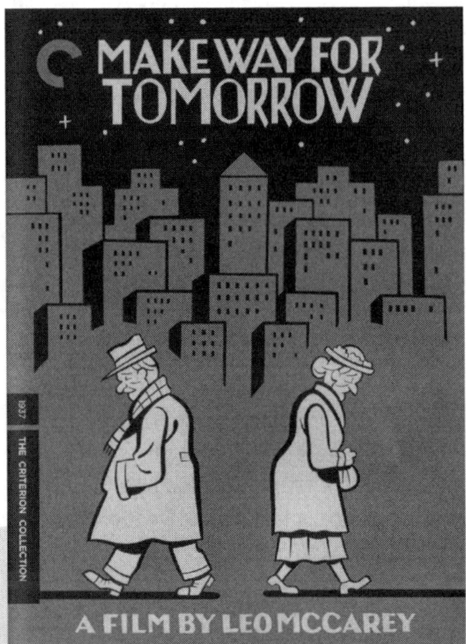

Make Way for Tomorrow (1937)
DVD DISTRIBUTED BY CRITERION FILMS, 2009

John Migliore

Long unavailable on any home video format and seldom revived, *Make Way for Tomorrow* (1937) seems to be that rare example of a highly regarded film whose scarcity was due to its subject matter and lack of star power rather than copyright issues or any of the standard reasons for a film's disappearance into obscurity. Though the problems of the elderly and the often tense dynamic between parents and their adult children remain universal subjects, they have never been an easy sell at the box office or in American culture as a whole. Criterion's release of Leo McCarey's meditation on family, marriage, and the fleeting glories and lasting indignities of old age provides a chance to evaluate both the film and its place within the director's output. Studiously apolitical, and making no overtly direct claims to social relevancy, the film nonetheless argues subtly and, in the end, painfully for attention to be paid.

The film's plot is simplicity itself. Married fifty years, Bark and Lucy Cooper (Victor Moore and Beulah Bondi), unable to make their mortgage payment, are forced to leave their home. Dreading the idea of going to a so-called rest home, which would require them to permanently separate, they each move in with one of their children's families. This, too, requires them to be several hundred miles apart, a state that they tell themselves will be temporary. As weeks go by, the tensions occasioned by generational friction, small spaces, and the accretion of assorted grievances, perceived and actual, mount. Eventually, it becomes clear that Bark and Lucy will never be able to live together again. Then, as now, few are willing to hire a man in his late sixties, and none of the children, for a variety of reasons, both selfish and practical, are willing to take them in. He will go off to a daughter in California, and she pretends to welcome the prospect of life in a home for the aged. After a last, poignant afternoon spent in New York revisiting the sites of their honeymoon, the film ends with the couple parting at the train station. With no independent income and at a time when long-distance travel was realistically available only to the well-off, we infer that they may not see each other again.

The film represented a gamble on the part of Paramount Studios. Having defined itself from the beginning as a place where directors held great sway, Paramount was predisposed to allow top filmmakers a calculated risk or two. Initially, their wager did not pay off. The combination of difficult subject matter, a cast composed entirely of character actors, and the decided lack of a happy outcome kept audiences away, and critical acclaim was by no means unanimous. McCarey apparently intended the film as a tribute to his father and was deeply pained by its reception. When accepting the Academy Award the following year for his direction of *The Awful Truth* (1937), his speech was gracious but brutally succinct: "Thank you very much, but you gave it to me for the wrong picture." Orson Welles said that *Make Way for*

Tomorrow "could make a stone sob" and wondered decades later at "the fact that here was this marvelous film . . . and nobody went!" Fellow directors continued to champion the film long after McCarey died and understood his reputation to have been partially eclipsed for a perceived alliance with the most reactionary wing of anti-Communism in Hollywood near the end of his career.

Make Way for Tomorrow also inspired *Tokyo Story* (1954), and in its pacing and tone, the links to director Ozu Yasujiro's examinations of human nature are evident in a willingness to observe a series of individually innocuous but collectively significant events unfold. Both directors share a humanistic outlook without excessive sentimentality. They are also similar in their ability to show us a wide range of simple, everyday people in whom we can, and indeed must, recognize ourselves. Watching this film, viewers are constantly led into a complicated response as the director and actors make us recognize our own families in the one they have created on-screen. This is particularly evident in a masterful extended sequence in which the Coopers' social-climbing daughter-in-law (Fay Bainter) conducts a bridge class as Lucy sits in her rocking chair interjecting comments to both Bainter and the room at large. Bainter and her students are at first visibly uncomfortable with Lucy's physical and verbal presence, just as we, as viewers, are also led to contemplate our exasperation with or discomfort toward older relatives. Then McCarey reverses the scene completely: Lucy takes a long-distance call from the ailing Bark, and her tenderness and longing to be with her husband have a visible effect on the audience both within and outside the film. Miraculously, McCarey keeps this from feeling manipulative and continues to successfully stage such moments in a series of similar set pieces.

Consistently throughout the film, characters respond in unexpected ways, upending our expectations and Hollywood conventions. Assuming that they must be secretly wealthy, a car salesman pitches the Coopers by taking them for a ride through New York City. We brace ourselves for anger and rejection when he finds out that they cannot afford to do more than look at the car. When the moment comes, disappointment flickers across his face, but he

pulls himself together and gallantly deposits them at their honeymoon hotel. Inside, finding that much has changed, they are introduced to the current manager, who, rather than giving them the politely abbreviated brush-off we expect, is genuinely invested in their memories and solicitous of their needs. Most crucially, McCarey does not demonize the Cooper children: in the main, they are recognizably flawed human beings, subject to doubts, insecurities, and spousal pressure. When the oldest and most sensitive son reckons in a single line of dialogue the cost of having pulled his parents apart, it is perhaps the most quietly devastating moment in a film full of them.

In navigating these tricky emotional shifts, the director is aided immeasurably by his cast, particularly Moore and Bondi, two veteran character actors here getting their only real opportunity at leading roles. They were, respectively, only sixty-one and forty-nine during filming, but our belief in the characters' advanced age is never shaken. Moore had played dramatic roles on Broadway but sustained an over thirty-year career on-screen, cast as the bumbling sidekick or comic drunk: this film represented the single time that the actor was handed a meaty dramatic part, and he is extremely touching. He uses a toned-down version of his patented irascibility and slightly distracted air to communicate Bart's injured but unbowed pride and uncertain attempts to master events beyond his control. Bondi, by contrast, played variations on this role for over fifty years but never had a vehicle with such space to achieve this level of characterization. Often required to make the viewer feel both discomfort and protectiveness in the same moment, she never makes these tonal shifts any more jarring than necessary. It is a masterful performance—and it is a bit painful to watch other, more truncated performances that catch faint echoes of her work here.

McCarey demonstrates that we cannot always, or even often, live up to the best in our natures. But above all, the film is a stark argument for the fact that finally, all we have is each other, and so it is in our best interest to try. McCarey considered a comedic version of this same idea in *The Awful Truth* and would rework the theme throughout the remainder of his career, though most of his films after the 1930s would center on communities created through patriotism and religious belief rather than the more secular but equally powerful plea for connection found in *Make Way for Tomorrow*.

Criterion has done a superlative transfer, presenting a beautifully clear image with no noticeable softness, speckling, or scratches. Working from the original 35mm negative as well as other best-available elements, the crispness and clarity add immeasurably to the sense of this as being a universal story relevant to any time period, including our own. Supplements are interesting, especially for those unfamiliar with McCarey's work and the cultural climate of the film's release. The lack of participation from those directly connected with the production is sorely missed, although understandable, given the film's age. Peter Bogdanovich is interviewed on the disc, but McCarey's death in 1969 came just before the plethora of filmed interviews during the 1970s with directors, stars, and craftsmen from the studio system. The film also failed to benefit from the earlier wave of auterism because of its limited release in France, as Bertrand Tavernier notes in an essay reprinted in the booklet accompanying the DVD.

Bogdanovich provides a selective overview of McCarey's life, career, and responses of his peers to the film. The DVD lacks a commentary track, but this is ably balanced out by an extended conversation with jazz and popular culture essayist and critic Gary Giddins, who focuses mainly on the film as a cultural artifact. He notes that the film's release shortly after the passage of the Social Security Act would, within a few years, make it possible for many of the elderly to avoid the perils faced by the Coopers. Criterion has brought attention to many unsung titles over the years but rarely a mainstream American film as neglected as this, a portrait of the importance of strengthening familial and communal bonds that also, in a sense, speaks to the continuing need to provide preservation and access to films like this one.

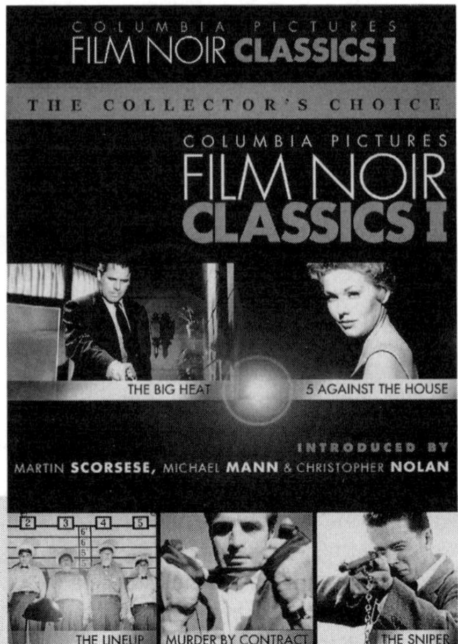

Columbia Pictures Film Noir Classics I
DVD DISTRIBUTED BY SONY PICTURES HOME ENTERTAINMENT, 2009

Columbia Pictures Film Noir Classics II
DVD DISTRIBUTED BY SONY PICTURES HOME ENTERTAINMENT, 2010

Columbia Classics Bad Girls of Film Noir Volume 1
DVD DISTRIBUTED BY SONY PICTURES HOME ENTERTAINMENT, 2010

Columbia Classics Bad Girls of Film Noir Volume 2
DVD DISTRIBUTED BY SONY PICTURES HOME ENTERTAINMENT, 2010

Ronald Wilson

There has long been a debate about what constitutes a B film and when it ceased to exist as a definable category. Much like the debates surrounding any film genre, movement, or historical periodization, its boundaries are elastic. Some scholars contend, for instance, that the B film is restricted to the Hollywood studio era and ended as an industrial practice with the Paramount Decree of 1948. Others limit the practice to the small Poverty Row studios, such as Republic, Monogram, and PRC, that relied on the B film to provide product to small, independent theaters. The problem of defining the B film is exacerbated when it is combined with the concept of film noir because both terms are accompanied by their own critical baggage. James Naremore defines B films noirs as "liminal products [that] occupy a borderland between generic thrillers and art movies."[1] Naremore's use of the term *liminal* seems especially appropriate as the category of film noir is continually expanding year to year, depending on either academic scholarship or DVD marketing strategies. Andrew Sarris further observes that "a disproportionate number of fondly remembered B pictures fall into the general category of the *film noir*. Somehow even mediocrity can become majestic when it is coupled with death."[2] The eighteen films in the recently released Columbia film noir DVD collections exemplify the majesty of mediocrity as it was developed at Columbia Studios in the 1950s. They also show how the B film noir was able to flourish in postwar Hollywood as an economic product that capitalized on crime and topical events.

One of the advantages that Columbia had in the post–Paramount Decree era was its status as a horizontally integrated minor studio. Because it had no exhibition venues to divest, it could adapt more easily to the changing economic environment. Columbia had been a prolific producer of B films, serials, and short subjects in the studio era. It was able to strategize by producing one or two A pictures, depending on finances in a given year, but the majority of its annual output consisted of B westerns, series, and short subjects. Harry and Jack Cohn once said of their business philosophy, "[We] want one good picture a year. That's [our] policy . . . and [we] won't let an exhibitor have it unless he takes the bread-and-butter product, the Boston Blackies, the Blondies, the low budget westerns and the rest of the junk we make."[3]

In the 1950s, Jack Cohn began to look more to independent production as a source for annual product, thereby diverting production costs to larger-budgeted prestige films. The production strategy of one or two big-budget-ed features supplemented by more modestly budgeted productions (generally forty films a year) continued. During the 1950s, some of Columbia's award-winning films included *From Here to Eternity* (1953), *On the Waterfront* (1954), and *Bridge on the River Kwai* (1957). But the majority of their output consisted of bread-and-butter films such as *Slaves of Babylon* (1953), *The Law vs. Billy the Kid* (1954), and *Creature with the Atom Brain* (1955) and many of the films contained in the Columbia noir collections. Sony had already begun marketing Columbia's postwar bread-and-butter product with the release of such DVD collections as the *Sam Katzman: Icons of Horror* collection, the *William Castle* collection, and the entire short subjects of the Three Stooges. It has now grouped together a disparate number of films in four separate collections under the aegis of noir. What the Sony's Columbia noir collections reveal is how B crime films developed during the 1950s through economic restraints that exemplified a certain tendency that came to be known as noir.

Martin Scorsese uses the expression *economy of means* in one of his introductions that make up part of the special features in *Columbia Pictures Film Noir Classics I*. Though he is referring to Irving Lerner's shooting style in *Murder by Contract* (1958), the expression is an apt one for all films in the four collections. Perhaps the most important criterion for B noir in particular, and the one that is best represented in these collections of Columbia films, is the films' economic imperative. Many had short shooting schedules, thereby making it a necessity to find alternative, less costly means of expression. Irving Lerner's *City of Fear* (1959), for instance, was shot in seven days. *Murder by Contract,* which influenced Scorsese's *Taxi Driver* (1976), had a six-day shooting schedule. Hugo Haas's *One Girl's Confession* (1953) was produced in twelve days, which seems exorbitant in comparison. But most of these Columbia films had three- to four-week shooting schedules, which provides an indication of their budgetary restraints.

Likewise, a number of these films utilize a significant amount of location photography (*The Glass Wall* [1953], *5 Against the House* [1955], *Nightfall* [1957], *The Sniper* [1952], *Murder by Contract, The Lineup* [1958]), helping to reduce costs. Several of the film directors represented in the collections were former B film graduates cum laude from the studio era and were trained in the economy of means through necessity. That these directors, held in high regard by many film noir enthusiasts, had previous technical expertise in B films is too often ignored when discussing their subsequent work. Phil Karlson (*5 Against the House, The Brothers Rico* [1957]), for instance, had worked at Monogram Studios directing Charlie Chan films. Jacques Tourneur *(Nightfall)* directed several notable horror films for producer Val Lewton at RKO (though these are highly regarded today, in the 1940s, they were little more than B films and prime examples of the economy of means). Don Siegel began as a montage editor at Warner Bros. and directed modestly budgeted B films there and at Republic. Edward Dmytryk directed such film series entries as *Confessions of Boston Blackie* (1941) and *The Falcon Strikes Back* (1943). This technical experience proved invaluable when the material they had to work with had budgetary constraints. In addition, many of the actors represented in the Columbia noir collections are character actors or leads that have yet to establish a screen presence such as Kim Novak, Aldo Ray, Vince Edwards, and Eli Wallach. Independent production is well represented here as well, including Stanley Kramer Productions *(The Sniper),* William Goetz *(The Brothers Rico),* Ivan Tors *(The Glass Wall),* and Hugo Hass *(One Girl's Confession).*

Significant to the look of the films contained in these collections is that they exhibit few of the visual motifs and stylistics that we typically associate with film noir. There is little use of chiaroscuro lighting, hardly any oblique camera angles, few flashbacks, and no expressionistic montage sequences. Instead, as Scorsese observes in his introduction to *The Brothers Rico,* there is a flatness to the image that can be attributed to a more objective style. These films showcase an objective view of reality that captures events as they unfold as well as characters' reactions to those events. Characters are framed objectively within their environments and in relation to others in a realistic manner. This objectivity is a contributing factor to the aesthetic development of the postwar crime film.

Another aesthetic development that is apparent in several of these films is their topicality. Unlike the crime fiction adaptations of classic noir, postwar noir often combined topical events with crime narratives. This is certainly the case with three of the films in these collections—*The Killer That Stalked New York* (1950), *The Glass Wall,* and *City of Fear* (1959). *The Killer That Stalked New York* was based on a 1948 *Cosmopolitan Magazine* article "Smallpox, the Killer That Stalks New York," which was inspired by a 1946 smallpox scare when millions of New Yorkers were provided with free vaccinations without creating a panic. The film obviously exploits that event by combining it with a diamond-smuggling operation, whose smuggler, Sheila Bennett (Evelyn Keyes), is also, unknowingly, smuggling smallpox into the city. In *The Glass Wall,* also shot in New York City, Vittorio Gassman (in his first American film) is an illegal refugee who goes into hiding to avoid deportation. The film exploits the plight of refugees under the guise of a criminal chase. Cold war paranoia over atomic radiation is fully exploited in Irving Lerner's *City of Fear,* in which escaped convict Vince Edwards believes he has a container filled with valuable heroin, when, in reality, it contains a radioactive isotope, Cobalt-13. The use of location shooting in these films and several others in this collection provides a topical realism to their situations and events. Phil Karlson's *5 Against the House,* for instance, is a heist film that takes place (at least for the heist itself) inside Harold's Club and Casino in Reno, Nevada, and that was shot, for the most part, in Reno and Las Vegas. The exploitative draw for this film was not the actors (most of whom were not then stars) but Harold's Club. San Francisco provides the location photography for both Edward Dmytryk's *The Sniper* and Don Siegel's *The Lineup* and helps establish an objective reality to their melodramatic narrative excesses. This objective style is indebted to the men who photographed it: Lucien Ballard *(City of Fear),* Joseph Biroc *(The Killer That Stalked New York, The Glass Wall),* and Burnett Guffey *(The Sniper, The Brothers Rico, Nightfall, Human Desire* [1954]).

The studio-bound work of Fritz Lang and Lewis Seiler also reveals an objective style that is controlled through framing and lighting. Lang's *The Big Heat* (1953) and *Human Desire* are both examples of meticulously fashioned classic Hollywood filmmaking, in which paranoia and claustrophobic environments are expressed through the characters and their relationship to the mise-en-scène. These two films reveal a postwar Lang who avoids expressionistic stylistics in favor of a more naturalistic view of a corrupt, vice-ridden world, in which violence can occur swiftly and without notice. There is very little of the virtuoso camera work typically associated with Lang's German or later Hollywood films, possibly a product of the restrictions of the studio system or a conscious effort by Lang to comment on the vulnerability and violence that lie beneath the surface of normalcy. Lotte Eisner refers to Lang's "rational camera," in which he strived for verisimilitude, demanding from his cameramen a newsreel-like authenticity.[4] The two films he made for Columbia are perfect examples of this objective style.

Though he is not as well known as Lang, the *Columbia Pictures Film Noir Classics* collections contain two films directed by Lewis Seiler, a well-trained action specialist of the studio era. Seiler began directing Tom Mix westerns in the 1920s, and some of his other genre work included *Crime School* (1938), *King of the Underworld* (1939), and *Guadalcanal Diary* (1943). Both *Women's Prison* (1955) and *Over-Exposed* (1956), contained in the *Bad Girls of Film Noir* collections, are studio-bound B films exploiting their female B stars. Seiler seems to be the B equivalent of Howard Hawks in his preference for a wide range of genres and action-oriented material. The B film's Marilyn Monroe, Cleo Moore, is featured in both these films as well as in Hugo Hass's *One Girl's Confession*. The inclusion of these films by Sony in a collection labeled "film noir" illustrates how that category has been expanded and exploited over time.

The two *Columbia Pictures Film Noir Classics* collections contain films that have been canonized as noir by many scholars and critics. My own well-worn copy of Alain Silver and Elizabeth Ward's 1979 *Film Noir: An Encyclopedic Reference* contains entries for most of the titles in both collections. Yet the *Bad Girls of Film Noir* collections warrant only two films with entries: *The Killer That Stalked New York* and *Night Editor* (1946). This somewhat problematizes the use of film noir as a category. Hugo Haas's *One Girl's Confession* is a case in point. The film, though it contains a crime, is little more than a B melodrama about a good girl turned bad. In fact, working titles of the film were "Story of a Bad Girl" and "Tough Girl." Hugo Haas specialized in this type of domestic melodrama, directing such B films as *Pickup* (1951), *Thy Neighbor's Wife* (1953), and *The Other Woman* (1954), all of which starred Haas's muse, Cleo Moore. Haas has often been referred to as the "foreign Ed Wood" (he was a Czech émigré), which emphasizes not only his low-budget production values and pedantic directing style but also that Haas, like Wood, was a true B film auteur: he produced, wrote, directed, and acted in his own films. Ed Wood's name is rarely invoked in connection with film noir, and I believe this may be the first time that Hugo Haas has been classified as such. Regardless, the inclusion by Sony of these films and other melodramas such as *Two of a Kind* (1951) and *Bad for Each Other* (1953) begs one to ask what really constitutes a noir film.

I can understand the noir connection with regard to the black-and-white cinematography of Joseph Biroc in the aforementioned *The Killer That Stalked New York* and *The Glass Wall,* but it brings into question the dimensions of the term *film noir* itself in relation to the other films in these two collections. As stated previously, the term is elastic, allowing for an expansion of its canon of films each year. It also has become a marketing ploy targeted at DVD enthusiasts. With the demise of the Fox Film Noir series, the standard has been somewhat taken up by smaller niche distributors such as Olive Films, with its recent releases of several Paramount films noirs, and the Warner Archives made-on-demand selection of crime titles, many of which are considered noir (though the Warner Archives does not use this category on its Web site; the films are listed as crime films). Sony has found a way to package not only "legitimate" films noirs but also many films that could not have been packaged in any other way. The time is not yet ripe for a "Hugo Haas Collection" or a "Cleo Moore Melodramas" box set, so the alternative is to exploitatively sell them, much like they would have been exploited in their original release, featuring their bad-girl image and connecting that with film noir.

The special features provided by Sony Pictures include some perceptive introductions by Scorsese on *Murder by Contract, The Sniper, The Big Heat,* and *The Brothers Rico.* Scorsese discusses not only the production background and visual style for these films but also their exhibition contexts. He explains, for instance, how *Murder by Contract* was originally double-billed with the film *The Journey* (1959), by Anatole Litvak. Michael Mann also provides an introduction to *The Big Heat,* and the sets include two features with Christopher Nolan on the influence of film noir and so-called pulp paranoia. Actress Emily Mortimer provides an introduction to Fritz Lang's *Human Desire,* discussing some of the film's themes and visual motifs. The inclusion of these features with these particular filmmakers highlights the extent of the influence noir continues to have on contemporary filmmaking. The audio commentary on both *The Lineup* and *The Sniper,* by James Ellroy and Eddie Muller, though entertaining, provides little in the way of substantial film criticism; instead, it details minutiae on film locations and the personal lives of little-known character actors and seems worthy more of the cult fan rather than the film scholar.

Theatrical trailers are also included on all of the collections and provide some insight into how these films were marketed to their audiences. This proves especially enlightening with the trailers included in the *Bad Girls of Film Noir* collections. Trailers for *Women's Prison* and *Over-Exposed* emphasize the sensational aspects of both films. "2489—A Dame with Curves Can Always Find an Angle—Even in Jail!" is the superimposed tagline over Cleo Moore pushing a prison laundry cart. The title of the film *Over-Exposed* is conveniently presented over a shot of Cleo Moore in a revealing outfit, followed by the tagline "The Camera Queen of the Clip Joints." The sensational tabloid crime connection helped to sell these films to audiences and provide them with a sensibility that now validates their categorization as film noir. Naremore has stated that "whenever we list any movie under the noir rubric, we do little more than invoke a network of ideas as a makeshift organization principle, in place of an author, a studio, a time period, or a national cinema. By such means, we can discuss an otherwise miscellaneous string of pictures, establishing similarities and differences among them."[5] Both Sony Pictures's *Columbia Pictures Film Noir*

Classics and *Bad Girls of Film Noir* collections have provided insight into a group of films that illustrate the flexibility and range of noir as it was produced and distributed by Columbia Studios in postwar America.

NOTES

1. James Naremore, *More Than Night: Film Noir and Its Contexts* (Los Angeles: University of California Press, 1998), 139.
2. Andrew Sarris, "The Beatitude of the 'B' Picture," in *Kings of the Bs: An Anthology of Film History and Criticism,* ed. Todd McCarthy and Charles Flynn (New York: A. P. Dutton, 1975), 49.
3. Douglas Gomery, *The Hollywood Studio System* (London: BFI, 2005), 166.
4. Lotte Eisner, *Fritz Lang* (New York: Da Capo Press), 373.
5. Naremore, *More Than Night,* 276.

Conferences and Festivals

Seventh Orphan Film Symposium
APRIL 7–10, 2010, NEW YORK

Daniel Eagan

A change in venue to Manhattan's West Side marked the latest evolution of the Orphan Film Symposium, whose seventh edition was held from April 7 to 10, 2010. Staged at the former Chelsea West Cinema, the gathering featured eighty films from seventeen countries, with eighty presenters discussing moving images depicting everything from gunrunning to repatriation to slapstick techniques in Zimbabwe. On everyone's mind were the dismaying economics of film preservation in an increasingly digital world.

By definition a deliberately eclectic assembly of film, the symposium drew from archives, museums, schools, and laboratories. Filmmakers ranged from Orson Welles to traveling amateurs, with work from Georges Méliès, jazz provocateur Edward Bland, animator Norman McLaren, and journeyman producer and director Bud Pollard. Several "firsts" were screened: the first film shot in Wales, the first fiction film from Great Britain, and the first releases from the Jamaica Film Unit. The audience could not have been more responsive: this was a crowd that even applauded a collection of studio logos assembled into a trailer for the symposium.

After an opening night screening that juxtaposed pornography from the Kinsey Institute collection and *Film ist. a Girl & a Gun* from found-footage expert Gustav Deutsch, the symposium proper began with Stefan Drößler's presentation of the fourth episode of *Orson Welles' Sketch Book*. Part of a television series Welles made for the BBC in 1955, it is a perfect example of an orphan film: the BBC contract called for one airing, the 35mm original elements no longer exist, a conflict between Welles's widow and daughter has prevented restoration work, and now much of the material is available on YouTube. What is the best way to preserve the series? Drößler, director of the Filmmuseum München, where a portion of Welles's work ended up, spoke about trying to protect the filmmaker's legacy—preventing the dissemination of outtakes, for example—while also finding funding for preserving the collection's magnetic stripe films before they exhibit signs of vinegar syndrome.

Welles is so well known that his work will always draw attention from potential sources of funding. Mona Simpson, who teaches video and digital media preservation in the Moving Image Archiving and Preservation (MIAP) program and at New York University, raised a more difficult economic problem while talking about every archivist's nightmare: a fire in the Ghana Broadcasting Corporation Audiovisual Library.

Funding is also a major problem for Paula Félix-Didier, director of the Museo del Cine Pablo Ducrós Hicken, a museum evicted from its former quarters in Buenos Aires. Founded in 1971, the museum includes over sixty thousand reels of film, 250 projectors, ancillary materials like a tinting guide to *The Cabinet of Dr. Caligari* (Robert Wiene, 1920), and the Manuel Peña Rodriguez collection, source of the elements that have been used for the expanded version of Fritz Lang's *Metropolis* (1927) as well as features, such as *Moy Syn* (1928), long believed lost.

Along with a 1969 newsreel documentary covering popular unrest in Argentina, Félix-Didier screened some examples of cartoons made for the 1940s home market in 16mm Cinepavision, "the toy that makes movies." These two genres—documentary footage of uprisings and animation from underappreciated studios and producers—turned into unstated themes for the symposium. Greg Wilsbacher, curator of Newsfilm Collections at the University of South Carolina's Moving Image Research Collection (USC MIRC), screened the only known visual record of refugee camps in Shanghai, filmed in 1937 after the Japanese invasion. Jirí Hornícek, head of the Film Historians Department at the National Film Archive in Prague, showed clandestine footage shot during the Soviet invasion in 1968. Art historian Juan Salas introduced *With the Abraham Lincoln Brigade in Spain* (1937–38), Henri Cartier-Bresson's first film. While researching the recently discovered "Mexican Suitcase," a cache of forty-five hundred still photography negatives documenting the Spanish Civil War that went missing in 1939, Salas also connected the film and Cartier-Bresson's work in the Spanish Civil War to well-known war photographer Robert Capa.

Animation showed up at the symposium in many forms, from *Mutt and Jeff: On Strike* (a not-so-subtle swipe at conditions endemic to the industry produced in 1920) to the bizarre, politically incorrect, and delightful *Die Entdeckung Wiens am Nordpol,* a 1923 advertising cartoon that at one point ground polar bears into ice cream. Thursday night included a ceremony during which Danielle Ash and Jodie Mack received the Helen Hill Award, which honors the legacy of Hill's independent film career. This segment featured Ash's *Pigeon Dance* (2007) and *Pickles for Nickels* (2009), Mack's *Yardwork Is Hardwork* (2008), and Hill's *Scratch and Crow* (1995), recently selected for the National Film Registry. Members of Hill's family were present, and excerpts from a film about Hill's life were screened.

Throughout the symposium, the introductions and talks were filled with humor, enthusiasm, and dense amounts of information. At times the discussions were more interesting than the films they covered. Annette Melville of the National Film Preservation Foundation (NFPF) and Richard Abel of the University of Michigan spoke about Film Connection, the program to return and restore American films from Australia. Shortly after the symposium, the NFPF helped bring about the repatriation of films from New Zealand. Titles once considered lost, such as John Ford's *Upstream* (1927), will soon become available to the public. Charles Musser of Yale gave a very moving introduction to Max Glaband's *The Investigators* (1948), a short agitprop comedy decrying anti-Communist hysteria that was produced by the proto-indie Union Films. Musser spoke emotionally about the impact of the McCarthy-era blacklist on the filmmakers, some of whose descendants met each other in the audience for the first time.

The most energetic talk may have surrounded *The Cry of Jazz* (1959), a recently restored work by Edward Bland. Jonas Mekas, artistic director of Anthology Film Archives, introduced the film by talking about its "revolutionary originality, truth and energy. Everybody was struck, like cutting with a knife. Here it is, this is what jazz is all about." Bland later recounted how his film was received by the

public, in particular after a Cinema 16 screening on February 24, 1962, with Ralph Ellison and Nat Hentoff in attendance. "I expected everybody to be angry," Bland recalled. As for Ellison, "He hated it."

Over meals, at parties, in the theater lobby, and in bars and nightclubs, money was an inescapable topic. Mike Mashon, head of the Library of Congress Moving Image Section at the Packard Campus for Audio Visual Conservation, could talk about curatorial decisions as a form of triage, even while pointing to success stories such as his discovery of a pre–Production Code cut of *Baby Face* (1933). Over lunch on Thursday, Sam Kula gave a crash course in the economics of digital preservation. Vanessa Toulmin, founder and director of the National Fairground Archive at the University of Sheffield, bemoaned the difficulties she faced with the twelve nitrate films from 1894–95 that make up the George Williams collection. "It took four months to actually restore the films, and four years to sort out the legal issues," she said. "It came out to about thirteen thousand pounds, and that doesn't include copyright costs."

How much to spend on preservation has become almost as important a question as what to save. Is a 1933 infomercial about the Hapsburg laundry in Vienna as important as *Laconia Reel* (1923), a home movie by Claudia Lea Phelps that documents the first round-the-world tour sponsored by American Express? And how do they compare to 1980s videos of town hall meetings from Sisterna Sandinista de Television?

Symposium founder and organizer Dan Streible, who teaches film history and archival research at New York University's Department of Cinema Studies and in its MIAP program, addressed the problems and goals of preservation in this way: "The partnerships among archives, labs, filmmakers, and scholars drive the Orphan Film Project. To have a neglected film rediscovered, physically preserved, reformatted for good presentation, and put into a historical context for an audience—that's an ideal outcome."

The films that resonated most for me were those that provided windows, however dim or confusing, into a lost past. They were proof of how flimsy our heritage is, how hard it is to preserve. Unedited takes from a behind-the-

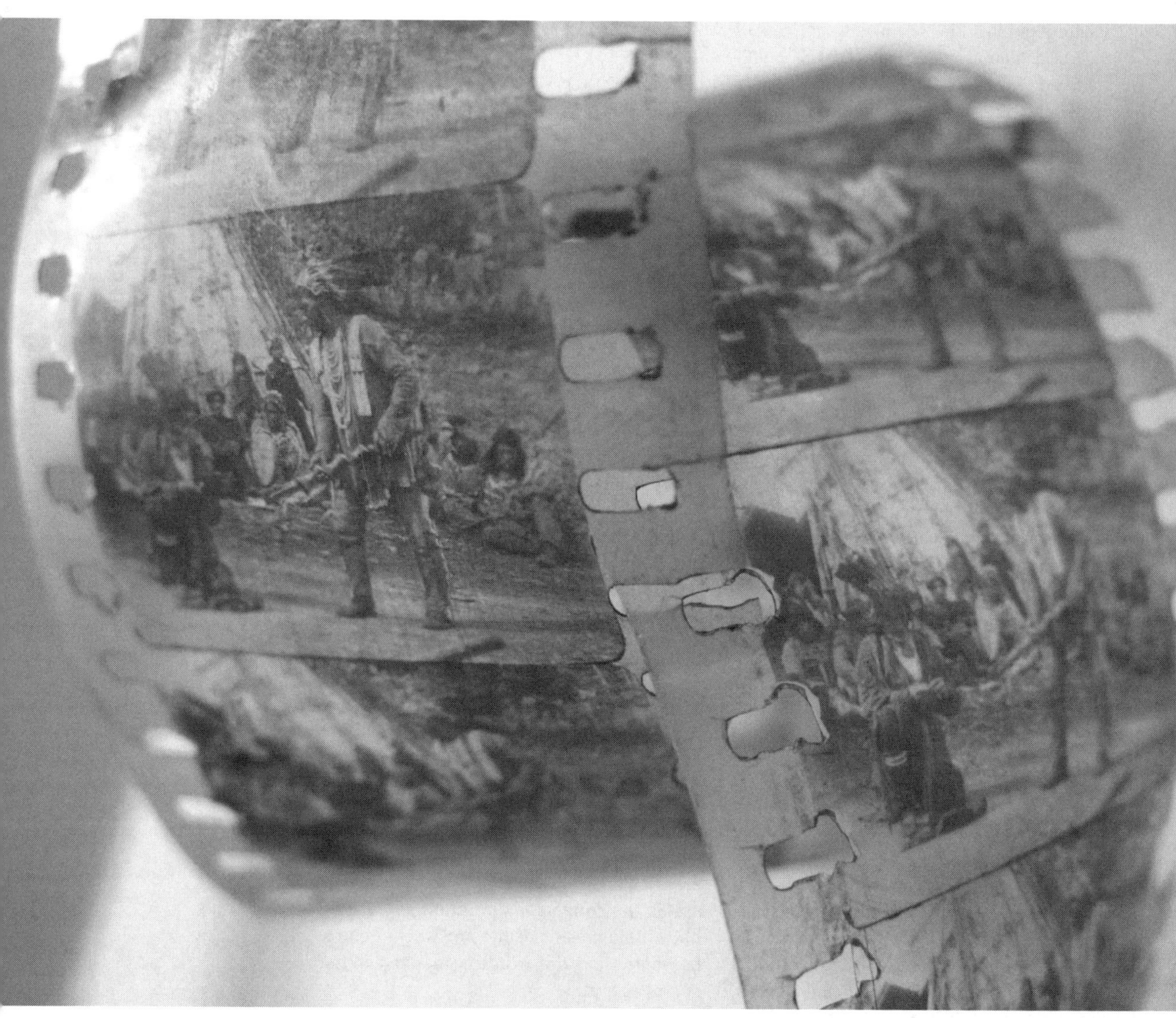

Frame detail taken during the restoration of *A Pictorial Story of Hiawatha* (shot in 1902–3). Photo courtesy Julia Nicoll, Colorlab.

scenes look at a Chinese movie studio, part of the Fox Movietone collection at the USC MIRC, captured performers and crew shooting a jazzy nightclub scene from an unidentified feature. The film segments from *A Pictorial Story of Hiawatha,* shot on Lake Ontario in 1903, first screened in 1904, and meticulously restored by Colorlab's Julia Nicoll, gave fresh insight into how Objiwe culture has been portrayed. *One Tenth of Our Nation,* a 1940 documentary that examined education for African Americans, showed how little our society has improved over the past seventy years. Archivist Rick Prelinger screened a new, high-definition transfer, from an original print, of *A Trip Down Market Street* (1906), a film of hypnotic beauty that was photographed from the front of the Market Street cable car in San Francisco. Thanks to the research of David Kiehn, which proves that the film was made immediately before the April 18, 1906, earthquake, it is now almost unbearably poignant as well.

Sadly, Callie Angell, curator of the Andy Warhol Film Project at the Whitney Museum of American Art, who presented *Uptight—David Susskind* (1966), passed away shortly after the symposium; attendee Sam Kula, a two-term president of the Association of Moving Image Archivists, died this past September; and New Zealand filmmaker Kathy Dudding succumbed to lung cancer in August. "Tracing the Flâneuse: New Zealand/Aotearoa," her presentation on women amateur filmmakers from the 1930s, showed the breadth of knowledge, compassion, and humor that is a hallmark of the Orphan Film Symposia. Though these orphanistas cannot be replaced, their work will be remembered, thanks in part to the opportunity this biannual symposium provides for people to unite around the battle to find, care for, and exhibit orphaned films.

The Eighth Orphan Film Symposium will take place April 11–14, 2012, at the Museum of the Moving Image in Astoria, New York. Its theme will be "Persuasion."

"Rescued and Regained": Il Cinema Ritrovato 2010
JUNE 26–JULY 3, 2010, BOLOGNA, ITALY

Margaret Parsons

Throughout its entire twenty-four years, Bologna's Il Cinema Ritrovato has never availed itself of fusty festival accessories like trailers or late-night parties for fabricating buzz, nor has this venerable festival ever fretted over off years during which the lineup suffered because pickings were somehow slimmer than usual. Since Bologna's mandate is the "recovered and restored," Il Cinema Ritrovato could be called an event for historians and archivists, but in fact, it is much more—a compelling and comfortable festival for any cineast with curiosity, a taste for well-crafted programming, and a lust for a new find from the deep recesses of cinematic history.

If anything, the 2010 edition of Il Cinema Ritrovato was more vigorously programmed than usual and thus more gratifying for the scores of international curators, critics, conservators, archivists, scholars, and students who already regard the city of Bologna as a mecca for cinephiles. The presence of Cineteca di Bologna, one of Europe's leading cinematheques, and L'Immagine Ritrovato, the workshop responsible for many recent stellar restorations, has elevated this Emilia-Romagna town to special status. Its congenial surroundings, relaxed pace, Bolognese cuisine, and artisan entrepreneurs along the arcades generate another sort of appeal.

Screenings and formal presentations take place mainly in two adjacent theaters on the campus of the Cineteca and in a nearby 1950s widescreen palace called Cinema Arlecchino. Discussions, projections, and musical accompaniments for the silent film presentations are generally exceptional, another reason Ritrovato tends to outclass any rivals. Interestingly, the entire city appears to celebrate cinema—Teatro Comunale di Bologna, the town's opera house, occasionally offers cine-concerts, while Piazza Maggiore, in the heart of the historic district, has nightly open-air restoration screenings that attract thousands.

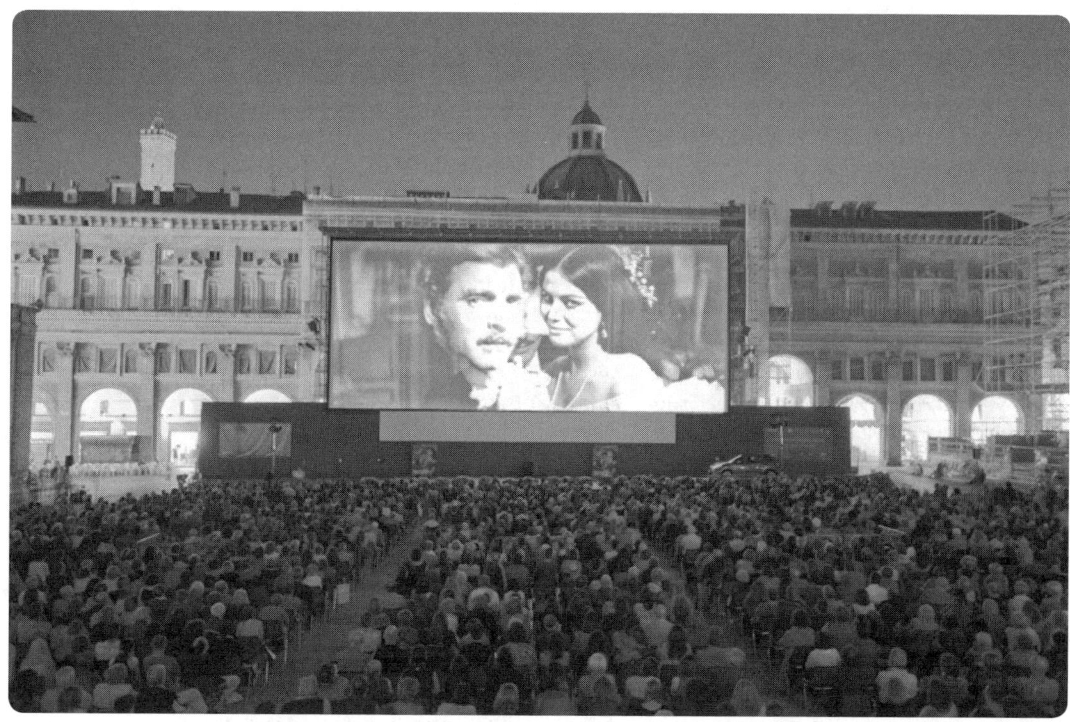

Bologna's Piazza Maggiore during a festival screening: *Il Gattopardo—Piazza 1*. Photo courtesy Piazza Maggiore e il pubblico del *Il Cinema Ritrovato (Bologna 2010).*

2010 PROGRAM HIGHLIGHTS

"Il Primo John Ford," a mind-bending series of twenty-nine early films (twenty-three silents and six sound films, some of them fragments) curated by Peter von Bagh and Guy Borlée in association with Schawn Belston and Caitlin Robertson, included a number of surprisingly good prints of several well-known master-works such as *Pilgrimage* (1933), *Four Sons* (1928), and *Three Bad Men* (1926). The latter, performed with full orchestra en plein air, was a Piazza Maggiore high point. There were also many lesser-known films and a few revelations such as *Up the River* (1930) and *Kentucky Pride* (1925). Ford's early work is not often discussed or taught, although these films illustrate well his natural inventiveness.

Possibly the greatest eye-opener at Ritrovato this year was "Albert Capellani: Un Cinema di Grandeur," twenty-four films structured by Mariann Lewinsky into eight programs spanning Capellani's career in France from 1906 to 1914 and concluding with the American-made *The Red Lantern* (this 1919 film functioned as a prelude for next year, when the director's American work, spanning 1915–22, will be shown). Capellani seemed at his best when directing the divas Alla Nazimova (in *The Red Lantern*) and the extraordinary Mistinguett, queen of the French music halls (in *La Glu,* 1913).

The two complementary sections organized by critic Goffredo Fofi and Cineteca di Bologna director Gian Luca Farinelli, "Hard Times, Italian Cinema, 1945–1949," and Ritrovato's artistic director Peter von Bagh, "Hard Times in Europe, 1946–1952," constituted their own mini *ritrovato*. These were both programs of surprising complexity, filled with intriguing rarities such as Alberto Cavalcanti's mood piece *They Made Me a Fugitive* (1947) and Renato Castellani's stirring neorealist take on the children of a marginal Roman neighborhood living in the shadow of the famous Basilica of San Giovanni in Laterano, *Under the Sun of Rome* (1947).

A highlight of every Cinema Ritrovato, "Cento anni fa" ("A Hundred Years Ago"), was curated this year by a number of specialists, including Mariann Lewinsky, Martine Offroy, Dominique Païni, Nikolaus Wostry, Giovanni Lasi, Luigi Virgolin, Manuela Padoan, and Celine Gailleurd. Any program representing so many perspectives and consisting of so many short films—over sixty prints from sixteen collections—is understandably very difficult to pull together. The careful organization this year paid off, as there was a distinct sense of historical tempo proceeding from "1910: A Year of Stars and Directors" to "The Future of Short Films: News, Science, Laughter," and so on, as well as a focus on geographical idiosyncrasy in "The Danish Medium Length Film" and "A Tale of Two Cities: Vienna and Prague."

"Pierre Etaix, the Clown's Poetry," a retrospective that garnered just modest praise from many attendees, was nevertheless a choice bit of revival programming. Etaix, an Algerian-born French entertainer whose sketches were at times contrasted unfairly with Jacque Tati's oeuvre, was a polished comic craftsman who possessed a slyly surreal sensibility. Jean-Claude Carrière was a close friend and cowrote a number of screenplays for the films of Etaix.

Reflecting on interactions between the object (or artifact) of cinema and the newer enhanced technologies has been customary at recent Ritrovato festivals. This year was no exception, and the section titled "Searching for Color in Films" included several cases in point. A highlight was a 4K Digital Cinema Initiative Package (DCP) presentation of *The Leopard* (Visconti, 1963). For this new restoration, with intensified color, the original camera negatives had been scanned at 8K. Attendees were also treated to a digitally restored 35mm presentation of the excellent but often underrated Delmer Daves western *Jubal* (1956). This restored 35mm print replicated the look of the original grain as well as the original 2:55 aspect ratio. Beautiful new digitally restored 35mm prints of *Picnic* (Joshua Logan, 1955) and *African Queen* (John Huston, 1951) rounded out the section.

World Cinema Foundation, the nonprofit organization established by Martin Scorsese several years back to preserve and restore neglected films, especially films representing nations that might lack financial and technical know-how, was present with revivals that included a rare 1939 André De Toth Hungarian feature, *Two Girls on the Street,* with some amazing vintage footage of Budapest; *Mest,* a 1989 Kazak feature; Ritwik Ghatak's 1973 classic *A River Called Titas,* a beautiful elegy about a dying river culture; and . . . *But Film Is My Mistress* (Stig Björkman, 2010), a new portrait of Ingmar Bergman's persona as a working filmmaker, culled from offstage footage of the master in action.

Speaking of offstage, there was a lot of informal discussion this year about DCP projections in the Piazza Maggiore. Several of the outdoor projections were high-resolution digital cinema and not traditional 35mm film prints. While still a staunch traditionalist, I have to admit that *Boudu Saved from Drowning* (Jean Renoir, 1932) never looked better than it did there in a 4K DCP restoration—but is it really the same movie now? How oddly paradoxical that the "Soirée Lumiere"—a thematic compilation of short works from the brothers, presented in Piazza Maggiore and narrated live by Institute Lumière director Thierry Frémaux—should be projected in 4K. Thus the famous innovators and showmen whose nineteenth- and early-twentieth-century experiments with the Cinematographe, the autochrome, and even 3-D technology changed the course of history were exhibited to a crowd of thousands in the format that will soon transform the experience of twenty-first-century moviegoing.

A newly resurrected 1971 work by Ingram Bergman, *The Touch,* starring Bibi Andersson, Max von Sydow, and Elliott Gould and released in the 1970s by ABC/Disney only as an English-language film (with the voice of Bibi and Max dubbed in English), was finally brought back in the two-language version intended by Bergman. Among the other "Ritrovati and Restaurati" ("Recovered and Restored") was an extraordinary 1965 film with Jacques Perrin and Bruno Cremer (camera by Raoul Coutard) on the Indochina War, *The 317th Platoon,* directed by Pierre Schoendoerffer. This was a find (no

English subtitles, alas) that I hope might have at least limited exposure in some U.S. venues.

A highly anticipated feature of Ritrovato is always the dossier section, which offers an in-depth focus on specific filmmakers and distinctive issues led by scholars and sometimes by famous and well-versed personalities such as close friends or relatives of filmmakers. This year's principal dossiers were on Federico Fellini (the latter in conjunction with a concurrent exhibition at Bologna's modern art museum) and Jean-Luc Godard, in the form of a session devoted to his Centre Pompidou exhibition several years ago. Interesting dossiers were also devoted to director Alessandro Blasetti, actor–director André Labarthe, film critic Michel Ciment, and actor–director Jean Douchet.

Cecilia Cenciarelli and Kevin Brownlow organized "Dossier Florey," this year's entry to the ongoing Progetto Chaplin (the Bologna Cineteca is now the critical center for Chaplin's legacy, restoring his films and housing the primary archival collection of his papers and photographs). Besides their illuminating discussion of Robert Florey (assistant director on *Monsieur Verdoux* [1947] and always a sensi-tive observer of Charlot), the dossier included screenings of Florey's *The Life and Death of 9413, A Hollywood Extra* (1928), *Murders in the Rue Morgue* (1932), and *The Beast with Five Fingers* (1946).

The emotional appeal of this festival is something akin to the pleasure of experiencing the artisanal—a fine product crafted in a traditional way by a limited number of hands, with great care and equanimity. Perhaps it was no mere coincidence that on two mornings of Ritrovato, there was a simultaneous "slow food" event going on immediately adjacent to the Cineteca theaters. So three cheers for artistic director Peter von Bagh, Cineteca director Gian Luca Farinelli, program manager Guy Borlée, and the entire staff of Cineteca di Bologna for a marvelous eight days—arguably the best time I spend at festivals all year long. When Peter was asked, in private conversation, what, if anything, he would do to celebrate Ritrovato's twenty-fifth anniversary next year, he answered, "Nothing special. . . . It will be like any other year, no difference." I can only interpret this remark as typical Finnish reticence on what will add up to another extraordinary event, Il Cinema Ritrovato 2011.

Contributors

Robbins Barstow made many amateur films, the majority of which focused on his family travels. In 2008, his *Disneyland Dream* (1956), an account of his family's trip to the theme park, was added to the National Film Registry for the Library of Congress. Other films include *Tarzan and the Rocky Gorge* (1936), *Family Camping through Forty-eight States* (1961), and a series of advocacy films on saving the whales. The longtime resident of Wethersfield, Connecticut, served as director of professional development for the Connecticut Education Association. He died on November 7, 2010, at the age of ninety-one.

Karen Cariani is the director of the WGBH Media Library and Archives. She has over twenty years of production, archive, and project management experience, having worked on numerous award-winning historical documentaries, including *MacArthur, Rock and Roll, The Kennedys, Nixon,* and *War and Peace in the Nuclear Age.* She has been project director for WGBH's Teachers' Domain, an online collection of multimedia resources for K–12 classrooms; for WGBH Open Vault, a digital library for the WGBH Archives; for the WGBH Mellon Digital Library prototype project; for the Institute of Museum and Library Service–funded WGBH Vietnam digital library; and for the development and implementation of the WGBH Digital Asset Management system. She is currently overseeing the Corporation for Public Broadcasting American Archive Inventory Project. She served two terms (2001–5) on the Board of Directors of the Association of Moving Image Archivists (AMIA). She was cochair of the AMIA Local Television Task Force and project director of the guidebook *Local Television: A Guide to Saving Our Heritage* (2004).

Ashish Chadha is an assistant professor of film media at the University of Rhode Island. He has a PhD in cultural anthropology from Stanford University and has previously taught at Yale University. He has also been making films in India for the past fifteen years.

Robert Dirig is the college archivist at Art Center College of Design. He holds an MLIS from the Department of Information Studies at the University of California, Los Angeles.

Daniel Eagan is the author of *America's Film Legacy* (2009), a guide to the titles in the National Film Registry. A companion volume, covering the movies added to the registry in 2009 and 2010, will be published in September 2011.

Ray Edmondson, the former deputy director and current curator emeritus of the National Film and Sound Archive of Australia, is the principal of Archive Associates, a consultancy company. He presently leads the Association of Moving Image Archivists' Advocacy Task Force and previously cochaired its International Outreach Task Force. Since 1996, he has been involved in UNESCO's Memory of the World Program, authoring its current "General Guidelines" and serving in several roles on its Australian and international committees; since 2005, he has chaired its Asia Pacific Regional Committee. He writes, speaks, and teaches internationally; his latest monograph is *Audiovisual Archiving: Philosophy and Principles* (2004).

Kate Fortmueller is a PhD student in critical studies at the University of Southern California. Her research interests include issues of labor, unions, background actors, and location shooting.

Giovanna Fossati is head curator at EYE Film Institute Netherlands (formerly known as Nederlands Filmmuseum). She holds a PhD in media and culture studies from Utrecht University and teaches in the MA Preservation and Presentation of the Moving Image Program at the University of Amsterdam. Her recent publications include "The Restoration of *Beyond the Rocks*," in *Beyond the Rocks* (1922; DVD release, 2006); "YouTube as a Mirror Maze," in *The YouTube Reader* (edited by Pelle Snickars and Patrick Vonderau, 2009); and the book *From Grain to Pixel: The Archival Life of Film in Transition* (2009).

Josh Glick is a PhD candidate at Yale University in the Film Studies and American Studies programs. Before coming to Yale, he worked in the Library of Congress's Motion Picture, Broadcasting, and Recorded Sound Division and as a paralegal in the law firm Storch, Amini, and Munves, PC. His academic interests are focused on the relationship between cinema and urban environments, American documentary film, and historical representation through cinema.

Jan-Christopher Horak is director of the UCLA Film & Television Archive and professor of critical studies. He was formerly director of archives and collections at Universal Studios; director of the Munich Filmmuseum; and senior curator at the George Eastman House. He earned his PhD from Westfaelische Wilhelms-Universität in Muenster, Germany. His publications include *Making Images Move: Photographers and Avant-Garde Cinema* (1997), *Lovers of Cinema: The First American Film Avant-Garde 1919–1945* (1995), and *The Dream Merchants: Making and Selling Films in Hollywood's Golden Age* (1989). He has also published over 250 articles and reviews in English, German, French, Italian, Dutch, Spanish, Hungarian, Czech, Swedish, and Hebrew.

Martin L. Johnson is a doctoral candidate in cinema studies at New York University. His research is on the production and theatrical exhibition of local films from the 1910s to the 1940s in the United States.

Sam Kula was born in Montreal, Canada, in 1932. He trained as an archivist in the Manuscript Division of what is now the Library and Archives of Canada (LAC) for three years before leaving for London, where he trained as a film archivist as deputy curator at the National Film and Television Archive of BFI. In 1968, he joined the newly established American Film Institute as its first archivist and assistant director. In 1973, he returned to Canada to establish the National Film and Television Archives at LAC. He retired in 1998. He was a founding member of AV Preservation Trust in Canada and was a member of the board until the trust was wound up in 2010. He served on the executive board of the Association of Moving Image Archivists from 1995 to 2003 and as president from 1999 to 2003. He was an archival consultant specializing in the monetary appraisal of audiovisual records and the author of *Appraising Moving Images* (2003). He died on September 8, 2010.

John Migliore is the archivist at the Kitchen in New York City. He is a graduate of the Moving Image Archiving and Preservation Program at New York University and has worked at MoMA and the Film Foundation.

William T. Murphy is retired from the National Archives and Records Administration (NARA), and as a consultant, he assesses audiovisual collections and provides research services for television documentary productions based on archival sources. He is the author of *Robert Flaherty: A Guide to References and Resources* (1978) and *The Current Preservation Status of American Television and Video* (5 vols., 1997). The Association of Moving Image Archivists elected him its founding president and presented him with its Silver Light Award. He is also a recipient of the International Documentary Association's Preservation and Scholarship Award. Since leaving NARA, he has worked on numerous television productions, and he has presented documentary programs in the Czech Republic and Lithuania on behalf of the State Department and the American Documentary Showcase.

Devin Orgeron is associate professor of film studies at North Carolina State University. He is the author of *Road Movies* (2007), and his articles have appeared in *Cinema Journal*, *The Velvet Light Trap*, *Film Quarterly*, and *The Moving Image*. Devin is currently writing a book about contemporary American directors, such as Errol Morris and Spike Jonze, who also work in commercial advertising. He is the coeditor of *Learning with the Lights Off: A Reader in Educational Film* (with Marsha Orgeron and Dan Streible, forthcoming).

Marsha Orgeron is associate professor of film studies at North Carolina State University. She is author of *Hollywood Ambitions: Celebrity in the Movie Age* (2008) and a dozen articles in books and journals such as *Film Quarterly*, *The Moving Image*, *Cinema Journal*, *Quarterly Review of Film and Video*, and *Historical Journal of Film, Radio, and Television*. She is currently at work on a book about director Sam Fuller's war films, beginning with the 16mm amateur footage he shot of Falkenau concentration camp at the close of World War II. She is coeditor of *Learning with the Lights Off: A Reader in Educational Film* (with Devin Orgeron and Dan Streible, forthcoming).

Margaret Parsons is founder and head of the Film Department at the National Gallery of Art, Washington, D.C., an exhibition program as well as a library of documentary film material about the arts. She has served as a trustee of the Flaherty Seminar and has been an advisor to the Getty Trust's Program for Art on Film, the Environmental Film Festival, the Maryland State Arts Council, and the Smithsonian Folklife Festival. She has served on a number of international festival juries and, in addition to film, writes about outsider and self-taught artists.

Louis Pelletier is a PhD candidate at Concordia University, where he is currently working on a dissertation on film exhibition in Montreal. He is research coordinator of the Canadian Educational, Sponsored, and Industrial Film Project as well as of the early cinema research group GRAFICS. He has published on silent cinema and film exhibition in *Film History*, *Living Pictures*, and *Cinemas*.

Wendy Ann Shay has been the deputy chair and audiovisual archivist at the Archives Center, National Museum of American History, Smithsonian Institution, since 2005. She began working in the field of moving image archiving in November 1983, when she was hired to develop a system for cataloging anthropological film at the Human Studies Film Archives. Ms. Shay ultimately became the director of the Human Studies Film Archives prior to assuming the audiovisual archivist position at the Archives Center in January 1992. With degrees in folklore, museum studies, and anthropology from Indiana University (BA) and Cooperstown Graduate Program of the State University College of Oneonta (MA), Ms. Shay did not plan to become an audiovisual archivist. However, she fell in love with the work and the field. Currently president, Ms. Shay was one of the creating members of the Association of Moving Image Archivists.

Eric Smoodin is professor of American studies and film studies at the University of California, Davis. His most recent books are *Regarding Frank Capra: Audience, Celebrity, and American Film Studies, 1930–1960* (2004) and *Looking Past the Screen: Case Studies in American Film History and Method* (coedited with Jon Lewis, 2007).

Sarah Street is professor of film at the University of Bristol. Her major areas of research are British cinema history; the politics and economics of the contemporary film industry; aspects of costume and cinema, including work on Hitchcock; set design; and color film. Her publications include *British National Cinema* (1997; 2nd ed., 2009), *Costume and Cinema* (2001), *British Cinema in Documents* (2000), *European Cinema* (coedited with Jill Forbes, 2000), *Moving Performance: British Stage and Screen* (coedited with Linda Fitzsimmons, 2000), *Transatlantic Crossings: British Feature Films in the USA* (2002), *The Titanic in Myth and Memory* (coedited with Tim Bergfelder, 2004), *Black Narcissus* (2005), *Queer Screen: The Queer Reader* (coedited with Jackie Stacey, 2007), and *Film Architecture and the Transnational Imagination: Set Design in 1930s European Cinema* (coauthored with Tim Bergfelder and Sue Harris, 2007). She is completing work on a project on the impact of color technologies on British cinema.

Katie Trainor is the film collections manager at MoMA. She is a graduate of the L. Jeffrey Selznick School of Film Preservation. She is also one of the cofounders of the Center for Home Movies. She is an active member of the Association of Moving Image Archivists and has been organizing the Archival Screening Night for the past ten years. She continues to be active as a motion picture projectionist at several select film festivals in the United States.

Ronald Wilson is a lecturer with the Graduate Writing Program at the University of Kansas. He has published reviews with *Film Quarterly, The Journal of American Studies, The Historical Journal of Film, Radio, and Television,* and *The Quarterly Review of Film and Television.* He is currently completing a manuscript on the television series *The Untouchables.*